MODEL
RAILROADING
IS
FUN

And more than a half million hobbyists have found that this book makes it even *more* fun! You're now reading the fifth edition of MODEL RAILROADING—a *new* edition, bigger and richer than any other manual ever published . . .

The quickest glance through its pages will show you how comprehensive a volume it is: you learn from step-by-step drawings, photographs, and text how to re-create the whole fascinating world of passenger and freight railroading.

You learn how to organize and conduct a model railroading club; the values of model railroading as a civic project. It's crammed with instructions on landscaping; wiring for realistic operation; new, practical, tested track-layouts; exciting information on the three types of Lionel track, including the new, fabulously real Super "O" gauge; how to make models for your pike. Open it, use it, read it—the ideas are almost inexhaustible!

Bantam Books and Lionel's staff of experts have made this book your key to tops in authenticity and tops in fun in model railroading!

Dedicated to

J. Lionel Cowen

MODEL RAILROADING

Prepared

by the

Editorial Staff

of the

Lionel Corporation

Greenberg Publishing Company
7566 Main Street
Sykesville, MD 21784
301-795-7447

Manufactured in the United States of America

Greenberg Publishing Company, Inc. offers the world's largest selection of Lionel, American Flyer, LGB, Marx, Ives, and other toy train publications, as well as a selection of books on model and prototype railroading, dollhouse building, and toys. If you would like a copy of our current catalogue, please write to request one.

Greenberg Shows, Inc. sponsors the world's largest public model railroad shows. The shows feature extravagant operating model railroads for O, Standard, HO, N, Z and 1 Gauges, as well as a huge marketplace for buying and selling model and toy trains, layout accessories and railroadiana, in addition to a large selection of miniatures and dollhouse building materials. Shows are currently offered in metropolitan Baltimore, Boston, Ft. Lauderdale, Pittsburgh; Virginia Beach; Edison, Cherry Hill and Teaneck in New Jersey; Long Island in New York, New Orleans, Philadelphia, Richmond, and Tampa. To receive our current show listing, please send a self-addressed stamped envelope marked *Train Show Schedule* to the address above.

ISBN 0-89778-178-3

A Message from
Richard P. Kughn

Lionel trains have captured a special place in the hearts and minds of America. What boy or girl did not glory in the idea — as I did — of owning and operating a powerful, colorful train set? And tell me, what parent did not feel that the ultimate Christmas gift for his child was an operating Lionel setup?

Railroad enthusiasts the world over have enjoyed the established Lionel tradition of model train operating and collecting for ninety years. That's right. This year, we're celebrating our ninetieth birthday, which I'm sure you'll agree is no small feat for a toy or a toy company!

And once you read this book, a reprint of the 1958 edition of **MODEL RAILROADING**, you'll see for yourself how our traditions of the past — consistency, continuity and innovation — still apply today.

Isn't it nice to know that Lionel trains created in the 1920s, 1930s and 1950s can be operated today on the same track, using the same power supply, as many 1990 models? Maybe this uniformity is the reason many Lionel trains are now operated by fourth-generation owners — passed by loving hands from parents to children, from children to grandchildren, and so on. And along with the gift goes the admonishments of how to best care for and preserve this precious family heirloom.

Lionel trains fire the imagination of children and adults alike, and creatively interpret the developments and milestones in the railroad industry. Once you get your hands on the latest Lionel technology — like the GP-9 Rail Scope with a miniature video transmitter inside the cab — you instantly become part of Lionel's family tradition!

I'm sure you'll agree with me that **MODEL RAILROADING**, initially published in 1950 and last available in 1961, offers plenty of good advice and friendly encouragement. And as we all know, this information is as important today as it was forty years ago.

Today, Lionel makes trains in four different sizes: traditional O Gauge, classic large Standard Gauge, new Large Gauge, and S Gauge. Although this book was written for the O Gauge operator, its nuts-and-bolts information and how-to-fix-it advice will be helpful to all Lionel operators.

Carrying on the Lionel tradition conveys a special responsibility and a great honor. To paraphrase founder Joshua Lionel Cowen, welcome new and current members of the electric train-operating fraternity, good luck, and have fun with this most fascinating hobby.

Richard P. Kughn
Chairman of the Board
LIONEL TRAINS, INC.
September, 1990

CONTENTS

INTRODUCTION

I know you are going to enjoy this newly revised and enlarged edition of the up-to-the-minute book that has guided hundreds of thousands of people to the pleasures of model railroading.

In my fifty-eight years of building miniature electric trains I have never discovered a more fascinating hobby.

When I started the manufacture of electric trains 58 years ago, miniature trains had very little resemblance to the beautifully scale-detailed models we manufacture today. In the intervening years tremendous progress has been made. Today the model railroad enthusiast, with the equipment now available, can construct and operate the most modern railroad system—controlling and directing his trains by the magic of electronic remote control.

Now you can enjoy the thrill of sitting at the control throttles of your model set—complete master of a miniature railroad system that performs all the functions of a real one. By remote control you can blow the whistle of your locomotive, increase or decrease its speed, stop and reverse it—you can "make up" trains, guide them through intricate switching systems, sidings and spurs, load and unload cars, operate roadside equipment. You become, at one time, engineer, brakeman, conductor, yardmaster, dispatcher, as well as owner and general manager.

Naturally you'll want to match the realism of your model outfit with a fitting background, scenic surroundings as lifelike as the perfection of the trains themselves. You will spend many a pleasant hour, planning and building a little world of your own with its villages, mountains, prairies, rivers, all linked together, as our country is, by the vital network of railroads.

The fascination of model railroading—the urge to build and operate a miniature railroad system—is typically American. Each individual has the opportunity to inject his own personality into his work, to create a railroad system unlike any other one in the world.

To those of you who are joining us, and those who are already members of our fraternity of model railroad fans, I wish the very best of luck, and at least some measure of the happiness I have had in my 58 years as a builder of model electric trains.

JOSHUA LIONEL COWEN
Chairman of the Board, The Lionel Corporation

THE OLD The most romantic era in railroading was the one dominated by the old wood-stoked and coal-burning steam locomotives. Many model railroaders today still build these old-type trains, using motors, driving gear and trucks of modern-type rolling stock.

THE NEW The tendency nowadays is to convert model pikes to Diesel operation, with high-speed freights and passengers with stream-lined cars and realistic horns.

WHAT AND WHY

M ODEL RAILROADING comes very close to being an all-embracing hobby. It can be tackled in so many different ways that every person can find pleasure in it. And every person can find use for his particular skills.

Every useful or necessary ability in model railroading can be learned from the bottom up. A railroad is built a bit at a time, and so are the necessary skills.

Yet in model railroading each person can express himself by building, by inventing, by creating. Best of all, model railroaders get to see their work in operation. They control their tiny empires completely.

Near at hand a little freight train scurries into a siding, a switch is thrown, and the fast freight passes safely by with screaming whistle. A moment later it curves off into the hills, and not a minute afterwards a sleek passenger train glides past in the opposite direction pulled by an effortless Diesel engine. Only then does the little way freight pull out of the siding and resume its delivery of cars on sidings here and there along the line.

The operation of such an accurate model railroad is fascinating. What is more, it parallels the operation of a real road. The person who operates the small road does work that would be done by a dozen or more persons on a real railroad. And to run his creation smoothly he must have skill, experience, and knowledge.

This book provides any model railroader with the know-how for building a permanent, table-mounted layout. A few tools, a few dollars, a bit of patience, and some available space are the only requirements.

The railroading described here cannot be done on the living-room floor with track hauled from some drawer or closet; but it can be done rather easily if a building plan is made and followed. Before beginning to plan—which is considered in the next chapter—there are a few basic points to be understood.

The terms "scale" and "gauge" often confuse experienced railroaders. "Scale" refers to the relation in size between a model (or drawing) and the real thing (called the "prototype"). In model railroading, the most commonly used scale used is ¼" to 1'. This means that each part of the model is 1/48 the size of the original. That includes the distance between the wheel flanges, and this is where "gauge" comes in.

Gauge refers to the distance between the heads of the rails, nothing else. Real railroad standard gauge is 4' 8½", so that in ¼" scale the gauge is very nearly 1¼". All 1¼" gauge is called "0" gauge, as in the drawing on this page.

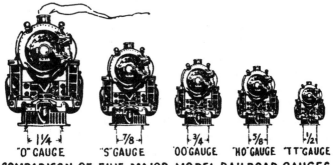

| ⊢ 1¼ ⊣ | ⊢7/8⊣ | ⊢3/4⊣ | ⊢5/8⊣ | ⊢1/2⊣ |
| "O" GAUGE | "S" GAUGE | "OO" GAUGE | "HO" GAUGE | "TT" GAUGE |

COMPARISON OF FIVE MAJOR MODEL RAILROAD GAUGES

The drawing shows the relative sizes of "0," "S," "00," "H0" and "TT" gauges. If you are planning to become a railroader, take care in choosing which gauge is going to be the right one for you, for once you have started with one of them it will be difficult to change, as they cannot be used together. When choosing, keep in mind that the smaller the model, the more delicately it is made, and caring for them, laying track and other operations are more exacting.

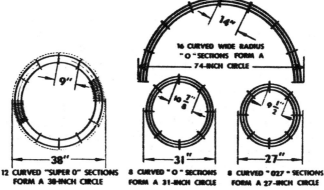

16 CURVED WIDE RADIUS "O" SECTIONS FORM A 74-INCH CIRCLE

12 CURVED "SUPER O" SECTIONS FORM A 38-INCH CIRCLE

8 CURVED "O" SECTIONS FORM A 31-INCH CIRCLE

8 CURVED "027" SECTIONS FORM A 27-INCH CIRCLE

The Lionel Corporation makes "O" and "HO" gauge equipment and in the 1930's it made "OO" as well. Actually, Lionel's "O" gauge track is available in four different varieties illustrated above: "O", "O27", "072" and the new Super "O". Popular "027" is the light-weight track furnished with lower-priced train outfits. "O" track is heavier and used to be provided with the more expensive outfits before being replaced by Super "O". "072" track curves mate with the regular "O" track but have a wider radius.

In making the changeover to Super "O" track Lionel was careful to design a series of transition pins and clips so that the new track could be mated with either "O" or "027" track components. This makes it possible for model railroaders to convert to the more attractive Super "O" track without undue strain on the budget.

Planning a Permanent Layout

Many boys receive their first train at Christmas time. It is natural that they set them up for quick operation.

Although some of these new sets are dismantled and put away in the attic after the holidays, a great many become the beginning of complete model train empires. Planning and constructing model train layouts is not only lots of fun, but it's character-building. It takes straight thinking and imagination to plot a whole railroad system and build it from the ground up. And it's good to know that while you're building you're building for a lifetime of happiness.

Instead of the confusion pictured below, imagine a corner of the cellar, a spare room, or an attic with a permanently mounted table. There are hills, roads, cars, and buildings. The railroad curves in and out of the hills in what seem to be long runs. There is the suggestion of a city and its large terminal. There are villages. There are trackside industries.

It can be a breath-taking sight and one that will make many people say, "I would love to have that, but I couldn't ever make anything like it." To themselves they may add that they couldn't afford it.

Neither objection is very serious. No bit of work on a fine model railroad is so difficult that it can't be learned on the first or second try—it's just a matter of doing each little bit at a time, and in the end they all add up to something big and fine.

The financial problem is not serious either. Few, if any, model pikes were furnished with trains and equipment at

one time. As a matter of fact, it is better to spread out your purchases of equipment over a period of time, so that you can carefully select the items you need or want. The bigger items, such as locomotives and special accessories, can come on special occasions, but an extra car here and there, a bit of track, and other odds and ends can be gotten as required.

Even the space problem can be licked, and many an ingenious hobbyist has had his railroad in an apartment. He may have mounted it on casters to roll under a bed; he may have it built so that it folds into little more space than a card table. Architects frequently show a table folding against the wall when they draw an ideal playroom.

A minimum number of tools are required, although there are many that can be used. In fact, time is the one thing that is needed most. Naturally, time, too, can be spread out over the years, and one can always get a beginning road running in a few hours. But a full treatment with all the little extras will take quite a few hours of work.

And what hours they will be!

There will be all the fun of planning in the mind's eye and with pencil and paper. There will be the gathering of the discarded lumber that will make the table. The carpentry doesn't have to be expert, since it will eventually be completely covered anyway, but even the most inept hammer jockey will drive a pretty straight nail by the end of his first model pike.

And the wiring: it's amazing how many people who never fixed a light cord can hook wires to transformers, switches, lamps, and accessories and have them operate with perfection. And one of the advantages of working slowly is that, because units are added one at a time, the wiring is understood and remembered.

Then there is the pleasure of making model structures and painting them, making scenery and coloring it. Some modelers paint their own backdrops, and while they are not artists, they learn by trial and error until the work has a professional touch.

Of course, there are background scenes to be purchased in any model store. Buildings of all sorts can be bought and readily assembled. What one chooses to do depends upon interests and abilities. But never forget: there are no tricks to model railroading that can't be learned by anyone.

Model railroads such as those on pages 16 and 17 are not beyond the ability of anyone. They need not take too much space; they are not expensive.

With roads like these, the builder would very likely count on expanding them at some later time. One of the characteristics of modelers and model railroads is that they rarely remain static.

Like a real railroad, model railroads change. A real road changes to meet new traffic needs. Industries grow up in one area, while in another region the mines become unproductive and traffic dwindles. Railroads are constantly ripping up track and re-laying it somewhere else.

On a model railroad, traffic needs are imaginary, but the needs and desires of the operator are very real, and track is being ripped up and re-laid just as on a real road. And just like a real road, the model road has a constant growth. New buildings are added, new industries appear. Many of them require new trackage.

As a model railroader, you should keep in mind that you need not build a perfect model railroad that will never change. Changes are part of the fun.

And now, before jumping into the "how" of miniature railroading, there is one other point to remember.

Even the finest model railroad layout will not run itself. It takes a person to make it come to life. The more

On this and the following page are shown three simple and inexpensive layouts that can be quickly and easily built. Enough track, switches and accessories are included to provide hours of entertainment.

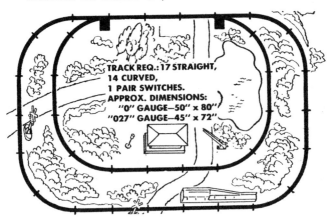

TRACK REQ.: 17 STRAIGHT,
14 CURVED,
1 PAIR SWITCHES.
APPROX. DIMENSIONS:
"0" GAUGE—50" x 80"
"027" GAUGE—45" x 72"

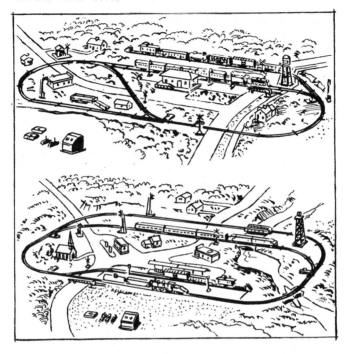

that person knows and applies real railroading to model railroading, the more purposeful the hobby will be and the more fun. It can be fun, the greatest fun in the world, if it is organized along the general lines followed through the rest of this book.

But if it is disorganized and aimless and trains run hither and yon without meaning, then little has been accomplished except to move the confusion of the floor up onto a table.

By following the simple rules and ideas that have made the hobby entrancing to thousands upon thousands of hobbyists, you can join their ranks. Most of those ideas are included here, but hobbyists are an inventive group, and by the time this book appears there will be new ideas expanding on the basic rules stated here.

And so: To work!

Model railroaders who accumulate equipment throughout the years often wind up with "solid trains" of coal cars, "reefers" and others. Shown above is a "solid train" of cattle cars in an appropriate setting. Shown below is a sketch of a cattle "way station."

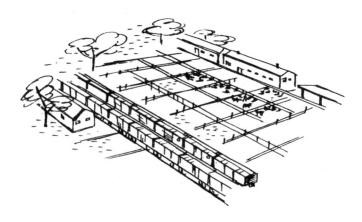

BUILDING
YOUR OWN
MODEL RAILROAD

CHAPTER TWO

MODEL RAILROADING will be fun for you. In your spare evenings you can have the thrill of creating an empire. And when you have visitors, you can demonstrate your control and operation of a busy railroad.

First, of course, there will be some planning to do. This, too, is a fascinating part of model railroading. The only limits in the planning stage are your space and your imagination. You can plan and dream of the vastest road ever built—and you can figure how a modest beginning might lead you through the years to that grand plan.

All you need for planning is paper, pencil and ruler at this time. Later you will make detailed plans and need other devices, but right now, let your plan be loose and imaginative.

In making your plan, keep two things in mind. First, you must know the space available, since that will probably not change. Second, select the type of railroad you would most like to have and plan towards it.

Notice that nothing is said about money or present equipment. That is because it is usually best to plan the railroad you would like to have eventually—then come back to the things you can have right now. In this way you

Half of a two-car garage can be used to build a model railroad.

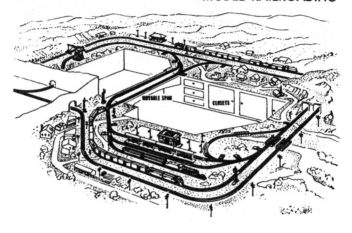

This cellar layout makes use of broken-up areas and takes increased interest from them. Storage space is retained under the layout tables.

can someday arrive at a splendid road even though you may start with nothing but a loop and a siding. Your long-range plan will save hours of work in revising the layout later.

If you live in a house, you will probably have a choice between the cellar, a room or corner, the attic, or one side of a two-car garage. If the cellar is dry and reasonably warm, by all means put the road there. There will be obstructions in the shape of posts, meters, and furnaces, but these can all be gotten around easily. The attic is next best if it is dry and does not get too hot or too cold (however, many new homes have very shallow attics not suited for model railroads).

Even in an apartment, though, a railroad can fold up against a wall (with an attractive map on the underside) or can slide under a bed. It can also be made in three or four sections which are stowed away in two or three minutes in a closet corner.

One apartment railroader used two boards 3½' square, and on each one he had a terminal. A box of extra track let him put one terminal in one room and the other in the next. With careful handling, two operators could keep two trains running on schedule, and they could set up and dismount the whole road in less than five minutes. Not an ideal solution—but a very good one.

When the space is selected, make a very careful drawing of it, showing each obstruction. A large piece of wrapping paper will enable you to make a large, scale drawing in which 1″ on the drawing equals 1′ of the actual space. If there are overhead obstructions, show the height above the floor.

This attic road does not yet have scenery, but shows the tablework and also demonstrates the necessity of having it placed against the wall. Table supports should be strong enough to support trains and scenery.

Usually, an "around-the-room" layout (page 20) which lies against three or four of the walls will give more variety than one in the center of the room. The two roads shown on this and the next page have variety and interest, and give an impression of greater size.

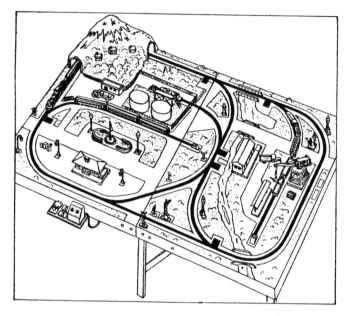

This ping-pong-size table has room for an interesting, active railroad. Scenery may be painted on movable cardboard sheets.

A center-of-the room layout, as shown here, has the advantage of accessibility and it is easier to assemble than the around-the-room type.

Usually it is a matter of choice which layout shall be made. However, in an attic with slanting ceilings, avoid a layout in the center of the room. Obviously, it would require the operator and any onlookers to stand near the walls and to be hunched over. In that sort of room, a layout should be against the wall.

In a cellar, the wall railroad will help to hide rough stone walls or unpainted cinder block or cement block foundations. It has the advantage of making the cellar more attractive with extra painting.

Usually, an around-the-room layout is worth the extra trouble involved in making it. It pays off in fun, in appearance, and in its ability to be expanded whenever desired

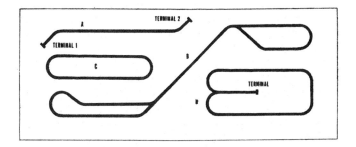

The four basic track plans: A is point-to-point; B is point-to-point
with loops; C is continuous; and D is the home-and-back type of road.
Many layouts are a combination of these.

Planning Your Layout

In making preliminary plans, consider the four basic
types of track plans (above).

Type A, the point-to-point road, is the closest to real
railroads, which run from one city to another (no matter
what the distance or how many branches they have). This
sort of layout has the advantage of realism, especially if
turn-arounds are arranged at each end so that locomotives
and observation cars can be reversed. Naturally, it can be
looped back upon itself and run under and over until it is
hard to recognize on the model layout, but its nature remains the same—point-to-point.

Type B is also point-to-point, but has reversing loops at
each end. This avoids the switches necessary to make a
reversing wye and does not require a turntable, which is a
rather complex project to make at the very beginning. It
is, perhaps, the best approximation of a real road that can
be made with a minimum of equipment.

Type C is a continuous loop. It is rarely encountered in
real railroading (except in "connecting" lines operating
around cities), but with a sufficient number of twists and
tunnels it can be given a very realistic appearance with
good operation. When a layout completely encircles a
room or an area—using a hinged bridge to clear doorways—
the continuous loop is most often used.

Type D is a home-and-back layout, often used when space is greatly restricted. It can be very effective if artfully landscaped, and if the operator uses ingenuity and imagination. It is run just as the point-to-point road is run, but the deception is that the terminal becomes a different stop each time around. One terminal does the work of two!

Having decided upon the type of layout that fits your needs and your space—or perhaps on a combination of two types—make some small sketches of the area as close to proper scale as you can without a ruler. The sketch below will give you an idea of the preliminary sketches that will be transferred to a large, accurately scaled drawing.

When sketching, don't strive too hard; just draw roughly. Then with the sketch complete, visualize the route of one train. Then put a second train on, and finally a third—all in the mind's eye.

When a satisfactory layout sketch is made, start to transfer accurate track plans to your over-all scale drawing. Take the dimensions from the drawings on page 25, remembering that the Super "0" circle is made up of 12 curved sections, "0" and "027" eight each, while "072" requires 16 sections.

First sketches may be rough; later a detailed plan is needed.

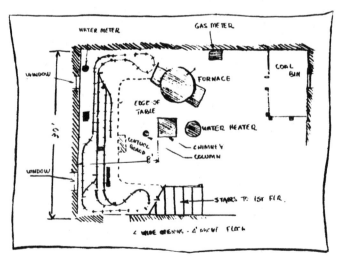

A switch is shaped as though a curved section were placed over a straight section, a useful tip in drawing. Use half-sections where necessary, and if needed, odd lengths may be made by cutting sections to the desired length with a fine hacksaw or even a coping saw.

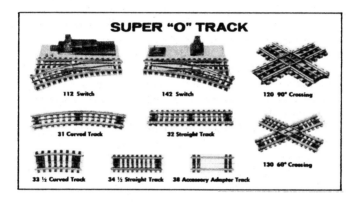

SUPER "O" TRACK

112 Switch   142 Switch   120 90° Crossing

31 Curved Track   32 Straight Track

33 ½ Curved Track   34 ½ Straight Track   38 Accessory Adapter Track   130 60° Crossing

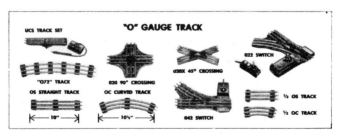

"O" GAUGE TRACK

UCS TRACK SET

"072" TRACK   020 90° CROSSING   020X 45° CROSSING   022 SWITCH

OS STRAIGHT TRACK   OC CURVED TRACK   042 SWITCH   ½ OS TRACK   ½ OC TRACK

|← 10" →| |← 10¾" →|

"O27" GAUGE TRACK

1122 SWITCH   260 BUMPER   1020 90° CROSSING   1022 SWITCH   1023 45° CROSSING

1018 STRAIGHT TRACK   1013 CURVED TRACK   6019 TRACK SET

|← 8¾" →| |← 9½" →|

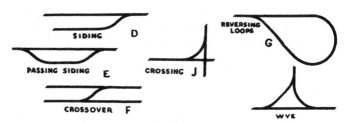

These are some of the simpler track plans used in real and model roads.

Templates may be made of cardboard in any scale that is desirable. By making templates with one, two, and three straight sections, and one, two, and three curved sections, an accurate layout can be made with very little waste time. You can get ready-made templates by writing to The Lionel Corp., Sager Place, Irvington, N. J. They will send some which can be cut out and used quite easily.

Using some of the track patterns shown above, you will be able to adapt your basic sketch to the accurate plan. Later you may want more complex trackwork, but for a starter, these should do.

In the next few pages, some very practical layouts are shown. They were developed just as outlined above, and by carefully following the trackwork you can see how each could be begun with a pair of switches and minimum track.

The pike shown below is a point-to-point road curved back on itself to give length. Other sidings and cut-offs

This point-to-point plan is patterned directly after most real roads.

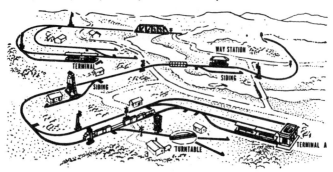

can be added in time. Notice that only one terminal provides a turn-around for locomotives. In time a short wye or a loop will be added to the other terminal. Note also

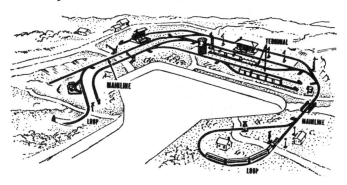

This point-to-point system has two reversing loops, is easy to operate.

that the passing siding is necessary at the way station so that opposing trains can pass in route. This layout is about half developed in its present state: it can be started with less material; it still needs additional work to be complete.

On this page is a point-to-point road with loops and a large through station. This station is similar in nature to New York's Pennsylvania Station, while those on the facing page resemble New York's Grand Central Terminal. Notice that this road provides a variety of action, that a number of trains can operate at one time, that there is plenty of opportunity to expand both in scenery and trackage. Yet it is a complete road at the moment, ready to run.

On this road a long siding runs from the station. In time, this can become a branch line with trains operating out to a new terminal to be installed later. This may be done by allowing the track to drop under the loop and run around in a slow rise to the right-hand corner of the room, and in time that branch might be tied in with the nearest loop, providing for a further variety of routing and operation.

While the road has advantages as it is, in the future it may be desirable to put in a track which jumps over the

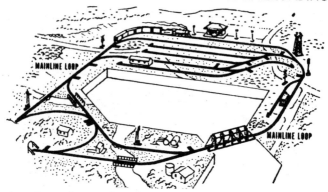

A continuous loop road can have many variations in or out of the loop. One shown here has many sidings and a double reversing loop.

gap between the two loops and forms a large continuous loop such as the one shown on this page (above). This will require a bridge or narrow scenic section which is hinged and can be raised for entering and leaving the room.

While such a bridge is not a tremendous task, it does take time and accuracy to build it, and it may be a good idea to leave it as a project for later development.

Where a continuous loop is used, some provision for reversing direction should be included, and in this illustration it is done by having a double loop tied into the main-line loop. Take a moment with a pencil and trace out the surprising variety of routes that a train can take on the main line because of the double loop in the near left-hand corner. Notice also that the station has a passing siding so arranged that there are several internal sidings, a common railroad device. In this case, too, a fully operating road is provided, but there is unlimited opportunity for expansion, especially if a mountain division should be added afterwards. We will show this later.

In a sense, the home-and-back road is a variation of the continuous loop, for it is really a large loop with one terminal located either inside the loop or along one outside track. It combines the features of the point-to-point and the continuous loop and one variation is shown next.

Basically, the layout shown on page 29 is nothing but a

big loop with a long siding running from it. But there are three interesting features of the layout pictured here that transform it from a rudimentary layout to an interesting operating road.

First, consider the loop that is located inside the main loop. Trace out a few routes and see the variety of runs the trains can make. The variety will do two things: fool the onlooker into seeing a large, long, and widely diversified road; and enable you to change the direction of entire trains while running. The loop gives you variation in running over the main-line trackage.

Second, notice the crossover in the lower right-hand corner, at the terminal. This is good prototype planning. It enables a double-ended locomotive, such as the Diesel shown here, to drop the cars at the station, run ahead, back out on the other track, and finally come up to the other end of the cars. Thus, it is ready to begin a new run

This home-and-back road also contains a reversing loop with a crossing.

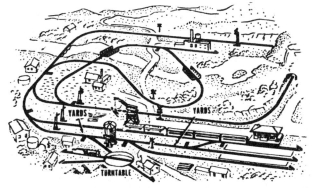

as soon as the imaginary train crew has moved through the cars and reversed the seats.

Third, notice the turntable. In the case of big steam engines, they can be backed out of the terminal just as the other locomotive was, then run onto the turntable. Here the direction can be reversed and the loco run onto any of the tracks for a new run. Such a turntable may be powered by a motor or by hand.

A double-track line is especially adaptable when used with accessories.

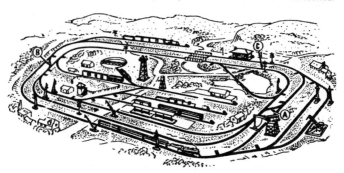

These four layouts cover the basic types of the point-to-point road, point-to-point with loops, continuous loop, and the home-and-back road. No matter how complex, any railroad, whether real or model, is a variation of one of these, or a combination of two or more of them.

Multiple Track Layouts and Grades

Most large railroads have double-track main lines. It does not always follow that the model railroader should work towards a double-track line as the ideal arrangement, but in many cases it will be desirable.

A double-track line should be fairly large in terms of space, otherwise the added track looks unnecessary or even gives a cluttered appearance. Also, a double-track line is made for heavy traffic and therefore must have larger yards and more sidings and rolling equipment. If desired, it can be set as a final goal for a single operator; or it can be a logical beginning when two or more people are working together pooling their material, skill, and time.

On the layout pictured at the top of page, the cross-overs marked A and B are important; they are the only way of transferring a train from one track to the other. Essentially, this is a home-and-back road with the terminal in the center of the loop. With the loop that is part of the central trackage, whole trains can be turned. Meanwhile a turntable cares for locos that need reversing.

Passing tracks and sidings marked G provide for operation of several trains at once. A large section of industrial sidings, such as those on the right, means that a switch engine can be drilling a number of cars on the sidings while the main lines are busy. In that case, the switcher will occasionally pop onto the main track for a short time and then return, just as it does on a real road.

The loop C is provided in order to give a train a longer run without having to pull into the same terminal it left only a moment ago.

By now, it can be seen that one of the essentials of model railroading is a sort of genial deception. Even the largest clubs can hardly approach the scale length of a very short real railroad. But deception is employed. A few rolling hills built up over Loop C would mean that a train could be run under the hills and left to sit for a few minutes while other trains passed. Then, quite suddenly the train comes to life, emerges—but in a different direction.

All this is quite apparent now, but imagine how it would strike an onlooker who had never seen the plan and did not know the loop was there. With these and a few other

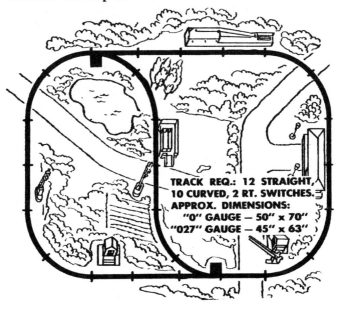

TRACK REQ.: 12 STRAIGHT, 10 CURVED, 2 RT. SWITCHES. APPROX. DIMENSIONS: "O" GAUGE — 50" x 70" "027" GAUGE — 45" x 63"

tricks, a variety of concealments can be worked so that
schedules are realistically long and operations are convincingly real—even to the operator who invented the tricks!

Where a grade is added to enable a train to duck under
the table or to run through some concealing mountains,
the illusion is all the greater. Such artistry, like all the rest,
needs only the application of time. There is no complicated carpentry, and the wiring is simple, but it will help
if such plans are considered when making the first plan of
action.

This brings us to the layout that offers just about everything. Here one can run trains for an entire evening without ever having a train repeat itself. Trains will run on
different divisions, will carry loads in opposite directions.
Peddler freights will trundle along, dropping into sidings
to allow superior trains to pass. Here a new problem can
be introduced: How can you run a wrecking train to accidents on the layout with a minimum amount of inter-
ference, even though some tracks are blocked?

A bit of time spent in figuring out the advantages of
such a layout will benefit you greatly—may even show you
why you want to plan towards such a road.

If you do plan a road with grades at this time, remem-

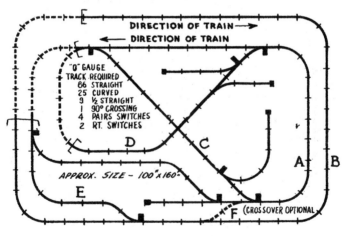

This plan of the road opposite shows hidden trackage by dotted lines.

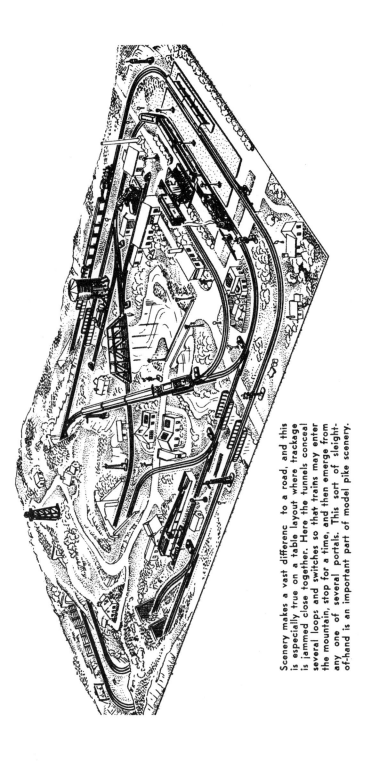

Scenery makes a vast differenc to a road, and this is especially true on a table layout where trackage is jammed close together. Here the tunnels conceal several loops and switches so that trains may enter the mountain, stop for a time, and then emerge from any one of several portals. This sort of sleight-of-hand is an important part of model pike scenery.

ber several points. Grades should be no steeper than ½"
rise or fall to each section of track, gentler if possible. Lionel's twin-motored Magne-Traction locomotives will climb
a grade much steeper than this with a full load of cars, but
try to minimize the grade in any case and avoid abrupt
changes in grade. The change in grade should not be
greater than 2½%. In other words, it should take at least
three track sections to obtain the transition between level
track and a grade as steep as ½" per section.

Lionel's No. 110 Trestle Set takes care of this requirement automatically but if you are constructing your own
grades check the operation of your rolling stock carefully
to see that the pilots of your steam locomotives do not
short out on the center rail and that the couplers remain
in reasonably good alignment at the points where your
grade changes.

On these two pages can be seen variations of two-level
roads that offer new and different possibilities. Both of
them have long tunnels that can conceal a train for long
periods while other action is so exciting that they are almost forgotten. A switch or two adroitly concealed (but
left so that it can be reached in case of trouble) would
change operations even further by allowing a train to
change from tunnel to tunnel. Thus, a train could emerge
at some completely unpredictable spot.

Both of these layouts show that a model railroad is built
in a manner opposite to that in which a real railroad is
built. The real road must take the land as it finds it and

A road with grades poses problems, but the work pays handsome rewards.

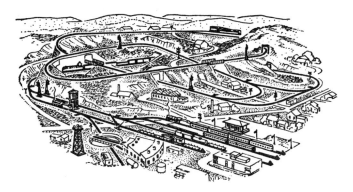

Grades make a pike more interesting, but cannot be done in a small space. Layout shown here rises to 3 levels and is equipped with switches to give continuous operation.

build around it somehow. As model railroaders, we build a railroad and then tailor the landscape and the cities to fit the pike.

To be sure, the features of the landscape should be those that a railroad would normally meet, and they must be handled as a railroad would handle them. Properly done, they not only enhance the appearance, but they actually aid operation by giving reality to what at first appears to be nothing but a maze.

On all of the layouts shown, one of the most important features has been the terminal and its yards.

Model Railroad Yards and Terminals

On a real railroad, a yard is any track or set of tracks that serves to (1) store engines or cars, (2) allow for making up or breaking down of trains, and (3) provide for receiving and dispatching of freight.

On a model railroad, yards do the same thing. The only differences will be that yards will be smaller and that in many cases one track will do two or three of the jobs mentioned above.

Still, for best results, a model railroad locomotive yard should be planned on the same theory as a big one. The only real difference between the two is that the model loco-

A careful study of this diagram will show the parts and plan of a typical compact railroad yard for freight and passenger operations. Check each point lettered on the drawing against the table; and trace the routes of the various kinds of trains.

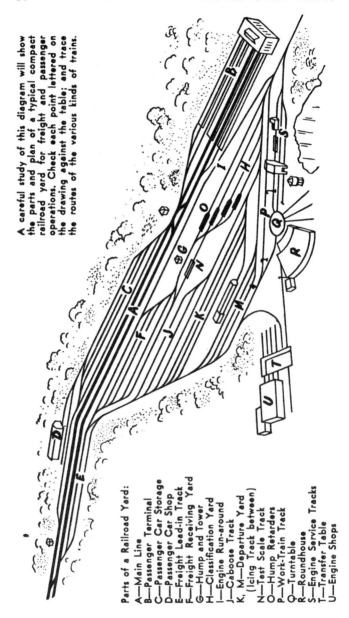

Parts of a Railroad Yard:

A—Main Line
B—Passenger Terminal
C—Passenger Car Storage
D—Passenger Car Shop
E—Freight Lead-in Track
F—Freight Receiving Yard
G—Hump and Tower
H—Classification Yard
I—Engine Run-around
J—Caboose Track
K, M—Departure Yard
    (Icing Track between)
N—Test Scale Track
O—Hump Retarders
P—Work-Train Track
Q—Turntable
R—Roundhouse
S—Engine Service Tracks
T—Transfer Table
U—Engine Shops

motive does not have to take on coal and water, nor does it dump ashes. Otherwise, they are quite similar.

On the opposite page is a diagram of a complete real railroad yard. For a real yard, it is compact. It fulfills all necessary functions. But for a model road, it would be too immense, and even the biggest club would tackle such a model with serious doubts.

The drawing can serve the purpose of showing how a yard works, and from that we can see the functions of a model yard. We can then design our own in the best possible way.

The heavy lines represent the main-line tracks; others should be traced until understood.

Notice that the drawing shows a terminal. Trains terminate at the station and can go no further, a situation which led to the joke about the woman who asked a New York Central conductor, "Does this train stop at Grand Central Terminal?" His answer: "If it doesn't, lady, there'll be one heck of a crash!"

A station, such as Pennsylvania Station in New York, could be made here by moving the building to one side and allowing the main-line tracks to continue on through. In one case the line terminates at that point, in the other the line continues on through.

Most of the yard opposite is self-explanatory. The hump, G, and the retarders, O, are a common sight today in classification yards. Instead of trains being broken up by shunting each car with a switcher, they are pushed up to the top of a rise. There the cars are cut loose one at a time to coast downhill and stop in the proper track. Naturally, the proper switches must be thrown, and also they must be stopped somehow.

Rather than have a brakeman on each car, electric retarders are used to slow the car at the proper time. In this way a train can be broken up and the cars rerouted in a very short time with very few men.

Humps have been built on model railroads; but they are hardly practical, and would serve only as exhibition pieces.

After fully knowing the drawing, try sketching roughly a plan for your own yard, making each of the divisions with only one track. Then, with a few combining moves, you will find that it is getting down to modeling size.

Opposite are drawings of three smaller yards connected with stations. Yard 1 shows a station with three through tracks, A, B, and C. Local trains terminate and originate on tracks marked D. An arriving train would pull into D and discharge passengers, then back to storage yard E and leave the cars there.

The locomotive moves to one of the standpipes F and takes on water, then to the wye and the ashpit marked I. From I, it can proceed to track J and await orders; the wye will serve as a turn-around.

Tracks G are freight tracks, called "house" tracks. Tracks H are "team" tracks for loading or unloading directly to or from trucks.

Layout 2 is a simpler station, but much of the plan is the same as in 1. Crossover A leads into track B. Track B is often omitted on model layouts, but on a real road it is very important. The left end of it is called the "lead" track and is so arranged that a loose car or runaway loco-motive cannot roll onto the main line. The opposite end is called the "safety spur" and serves the same purpose.

In the arrangement marked 3, one track serves as the entire yard area. Yard 3 demonstrates that, for a modeler, two switches can make an entire station and freight yard.

In the three drawings on this page and the drawing on page 36 there are all the elements of real yards. The parts of a yard may be differently located because of local con-ditions, but the parts themselves do not change.

Today, with the increasing use of Diesel engines, a new part has been added to most yards. One siding of the engine yard has stations for loading oil into the locomotives and platforms for cleaning and servicing the engines. These will be covered more thoroughly later.

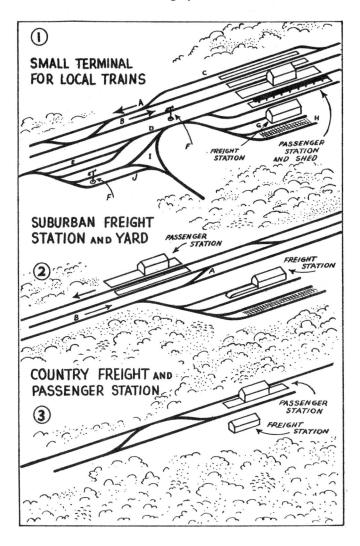

These are step-by-step directions for building a simple table-top railroad. The next chapter tells you how to build tables.

This layout, which is described on the following pages, requires 12 OS straight track, 3 1/2 OS straight track, 8 OC curved track, 1 pair 022 switches, 1 left 022 or 042 switch.

The table-top type of model railroad shown on this and following pages is easy—and fun—to build. This particular one measures 4 by 8 feet, because the platform is constructed of plywood and this is the usual size in which plywood sheets are sold. However, as mentioned, this is merely a suggestion, and you need not be confined to these dimensions. Consult the chapter on Tablework.

The first step, shown here, is the preliminary layout, sketched out with crayon on rough paper, or on the plywood itself. This preliminary sketchwork will include the

placement of scenery and accessories as well as your track scheme.

At this stage, tack your track down lightly—give your train a practice run to be sure it is going where you want it to go. Then you won't have to tear up roadbeds after you have landscaped. The practice-run system for new layouts is extremely important for layouts which include grades, overpasses, etc. because of necessary clearances.

Note that lake, brook, roads and accessory positions have been marked out. Position of the transformer has also been determined.

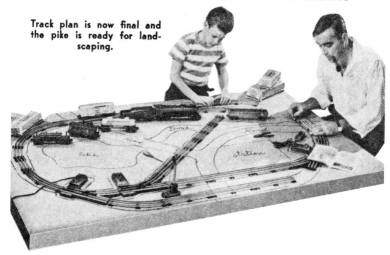

Track plan is now final and the pike is ready for landscaping.

When all members of the railroad system are satisfied with the preliminary sketch, remove all track and accessories before starting the landscaping. The common landscaping materials like sand and sawdust are much better applied before track is permanently laid.

As a railroad empire builder you have a wide-open choice of landscaping materials. You can buy ready-made materials in hobby stores or you can let your imagination run free and find things to use in the cellar, the attic, outdoors.

Plain sand makes excellent roadways (sprinkle a few pebbles around). A comb run through dried coffee grounds gives the appearance of plowed fields. Pieces of sponge, dipped in dye, will furnish bushes and trees. These and other materials will be described in the "Scenery" chapter of this book.

A "Do-it-yourself" Kit

A complete do-it-yourself landscaping kit No. 920 recently developed by the Lionel Display Department contains the materials used by these experts for building the amazingly lifelike train displays for large department stores and other model train dealers.

It contains a pair of molded tunnel portals, a 3' by 4' piece of special felt material for covering a mountain tunnel structure, an assortment of vari-colored "grass," dyed and treated lichen for making bushes, trees or hedges, realistic rock-like material, a quantity of dry glue and a set of special water colors.

The quantities of materials provided in one kit are sufficient to landscape a 4' by 8' layout. If your railroad is a good bit larger than that you can get a second kit or obtain additional supply of various materials from the Lionel Service Department.

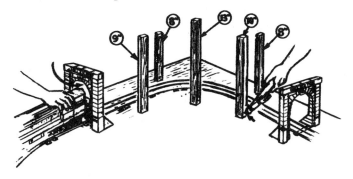

One method of framing out a mountain is to toe-nail vertical supports into the platform. This is also the time to check the operation of your rolling stock to see that all of it has adequate clearance through the tunnel.

Another way to frame a mountain is to use a couple of corrugated paper cartons. Cut off the bottom leaving enough material to bend out a
nailing strip. Cut out archways in the ends of the boxes and there you
are! Of course, the advice to check clearances still goes.

The general planning of the layout and the positioning
of the mountains and tunnel portals should be done as described on the preceding pages. To support the mountain,
toe-nail pieces of 1″ by 2″ into the platform and build a
general shape of the mountain from screening, or even from
heavy butcher wrapping paper or opened-up shopping bags.
The paper can be held to the uprights with thumb tacks.

The dry glue furnished with the kit is dissolved in 2
quarts of water. Let the mixture stand for about a half hour
until it is smooth and clear in color. The felt is then
soaked in the glue, wrung out as well as possible, and
draped loosely over the mountain form. Wads of newspaper roughly crumpled and inserted between the wrapping paper and the felt are used to simulate irregular
mountain terrain. The edges of the felt near the portals
are clipped to the portals with the steel clips provided for
this purpose.

When the felt has dried overnight it will be hard and
ready for painting. Not too much painting is necessary
because the rough, grey texture of the felt simulates ground
and bare rocks very well. The painting should be done by
daubing the colors with the end of a brush rather than by
trying to cover the surface completely. Clumps of multi-

colored lichen are glued to the surface here and there, and green and yellow sawdust sprinkled over the surface irregularly to give appearance of patches of grass and flowers.

The cement which remains is spread over the entire board, and grass sprinkled over the wet surface in generous amounts where lawns of green fields are desired. Rock is sprinkled at the bottoms of the steep mountain sides, along embankments, around streams or lakes and the base of tunnel portals where it might normally accumulate by rolling off the mountain side

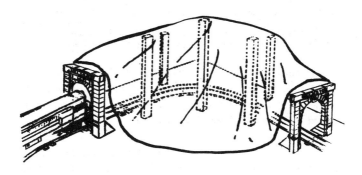

Here are the two final steps in your mountain building. First, the rough shape of the mountain is developed by tacking wrapping paper, etc., over the frame work. Next, glue-soaked felt is draped over the paper, with crumpled wads of newspaper inserted here and there between the two layers.

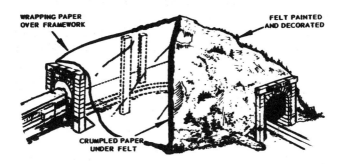

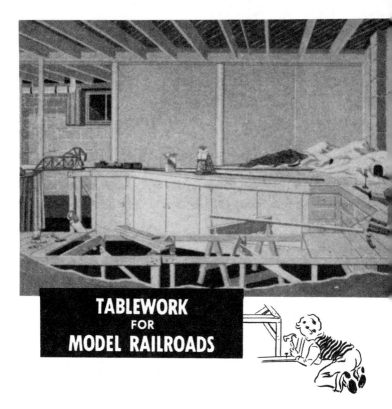

TABLEWORK
FOR
MODEL RAILROADS

CHAPTER THREE

TABLEWORK supplies the foundation for your railroad empire. It must be firm—steady enough to resist the vibrations set up by the trains. But it does not have to be made of heavy lumber, of new lumber, nor of expensive lumber.

The carpentry will place no great demands on anyone who can hammer home a nail. The rest can be learned.

The cellar layout shown above is a neat job by a good home carpenter. It is the sort of road that is aimed at. It is not the sort which one attempts at first unless unusually skilled.

In getting wood for your road, there are only two important rules: (1) don't get green wood, for it will warp and your tracks will be out of line forever, and (2) don't

Fig. I

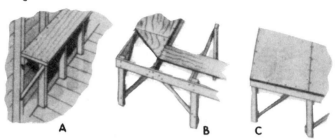

A   B   C

buy expensive wood, for there are better things to do with the money.

If you can't find second-hand wood around, try buying soft wood of odd sizes and lengths at a second-hand lumber yard. Otherwise, specify soft woods of the cheapest sort at a regular lumber yard. The chances are that you can scrape up nearly enough around the house.

Above, in Figure 1, are three methods of construction, one for the attic, two for table construction. You can see that if the wood is concealed by draperies or cabinets, there is no reason why it need be fine-grained or regular.

For top shelving on which tracks will rest, use dry wood that will not warp. Do not worry about knots, since these can be hidden by scenery. For solid surfaces such as table C, try getting second-hand plywood of ½″ thickness or

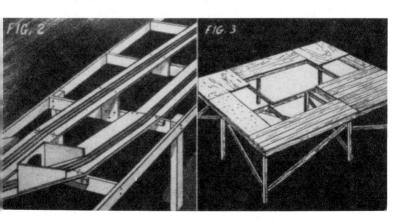

FIG. 2   FIG. 3

more. Shelving ¾″ thick, or shiplap, even heavy beaver-board or pressed wood will do. Surface parts may be odd-sized and fitted in place, especially in an irregular-shaped table.

Tablework need not be solid (see Fig. 2, page 47), and where rolling hills and streams are to be made, it is often better to avoid flat surfaces. If grades are planned, do not use solid surfaces except at stations, terminals, and yards.

Free-standing tables, not anchored to any walls, should be pinned to the floor with brackets if possible. Where floors are hardwood, the weight of the table will hold it in place fairly well.

Wall-type layouts in cellars present a slight problem in tying the wood to the floor and walls. With cinder block, one can drive nails directly into the block. With poured concrete or cement block, cut steel nails can be used by tapping gently and steadily with a heavy hammer. Lead plugs will hold screws quite well; any hardware dealer can supply them and tell you how to use them and a star drill.

The cut-away drawings on this page will explain them-selves. It can be seen that the system used in Fig. 4F, in which hangers from the rafters are used, is the simplest.

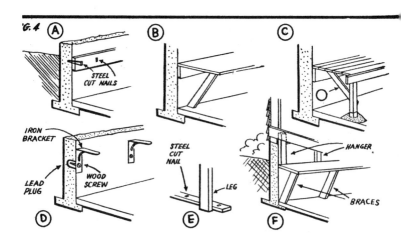

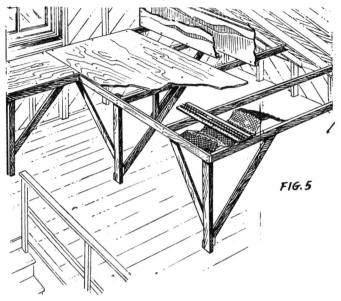

FIG. 5

However, it does require more lumber—which may be hard to come by.

The attic is far-and-away the easiest place to make a train table (see Fig. 5). When crosspieces are nailed directly to the rafters, a great deal of lumber and woodworking is eliminated. Also there is little prospect of the members working loose.

Unless you live far south, insulate the roof before putting up the trains. Otherwise, the attic will be too hot in summer and too cold in winter. The insulation can be bought in rolls and easily installed; it will pay off in general comfort throughout the house.

In making the table, the best rule about height is: the higher, the better. Avoid making tables too low, for there will be too much stooping and the view is not the best. However, if the layout is being built for children, the ideal height is about 30″.

The table above combines flat work and open work, the wire screen forming a base for contoured scenery. Allow space for backgrounds on all wall pikes.

In the illustration below, notice the use of flat areas for yards and where grades are joined. The wire screen will support plaster scenery that will give variety to the view.

Notice the rising trackboard. It is supported by an upright nailed to one of the crosspieces. If the underlying track is on a down grade from the level area, it will be necessary to depress the cross-bracing pieces so that their tops are at the low point of the trackage. This is wise, for if one track drops as the other rises, an overpass can be made in half the distance without increased grades.

A wide table of any sort poses a problem: how to reach every section of track. Derailments and wrecks will occur, and someone must get to them. In many cases the table may be sturdy enough to hold a person walking on it. But this means that utmost caution must be used never to step on track, shrubbery, or buildings.

An alternate system is to allow for "pop-ups." In some cases, where mountains or trackwork conceal it, a hole about 18″ in diameter can be left open and the operator

can crawl under the table and reach through. In other cases, a small section of table can be roughly hinged so that it can be lifted in trapdoor fashion. However it is done, the problem must be considered.

In cellar or attic, an around-the-room layout must allow an entrance for the operator and visitors. Occasionally an entire section is hinged and lifted. The pivot of the hinges must be exactly in line with the top of the tracks so that they match when lowered. At the free end, wedges or cupboard clasps must center the tracks. Copper contacts make the electrical circuits complete.

Most often, a one- or two-track bridge is used for entry

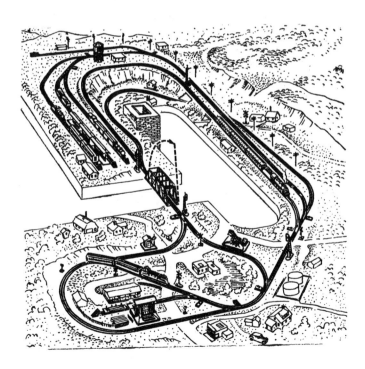

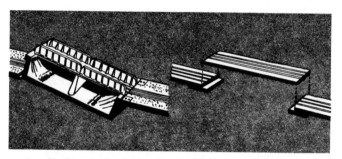

and exit. It can be hinged, or lifted out entirely, and it must be carefully made. Many fans wire the bridge so that trains cannot approach the spot when it is removed. This is done by having the bridge control all circuits.

Systems of hinging vary with the road and the builder, but many hobbyists like to have a latch so that the bridge will be held in an open position. This is handy when working and hauling material in and out.

However a table is built, its size and shape and type will be determined by the space available. But what if there is not space 4' x 6' or larger available?

In that case, space must be created. Even in a small apartment there is space which is not used. There is space under beds so that a layout 4½' x 6' can be kept there and taken out when needed. Accessories and tall buildings must be stowed away, and the rolling stock should be kept in a drawer or under a dust cover. But the main problem is licked as shown on the opposite page.

A folding layout can be made to take little more space than a card table and can be set up in a moment. Radio jack plugs make electrical connections between the two halves. The only problem to such a layout is that hinges must be carefully put on so that the track meets exactly each time.

Where a large wall area is available, a layout can be made and hinged so that it rises flat against the wall and is locked by hooks. The underside can be used as a bulletin board or a decorative space for pictures, or a map can be put on it and shellacked. In some cases, this has been done so that the layout rested on the bed when in use.

A wall-folding layout has the advantage of allowing storage space behind the board. It need not take up more than one foot of room area, and it could take less.

The ingenuity of model railroaders seeking to carry out their hobby is limitless; in one case a hobbyist raised his road against the ceiling with a rope-and-pulley arrangement. Another fan, Gene Fish, ran his track around the wall, just below the ceiling and from room to room of his apartment. This worked fine, even though he had to stand on a kitchen stool to see the trains.

We hope you can reach an easier solution.

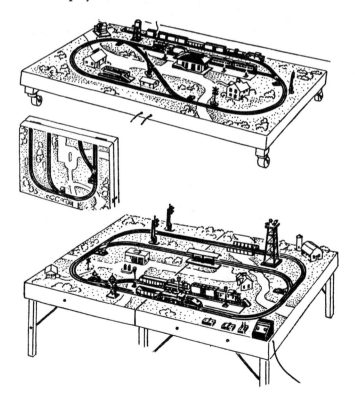

TRACKWORK

N^O MODEL LAYOUT is any better than its track. If the track is poorly laid, loose-fitting, and uneven, trains will not perform well—if at all. Surprising things can be done with the track; it is good when new. But for best results, it must be properly managed.

Before laying any track, inspect it closely—especially if it is not new. Discard broken or battered pieces. Replace missing pins, and tighten the ends by gripping the web of the rail with long-nose pliers. Wipe with cleaner or solvent of some sort, but avoid carbon tetrachloride—it can be extremely poisonous. In the case of badly rusted rails, sand lightly with 00 paper.

Rails are always fastened to trackboard or to tables with small round-head screws. Do not use nails. Not only will nails work loose in many cases, but they cannot be removed without battering the track.

On an open table such as the one below, track is screwed to boards 1″ x 4″. On curved sections, boards are fastened together and then cut with a keyhole saw to follow the curve of the track. Unquestionably, it is more work to lay out track in this way; but it will pay big dividends in the flexibility of your layout and the control of your landscape.

The advantages will be quite clear later when scenery is discussed, but even now it should be obvious that a valley cannot easily be cut into a solid table. Nor can streams be shown properly. There is further advantage in the track-work itself.

Your yards and your terminals will be on level pieces of board or plywood, just as real yards are generally on level ground. Suppose you want a mountain division high enough to cross over the lower level. There must be six inches difference in height of the tracks in order to clear the trains.

If you allow a half-inch rise to each foot (a very steep grade), it will take twelve feet to gain the six inches. However, let us consider the open table and its advantages.

Here you can let one track drop from the yard level while the other rises. Instead of taking twelve feet to clear each other, they need only six feet, since one will drop three inches while the other rises three inches.

In actual practice, a good rule is to take all of the space you can get to make your rise, especially as you will want to avoid grades with sharp curves. Curves add to the train load, and with a grade added to that, even a strong engine may have difficulty.

Also, do not start grades abruptly, but ease into them. Otherwise, the pilot—call it a cowcatcher if you prefer—will touch the center rail and will short-circuit the system.

When handling Lionel track, you must make certain that all connections are tight. Pins should be in place and firm. If pins are missing, buy new ones; or you can cut some finishing nails down to the proper length with a hack saw or coping saw. The square ends can be given a point with a file, and these will serve adequately.

Do buy some fiber pins, however. These will serve to keep rails lined up when you want to eliminate the electrical connection—a frequent problem. The air space (or

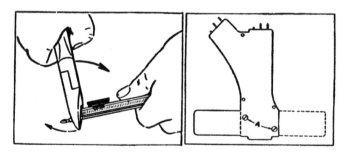

To pull track pins, clamp the cutting edge of pliers close to the track, gripping lightly. Hold the track and pivot against the pliers.

"Motors" on "0" gauge switches may be moved to either side; this will be an advantage when planning the yard and terminal tracks.

absence of any pin) is an adequate insulator, but it will allow the rails to be jogged out of line quite easily. Use matchsticks if fiber pins are not available.

When you are ready to apply the track to a board—and it should be carefully marked according to your plan—have a center line drawn for all straight sections and adjust the track so the center rail is on this line. Then with a light hammer and a finishing nail, tap a hole in the wood. Be very careful to hold the nail straight and the track steady. The nailhole will guide the screw into place. Do not tighten the screws too much or they will distort the ties, and cause a "wavy" track.

When a Lionel accessory, such as a semaphore, block signal, or crossing warning is used with an actuator, you must leave several lengths of track free on each side of the

Cutting track into smaller lengths will save you much juggling of your track layouts. Grip the track lightly in a vise, using wooden protectors, and saw with a fine hack saw or with a standard coping-saw blade.

pressure device. If necessary, though, long thin nails may be used which will allow the track to rise, but still prevent any sidewise motion.

If you combine "0" and "027" track, keep two things in mind: the "027" must be shimmed up almost ¼" to mate with the "0" gauge track; and the "0" gauge pins must be filed down in order to fit into the "027" track. While it poses some problems, many railroaders like to ease into their turns by using a section of "0" gauge track, two sections of "027," then another "0" section. This means a gradual tightening of the turn as trains enter it.

You can enhance the appearance of "0" and "027" track by adding extra ties between those affixed to sections. Super "0" track, with its closely-spaced, realistic ties does not require special work. It can be used with the other track by means of an adapter set made by Lionel.

Avoid banking curves if possible. It will distort the track, and if at all steep, the banking (properly called super-elevation) permits the locomotive to "straighten out" the cars by pulling them from the rails.

Wherever tracks parallel each other, allow a minimum of

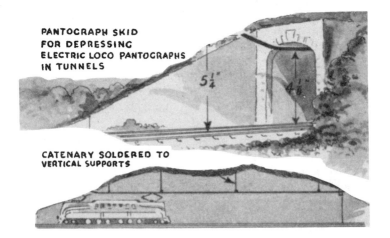

PANTOGRAPH SKID
FOR DEPRESSING
ELECTRIC LOCO PANTOGRAPHS
IN TUNNELS

$5\frac{1}{4}"$ $4\frac{1}{4}"$

CATENARY SOLDERED TO
VERTICAL SUPPORTS

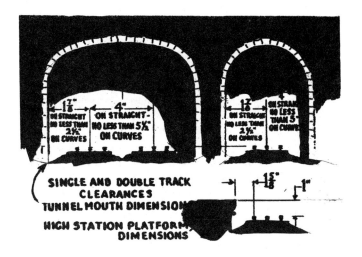

four inches between center rails. This is the least space that will avoid sideswiping. On turns, this should be expanded to six or seven inches because of the overhang of cars and locomotives.

Shown above is a chart of tunnel and platform clearances on straight track. Tunnel widths on curved tracks should be increased one inch on each side. Avoid platforms on curves, as they must be too far from track and will not look realistic. Pantograph skids, shown opposite, are required for tunnels too low to permit a GG-1 with raised pantograph to go through. Tunnels of this proportion are more realistic and worth the work of the skid. If you wish to eliminate them, the tunnel height must be raised.

Avoid such obvious traps as an RCS or UCS (remote control sections) butting against a curve. The reason is that cars or switching engines coming out of the curves may not have space to align their couplers.

BALLAST
GLUED

TRACK MOUNTED ON
RUBBER PADS WILL SILENCE
TRAINS

SILENCE OPERATION BY
MOUNTING TRACK ON
STRIPS OF BEAVER BOARD,
CUT AS ABOVE.

BALLAST
LOOSE OR GLUED

It is possible to eliminate much of the noise from your model railroad if that is desired. The problem comes from the fact that the train table often acts as a sounding board, almost as if the trains were running on a drumhead. The train table can be insulated in several ways, one of the easiest being to lay the track on strips of beaverboard. Cork or rubber mounting will do equally well, or better, but may be fairly expensive.

Properly handled, beaverboard can be quite realistic and add to the appearance of your track. By beveling the edges, and then painting flat black, a texture and shape much like standard ballast will be obtained.

Before ballasting the track, though, ties should be considered. On a large road these can be a bit of work; but even there, if the work is organized, they will not be too much trouble. They add greatly to track appearance.

Ties should be cut from ¼″ wood. They are ½″ wide by 2¼″ long. If possible, get ¼″ strips ½″ wide. Then mark and saw every 2¼″. Otherwise, rip a number of the ½″ strips, then cut a number of lengths at one time.

Stain them by cutting large numbers at one time and simply dropping them all into a bowl of dark stain. Move them around a bit and fish them out with a wire. Allow them to dry on scrap wood. See that each lies flat. They are fastened with small nails that do not split the wood.

There are many ways of making ballast. One is to shape each trackboard by beveling, then apply asphalt roofing paper to the board. This simulates the material quite well. Another possibility is to paint carefully the proper places with water glass or wall sizing, then sprinkle with very fine gravel. The gluey material holds the gravel, while it can be shaken or brushed from other sections.

A different approach is to make a mixture of sizing and gravel so that there is a light coating of the cement on each bit of gravel. Then this mixture can be applied. Before it dries, it is sprinkled with plain gravel so that the top layer is not shiny.

Even more simple is to use thick gray paint liberally applied, and to sprinkle the gravel onto it, pressing lightly. It will hold the gravel well enough to give texture to the

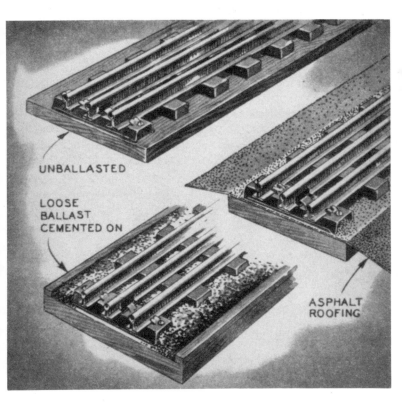

roadbed. In yards, ties can be omitted, and some asphalt paper applied up against the tracks; flaps may cover the metal ties. This will give the cindered appearance which yards get when the ties are completely submerged.

Below are illustrations of various track types. Notice that on the double-track line, a drainage ditch is provided between tracks. No drainage to speak of is provided in yard areas, and this follows railroad practice. Apparently the maintenance facilities around a large yard are so handy that the yards can always be righted if trouble develops. Then, too, tracks are constantly being shifted in yards, and while they carry heavy traffic, they do not carry it at high speeds and so can allow a bit of sagging or unevenness that could not be tolerated on the "high iron."

Sidings, too, do not carry fast traffic. Usually the switchers or way freights operate at a snail's pace—or more properly, a man's pace, to allow the brakeman to throw switches ahead of the train. Nobody seems to worry much about the condition of most sidings, and they frequently are overgrown with vegetation. Your sidings can parallel this

Super-O track with its closely-spaced ties needs only a little ballasting to look as real as life.

practice, so that instead of having ties and spruce, trimmed ballast, you may want to have the rails seem to sit on hard earth and buried ties. When you apply scenic effects to your road later, you can add grass and even weeds.

The scenery which you add later will solve certain problems, notably in operations, but it will bring others. If you intend to use track boards and scenery that includes tunnels, mountain divisions, and low level divisions, you must allow for operating errors later.

Especially where curves occur under mountains or other covered sections, derailments are possible. Even with the best equipment and control, accidents will happen. Usually, your locomotive will be powerful enough to run away with a string of cars if the voltage is turned too high. If it hits a curve at high speed, it will flip off. This is not a great problem, for one can crawl under the table and untangle it, or openings can be provided so that every spot can be reached.

However, don't forget that engines are damaged, often seriously, by being dropped to the floor. Wherever such a

Yard tracks have half covered ties. Unused sidings are often overgrown.

possibility exists, you should have guard rails or a false floor or a net of cloth to catch and hold the trains.

Switches present an added hazard under tunnels; avoid them if possible. They are a frequent cause of derailments, usually through the fault of the operators. If you must use them under tunnels, use fully automatic ones. As mentioned before, Lionel electrically operated switches, made for all types of track, have this non-derailing feature, which causes an approaching train to flip the switch automatically.

It is also possible to spring-load a manual switch. This can be done after disconnecting the lever, by using a very light spring to pull the switch point open (or closed). When a train comes through the other way, the flange pressure of the wheel will open the switch enough to allow free passage. Such work, however, is very delicate.

Test all track before you cover it or apply scenery to it. Operate trains frequently to locate any trouble. Good track means good operation.

ELECTRICITY and MODEL RAILROADS

CHAPTER FIVE

I T IS POSSIBLE to run a model railroad without knowing any more about electricity than a five-year-old knows. But—to run a large model road properly and to operate it well, it is best to understand some fundamentals.

This chapter will contain the minimum amount that you ought to know. You can go far beyond this level, but you should not make a large layout without this much knowledge, at least. There is a great deal that is not covered here, and you can go on experimenting and reading books and magazines.

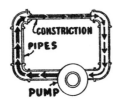
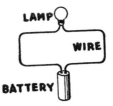

In its most elementary form, electricity is often compared to a flow of water through pipes, as shown here. Just as a pump can force water through pipes, even when constricted, so a battery forces electricity through wires to light a lamp. Instead of being measured in pounds per square inch, electricity's "pressure" is measured in volts. Instead of gallons per minute, electricity's "rate of flow" is measured in amperes, often called amps.

Another similarity of the systems above is that just as more water flows through a large pipe, so more electricity will flow through a large wire—the resistance is lower. Also, a rough, rusted pipe slows down water flow, and some materials slow down the electrical flow—the resistance is higher.

Resistance is important, for it allows three things to happen: (1) electricity is delivered to your home from long distances because of the low resistance of copper; (2) electricity lights lamps because high resistance makes tiny wires glow inside the lamp bulbs; and (3) electricity is confined wherever desired by the nearly total resistance of rubber, porcelain, and other insulators.

Every electrical circuit must have three parts: voltage, current, and resistance. The first two are provided by house wiring or a battery; the resistance is provided by a lamp bulb, a motor, or a heating element in an iron or toaster. If the resistance is reduced almost to zero—by allowing the wires of a circuit to touch without a major resistance—then too much current flows, and wires overheat because of the high amperage. In a home, this will blow out the fuses (if the fuse-box has been tampered with, it will often start a fire). In a battery system, it will drain the battery very quickly. Such low resistances are called *short circuits*.

The unit of resistance is called an *ohm*. Between ohms, amperes, and volts there is a constant arithmetical relationship. The formula is called Ohm's law, after the German scientist who discovered it. (Incidentally, volts are named for an Italian scientist named Volta, amperes for a French scientist name Ampère.)

In the formulae, V stands for volts, R stands for ohms (resistance), and I stands for amperes. The formulae:

(1) Amperes equal voltage divided by resistance—

$$I = \frac{V}{R}$$

(2) Voltage equals resistance multiplied by amperes—

$$V = R \times I$$

(3) Resistance equals voltage divided by amperes—

$$R = \frac{V}{I}$$

As can be seen, an ohm is the resistance of a conductor that will allow one ampere of current to flow when supplied with one volt of "pressure."

There are two different types of electrical current, both of which are encountered in model trains. Current from a battery is called *direct current* (D.C.). The name comes from the fact that the current flows in only one direction. Most house current is called *alternating current* (A.C.). This means that it pulsates back and forth, usually very rapidly. In most homes, *60 cycle* A.C. is used, which means that the current reverses itself 60 times each second. (Electricity travels at the speed of light, approximately 186,000 miles per second, and has no trouble at all covering the distance from your home to the power source in much less than 1/60th of a second.)

Alternating current has certain advantages in home use, one of which is that a *transformer* can be used to raise or lower the voltage.

Electrical power is measured in *watts*, which are an indication of how much work the electricity can do. Wattage is obtained by multiplying the volts times the amperes.

If we have a typical model locomotive motor which draws three amperes at twelve volts, we can now learn two things:

(1) $R = \dfrac{V}{I} = \dfrac{12}{3} = 4$ ohms of resistance.

(2) $V \times I = 12 \times 3 = 36$ watts of power.

If we raise the voltage, the power consumption will be

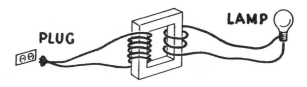

raised. This will show up in higher locomotive speeds.

A transformer is a device in which two coils of wire are wound around the same iron core but are not electrically connected. An elementary sort of transformer is shown on this page. Transformer action is dependent on the pulsating character of A.C., and it will not work on D.C. In fact, because of its low D.C. resistance, transformers may burn out if plugged into D.C.

Alternating current flowing through a coil around an iron bar sets up a magnetic field. As the current pulsates, it changes the poles of the field. This constantly changing field produces a voltage in the opposite, and unconnected, coil. This process is known as induction.

We have thus changed electrical energy into magnetic energy, and back into electrical energy. In doing this, we can change the characteristics of the current that emerges. Especially, we can change the voltage. If the two coil windings are equal in numbers of turns around the core, the input and output will be the same (except for a noticeable loss due to wastage by heating the windings and magnetizing the core). If the input and output are to be changed, the windings must be different in the number of turns around the cores.

In a model-train transformer, there are different taps to which wires can be attached, and these use differing numbers of turns. Therefore, they produce different voltages. Besides this, there is a metal finger attached to the controller handle or knob, and this finger slides along the coils tapping off a varying number of turns. Thus, voltage can be increased or decreased by the controller. It is this feature which gives flexibility to train control.

Transformer Power Rating

Like all electrical appliances used in the home, transformers are rated by watts. This is a requirement of the Underwriters Laboratories and is an indication of the amount of power that the equipment will draw from your household electrical wiring system.

While it is possible to calculate the wattages required by each current-using item in your railroad and compare the total to the total wattage supplied by the transformer, this process is not always easy because the wattage losses in the transformer itself are not constant but vary depending upon the design of the transformer and on the conditions under which it is operated. A simpler method is to add up the current in amperes required by your equipment and to compare the total to the maximum current which can be safely furnished by the transformer.

The following table lists the current which can be supplied by Lionel transformers for at least four hours of continous operation, under normal temperature conditions.

Transformers	Amperes
1015	2.5
1043-1053	3.0
1033-1044	4.0
LW	5.5
KW	8.0
TW	8.0
ZW	12.0

Knowing the current which can be supplied by the transformer you can check it against the requirements of your model railroad by adding up the current, in amperes, consumed by your equipment, counting 1¼ amperes for each motor, and $1/5$ amperes for each steadily burning lamp.

You do not need to figure in the power requirements of automatic couplers and operating cars, since the couplers draw current for only an instant and operating cars only when the train is not running. For the same reason, do not add power used by such accessories as coal elevators, log loaders and other operating devices which are put in action when the train is not running.

For example, if your outfit consists of a 5-car illuminated passenger train pulled by an "O" gauge twin-motored locomotive, and you have a pair of No. 022 switches, 4 lamp posts and a couple of block signals, it would need:

Equipment	Quantity	Current	Total
Motors	2	1.25	2.5
Headlights	2	.2	.4
Car lights (2 in each)	10	.2	2.0
Switch lights	2	.2	.4
Switch controllers	2	.2	.4
Block signal lights	2	.2	.4
		Total current	6.1 amps.

This would mean that your outfit would require a continuous current of approximately 6 amperes and would call for a KW or a TW transformer.

In order to keep losses as low as possible, the most efficient wiring should be used. This means that all connec-

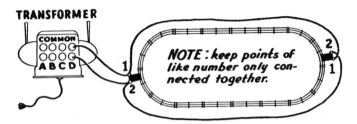

tions should be tight, trackpins solidly engaged. Wire of
sufficient size should be used. On a small layout, No. 22
wire will do, but on any large layouts, No. 18 or even
No. 16 wire should be used. (The smaller the number,
the larger the diameter of the wire.)

As shown in the illustration on the preceding page,
tracks are just extensions of the wires. They have a higher
resistance than copper wire, and consequently a long
stretch of track creates a problem of voltage drop. The
far side of a long layout may have so little voltage that

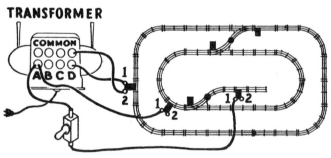

engines creep along, though they go nicely near the transformer connections. The solution is to run jumper wires
to the far side of the layout, and, since copper's resistance
is low, the voltage will be restored at the far end. In doing
this, take care that center rail connections are made to
the same wire—like rails must be connected to like terminals—otherwise a short circuit will result.

A train layout of any size at all will need to be sectionalized so that one train may be run while another is
halted at a terminal, yard, or siding, or on a different

track section. To do this, it is only necessary to insulate
the track section by using a fiber pin in the center rails

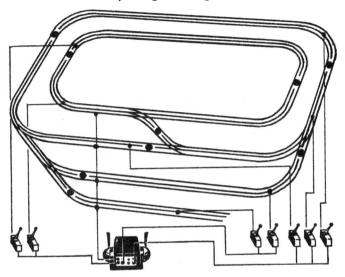

of the section to break the circuit. With the circuit broken
by fiber pins, it is then necessary to run a separate wire
to the isolated center rail. It should have its own controlling switch, or be on a separate section of a double-con-
trolled transformer, if one is being used.

Diagrams on these two pages show a simple sectionalized
layout and a complex sectionalized layout. Trace the wiring
until you understand the principle.

A handy system for wiring is to use wires with insulation of different colors. By using one color for center
rails, another for ground wires (outside rails), and other

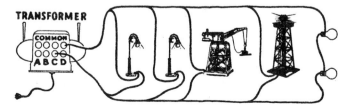

colors for accessories, you will have far less trouble tracing wires when you make additions or changes—or when you have electrical troubles.

It is recommended that tracks and accessories be wired to different posts. Since most accessories use 12-14 volts, they can be hooked up to the B or C posts of a heavy-duty transformer, and the arrangement can be as shown on p. 71. In the illustration, accessories are wired in *parallel*, and any one may be disconnected without breaking the circuit. The two lamps on the end wire are wired in *series*, and if one is unscrewed and disconnected, the other will go out, since the circuit has been broken. By placing two identical 6-volt lamps in series, they will equal one 12-volt lamp. If 18 volts are used on a line, three identical 6-volt lamps should be used. If these were placed in parallel, thus receiving the full 12-14 volts, they would burn out very quickly. These lamps can be used as indicators on your control panel.

Of course, the wires to accessories do not actually have to be laid parallel to each other—that is merely a schematic method of showing them. In practice, you can hook one wire of the accessories into a black wire used as a common ground. Another wire, perhaps brown in color, could be strung around the layout from the B or C transformer post, and the *hot wires* from accessories tied to it wherever convenient.

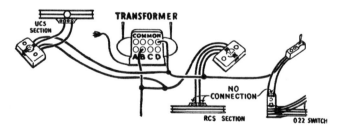

This hot lead can also be tapped for the fixed voltage plugs on automatic switches (the common ground for the switches is already made through the outside rail connection).

Since most accessories are powered by solenoids or motors (a solenoid being a tubular electro-magnet which operates an iron plunger), most of them can be wired in several ways. Usually they receive power directly from the tracks and cannot operate when the power is off. By following the plan above, they can be wired so that they operate directly from the transformer regardless of track power. This means that operating cars will work and switches can be moved without applying the main power to locomotives.

The technique is to ignore their ground connections and ground switches directly to the transformer, leaving

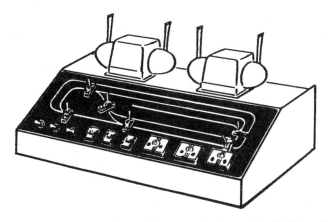

the center connection of the switch bare. On RCS and UCS tracks, both hot and ground wires are hooked to the transformer.

By now, you may have discovered by calculation or experience that you will have a large number of wires running to the various posts of your transformers. If so, it is time to make a control panel which will simplify wiring in the long run, which will enable you to expand easily at any time, and which puts all controls right at hand.

The front of your panel may be of whatever material you have at hand or find desirable. Masonite is excellent and easily workable, but plywood will do. As shown on the preceding page, a diagram of your tracks should be painted as a white line about ⅜″ wide. On every section that is controlled as a separate unit of track, drill a hole to allow a lamp to be inserted. Near the bulbs, another hole will allow toggle switches to be inserted, and these will control the energizing of the track and the lamps.

Below the diagram, fit in all switch controllers and accessory controls and RCS or UCS track controllers. Allow extra space for additions. Put the transformers at the top, on a level board if desired.

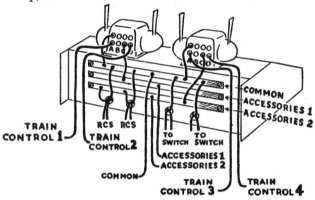

The back of the control board can be covered with a light panel that is easily removed, or it can be left exposed. On it are two or three long copper bars called *bus bars*. One of these is the common ground; the others are hot accessory outlets. Below the bars, holes are drilled to allow wires from the controllers to come through. All switch ground wires (the center ones) are run to the common bus bar, the others to the switch. RCS and UCS track have their hot and common wires hooked to the common bus bar and the hot bus bar as shown in the diagram on page 72.

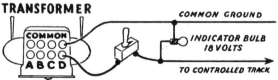

Meanwhile, various sections of track are hooked directly to the transformer posts, although a small bus bar could be used if desired. The best method of attaching wires is with solder, but holes drilled in the bus bars will enable you to twist the wires through, if soldering equipment is not to be had.

The diagram on p. 74 shows how control lights are used on the various sections of your track diagram. In this arrangement, the bulb will light when the section is energized, and at a glance, one can tell whether a stub track or siding has power. Main sections will also be wired the same way, except that in some cases the toggle switch may be omitted, since the transformer itself provides the on-off function.

The electrical systems discussed have been large ones in every case. Naturally, if you understand these, you can then make a smaller system. Remember, it is always wise to leave room for expansion.

Railroads, especially model ones, have a way of growing and growing—sometimes way beyond the original plans.

The Transformer for Your Railroad

Always remember that the transformer is the keystone of your model railroad. It delivers the electric power—if it's deficient, the pike just doesn't operate. Good transformers have built-in circuit breakers to guard against "shorts." They also have red warning lights to warn you of "shorts." If you are starting a small railroad with an idea of future expansion, check your local hobby dealer about the wattage that may be necessary for the expansion . . . particularly as it concerns railside accessories and operating equipment. If your dealer hasn't the information, it is usually contained in the catalog of the model train company.

SIGNALING and INTERLOCKING

CHAPTER SIX

Many model railroaders, good ones too, operate their roads by timetables and train orders. They have no great need for signaling, or they use small hand-thrown semaphores.

But as a road expands and as it comes nearer to real railroading, most modelers want an efficient and railroad-like signal system. Some will go even beyond this and interlock the system so that accidents are almost inconceivable.

All signal systems are based on the dividing of the road

into blocks. A block on a real railroad may be as short as half a mile or as long as ten miles. It is defined as a section of main-line trackage which cannot be occupied by more than one train except under special circumstances.

The length of a block will depend mostly upon the amount of traffic carried over the line. A passenger train coming up behind a slower freight will never be closer than one block. While the freight is in the block, a red signal will show behind it, and the passenger train must stop until the freight has passed into the next block or has moved onto a siding and closed the switch behind it.

The red signal may be controlled manually, automatically, or by interlocking.

The only manual blocks used today are run by the "controlled manual block system." The key word is "controlled," and it means that when any tower operator throws his signal, it affects the block ahead of him and the block behind him.

Such a system is shown below. It is in use by many clubs today, usually when there is a large membership to man the towers. A towerman is stationed at each signal. Of course, he may operate others too, but they would be similarly arranged, one set for each track or twin sets for a single track carrying two-way traffic.

The controlled manual block system below needs agreement by two operators to show a clear board; at right, a solenoid-operated semaphore.

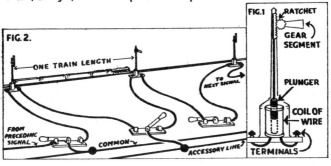

The signal itself is a simple solenoid, which requires only a lead wire and ground wire to operate it.

When no energy is supplied, the signal reads "stop." As can be seen, two towermen must agree in order to give a "go" signal. And when a towerman gives a go-ahead in his own block, he automatically throws the preceding signal to "stop." A set of buzzers enables towermen to communicate—two buzzes means to throw the double-pole switch left to give a clear signal in the approaching block. One buzz gives acknowledgment, a second buzz shows the train has arrived and is proceeding to the next block.

We can eliminate the men required if we make the system electrical. This is done by means of a "make-and-break" electrical switch operated by an electro-magnet—a device commonly called a "relay." Of the several makes generally available from distributors of radio and television parts the most suitable for model railroading are Potter & Brumfield MR Series and Guardian Series 200, both with 12 volt a.c. coils.

Now all that must be done is to make a track circuit

In "O" or "O27" insulate outside rail as above with adhesive tape and insulating pins. In Super "O" you can buy ready made insulated track No. 48 (straight) and No. 49 (curved).

which will energize the electro-magnet (which will move the switch—which moves the signal) and we have an automatic signal. And such a circuit is simplicity itself.

If we buy or make a piece of track with an insulated outside rail and connect it as shown at the top of page 79,

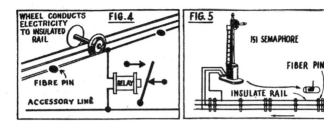

we find that anytime a train passes over the insulated rail it becomes live. The engine and car wheels have jumped over the insulation. Thus, if we want the train to activate a relay, we hook one relay wire to our accessory line and the other to the insulated rail. If nothing is on the track, the relay is dead; if anything passes the insulated rail, current flows through and the relay is immediately activated.

Such a relay can work our signals.

Before relay signaling is explained, it should be noted that an insulated rail can energize a Lionel semaphore signal without the use of any other devices.

A relay-operated system appears to be complex, but it offers definite advantages. Let us consider the diagrams below. By carefully tracing the flow of current, you will be able to see that in the top drawing the signal will give a

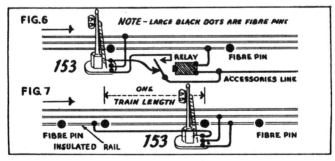

green indication to any approaching train. But when a train hits the insulated section, it energizes the relay and causes it to change the signal to red.

Without the relay, the lower drawing still serves in railroad-like manner. Here the signal is not lighted at all

until the train hits insulated section A. Then the signal
shows green. When the train has passed from A and onto
section B, the signal changes to red for any following
trains. You should realize that section B can be made as
long as necessary to protect the rear of the train.

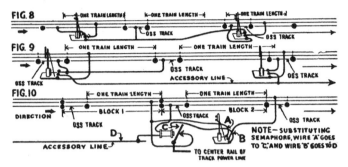

In many of these drawings you will see a section marked
"one train length." You will have to ascertain the average
length of your trains and leave it at that. When shorter
trains are run, the signal (shown on the preceding page)
will go out for a moment; longer trains will give a red
and green simultaneously.

The three drawings above are extensions of, or combinations of, the preceding signal circuits.

In the first drawing, a number of signals are used without relays. As a train touches section A, it turns the first
signal green. At section B, the first signal is turned to red,
and the second signal is turned to green. At section C,
the same wiring is still in effect. But at section D, the first
signal is no longer activated at all, and the second
signal is turned to red. Such a system might operate all
around a layout, with trains protected at all times.

The second drawing shows a similar system for the
semaphore signals, which are more simple than the signal
lights since they normally give a clear board without being
energized.

In the third drawing, trace the wiring carefully. It will
take a moment, and it may even require two or three tries,
but it should be clear in your mind. Under this system,

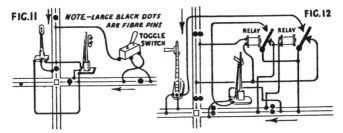

the action of the relay not only operates the signals, but it will automatically stop the train following. Thus, you can put two trains on one loop of track, and the second will never pile into the first even if the controls are untouched.

If you check the wiring closely, you may find that car lights will go out at times. This can be prevented by drawing the lamp current from the locomotive shoes instead of from the car shoes. However, it is not a serious problem if ignored.

Interlocking systems differ from signal systems. Automatic signal systems guard the same track, see page 80.

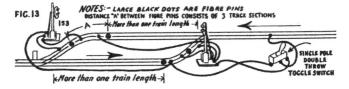

Interlocked systems are arranged so that if one track is live, a joining track is dead. Drawings on page 81 illustrate several possible applications, including a siding. On such a passing siding, a section is insulated at each end so that incoming trains clear the switches, then stop at the dead section. The single-pole, double-throw switch is set to stop the first train in; then the second train goes on through. After that, the first train can proceed whenever the SPDT switch is thrown.

The Lionel No. 450 Signal Bridge is 7½″ between bases and spans either single or double track as desired. It is pro-

vided with two red-green signals faced either way and can
be mounted in several positions on the bridge structure, depending on the indication wanted. If over single track the
two signals may be mounted over each other in center of

Figure, left, shows Lionel
No. 450 Signal Bridge
installed over two lines
of track. Below, left, is
same signal remounted
to operate trains both
ways on single track.
Bottom, right, shows sig-
nal set for two tracks
operating trains each a
different direction.

span, facing opposite directions. In two-train installations,
if bridge spans two "northbound" tracks both signals should
face "south." If one of the tracks is "southbound," the
signal over it should face "north."

Each signal is provided with a set of contact clamps on
the bottom of the bridge base so that the signals may be
wired to operate either independently or together. More
complicated operations may be developed by adding signals
No. 450L, which may be bought at your dealers, and
mounted as desired to handle four-way traffic.

If you wish both green lights or both red lights to go on
at the same time inter-connect the two No. 1 and also the
two No. 2 clips in the bridge bases. If you want reverse
indication (one red and one green) interchange the con

nections between the two bases (No. 1 clips to No. 2 clips).

For independent operation of the two signals two 153C contactors should be used as shown in Figure 15.

For manual control of either or both signals substitute any ordinary single pole, double throw switch for the automatic 153C contactor, as in Figure 16. For hooking up the bridge in connection with insulated track blocks used for two train operation see instructions on 153 Block Signals in your general instruction booklet.

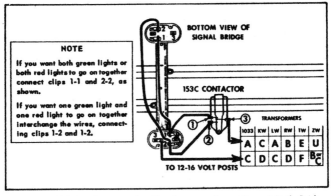

Figure 14—Wiring Diagram for Simultaneous Operation of Both Bridge Signals.

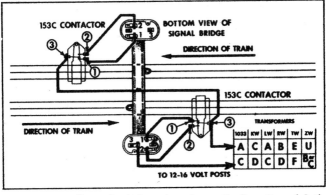

Figure 15—Installation for Independent Automatic Operation of Both Bridge Signals.

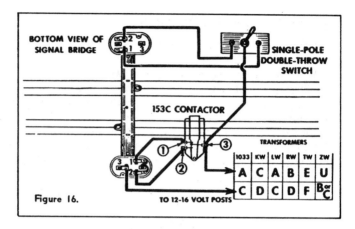

BOTTOM VIEW OF
SIGNAL BRIDGE

SINGLE-POLE
DOUBLE-THROW
SWITCH

153C CONTACTOR

TRANSFORMERS

1033	KW	LW	RW	TW	ZW
A	C	A	B	E	U
C	D	C	D	F	B or C

Figure 16.

TO 12-16 VOLT POSTS

Another type of train-control device available to model railroaders is No. 253 Block Signal and Control, which halts a train, then allows it to proceed after a few moments. A two-position signal is tied in with this operation, so that it appears the signal is controlling the train. The caution signal, which in three-position signals is indicated by the yellow light, is not used here. The normal aspect of the signal is red and the train reaching it stops each time. After a few seconds, the signal flashes green and the train proceeds.

In addition to three-indication and two-indication lights, another signaling device is sometimes used. This is the call-on signal described on the following page. Lionel's new No. 148 Dwarf Signal is ideal for the application as the green light is replaced by a yellow bulb.

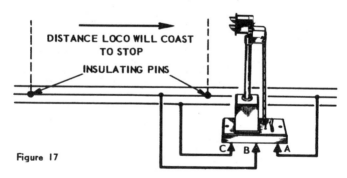

DISTANCE LOCO WILL COAST
TO STOP

INSULATING PINS

C   B   A

Figure 17

Usually, and always unless otherwise indicated, a red signal means stop. Without added information, an engineer cannot and must not pass a red light.

Added information may be given by a call-on signal. This will indicate a permissive red, and it may be given to a second section of a train. There are numerous other occasions when it may be used, most frequently near terminals or stations. (The only exception to a non-permissive red indication is on the rare occasion when a wrecking train is proceeding to an accident and must run through red lights.) When a call-on signal is used, a train will proceed with great caution, since something is blocking the track ahead.

We can adapt this call-on system to a model railroad. In the automatic system outlined previously, the most important thing was that a red signal automatically meant a dead section of track. The relay that gave the red indication also removed the current from third-rail trackage ahead of it.

In order to use a call-on system, we must first arrange to re-power the deadened third rail. The simplest and most complete method is shown below. Here a special button uses existing relays to reactivate the dead trackage.

Inserted in the system is a small signal showing red and yellow; this supplementary signal is the call-on. It is customarily placed below and slightly to one side of the main signal. Sometimes it is a dwarf signal, sometimes it is on a bracket jutting out to the right of the light standard.

By now it should be clear that signaling is no simple matter at all. There are, as a matter of fact, a number of other ways of indicating call-on signals, and some signal

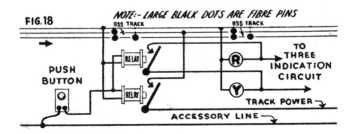

FIG. 18

NOTE:- LARGE BLACK DOTS ARE FIBRE PINS

FIG.19

systems us a lunar white light to indicate call-ons. On
other roads, certain lighting combinations not otherwise
used will give the call-on indication. If thorough coverage
of signaling is needed, a reference library must be con-
sulted for one of the standard works; all that is given here
is the most common model railroad usage.

Do not feel that lack of knowledge of railroad signal
systems brands you as an amateur. Even veteran engineers,
when traveling on a strange railroad, take a pilot aboard
to read the lights for them. Each major road has its own
system of lights, and only where two lines operate over the
same trackage, or where foreign trains customarily operate,
does an engineer of one road necessarily know the signals
of another.

Semaphores, on the other hand, are fairly standardized
as shown above. The train order board is a manual indication used at small stations or towers. In a vertical position
it means "no orders," but in a horizontal position it means
"proceed slowly to pick up orders." The orders will usually
be handed up on a hoop to the fireman as the train moves
by. The orders will cover any unusual departure from the
schedule.

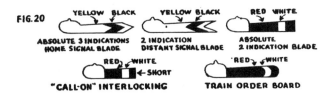

FIG.20

YELLOW BLACK   YELLOW BLACK   RED WHITE

ABSOLUTE 3 INDICATIONS   2 INDICATION   ABSOLUTE
HOME SIGNAL BLADE   DISTANT SIGNAL BLADE   2 INDICATION BLADE

RED   WHITE   RED   WHITE
                  ← SHORT

"CALL-ON" INTERLOCKING   TRAIN ORDER BOARD

Some typical signal placements are shown below and at the top of the opposite page. Where rail traffic keeps to the right, as on most U. S. roads, the signals are at the right so that they may be easily read as approached. Where multiple traffic exists, they will usually be mounted on a signal bridge and be directly over the track they control.

Below are some of the more recent signal innovations.

The Pennsylvania Railroad developed the position light by which the direction of the line of lights gives the signal. If one or more lights burn out, the signal can still operate. At all times, the signal can be read at a glance, and there is little chance of an engineer misreading the signal.

The Baltimore and Ohio Railroad uses a color position system which is similar, but with only two lamps for each position. Here there is double protection, since it is most unlikely for an engineer to misread both color and position.

The New York Central developed the searchlight signal, a penetrating light that strikes the engineer momentarily in the eyes. It is most difficult to ignore such a signal.

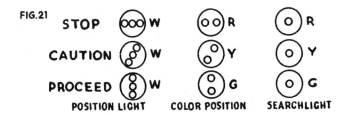

OPERATING

CHAPTER SEVEN

A MODEL RAILROAD that gives real pleasure to its owner should have three things: a good mechanical set-up; a good appearance; and varied, railroad-like operations.

None of these things will come immediately or without work. And none of them is fully separated from the others. Good trackwork and tablework, combined with careful wiring, make the mechanics of running trains a simple matter.

Good appearance is more than an aesthetic satisfaction —it will aid your operations.

By operating, of course, we do not mean the mere starting and stopping of trains. That is a mechanical matter. To model railroaders, operations cover the coordination and control of trains over the entire road during an entire running period.

To know operations, we will have to consider some facts about real railroads, how they run and how their operations apply to our model roads.

Railroads divide trains into as may as five classes. Some of these may be combined on a real road, and are even more likely to be combined on a small road. The classes are:

First Class: These are the crack trains of a line. Usually extra-fare trains, they are non-stop between major stations. The New York Central's *20th Century Limited* and the Santa Fe's *Chief* are examples. On a model railroad, this would be a streamlined set of cars pulled by the fastest locomotive.

Second Class: These are the passenger trains which make advertised connections between points on the road. They make limited stops at the larger cities or junctions along the main lines. On some roads, certain commuter trains which make limited stops are included in this class.

Third Class—This includes accommodation trains, the railroad term for trains making all stops along a route. If you have ever looked at a large passenger schedule, you will see that one or two trains a day fool along making every single stop. And it is amazing how many stops there are, though the through traveler is rarely conscious of them.

On most railroads, except for the very largest, the three classes above are combined into two. The combination depends on the type of traffic carried, but it can easily be seen that the first and second classes can be combined. Other roads might want to run one crack non-stop train, but other passenger traffic might justify only accommodation trains.

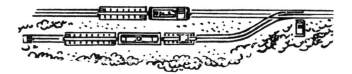

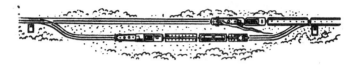

Fourth Class: Fast freight trains are included here. These are the express freights which whisk perishable commodities to major cities. They travel only from one major yard to another, and they do it with commendable speed. In addition to perishables, they will carry through shipments.

Fifth Class: The slow freights and way freights are the work-horses of the railroads. The difference is that the way freight goes only a few miles—usually well under a hundred—and sets out and picks up cars at private sidings. The slow freight travels between railroad yards, but covers all the small yards at junctions and stations. The slow freight travels on a schedule. The way freight has only travel orders, and hence on some roads is not considered fifth class, but is an extra.

Many railroads are so specialized that the classifications above are almost meaningless. A logging route may be a separate railroad, yet have only one passenger train a week. The coal branch of a main road may carry one accommodation train daily. On many short lines, there is only one mixed train daily—a train that serves all of the above purposes over the brief distance the road covers.

It is also obvious that most model railroads will have to make some compromises with the above classes. Large clubs can duplicate large road operations; small layouts can best duplicate smaller road layouts.

Even with a lesser railroad, or with a branch of a large road, deception is usually employed by the model railroader. One locomotive and one string of passenger cars may alternately serve as second- and third-class trains. A switch engine can double as a fifth-class train loco; and a freight engine may serve both fourth- and fifth-class trains. Thus three, or even two, locomotives can provide for all operations.

To know how this can be done, consider the way a real road moves its trains.

First- and second-class trains are made up in the passenger yards about an hour before train time. The diners have been serviced, and the club cars readied. Coaches, Pullmans and club and dining cars are moved to the proper track in the terminal or station. Meanwhile, baggage and mail cars are being readied on other tracks, then they are brought in and coupled up ahead of the other cars. Finally, the locomotive is backed into place and all lines attached.

At the proper time, the conductor will signal to the engineer and the train pulls out. The engineer is in charge as soon as the train moves, and he is controlled by the dispatcher, who must keep tracks clear for him. Once into a station and stopped, the train is in charge of the conductor, and the engineer will not go until he is given the signal.

When the train reaches its final destination, it is usually broken up in just the reverse of the order of making up.

During the trip, the first- or second-class train will have overtaken some passenger and some freight trains. In all cases they will have made way for it. Slow freights will have arranged to hole up in some convenient siding; fast freights will have cut off onto a long passing siding, and the accommodations will have been waiting at a station.

The accommodation train is made up in similar fashion, with the omission of the diner and club cars. There may be more baggage cars on it; the mail car may be left out. In some cases, the accommodation may carry milk cars, since even at its slow rate, it gives faster service than most freight trains. Along the road it makes every stop, often hardly gathering speed before it slacks off for the next stop.

Fourth-class trains are made up by yard switchers or by use of the hump in a main yard. Through shipments from major cities will have arrived, and locally originated shipments will be added. A locomotive, its size dependent on the load and the terrain, picks up the train, builds the air pressure and pulls out when the schedule and the conductor and dispatcher's signals say so. Once on the high iron, the engineer is in control and he retains control until a scheduled stop is made.

The slow freight and the way freight give way to everything on the railroad. The way freight has no rights at all, no set schedule. Yet it is, to most experienced model railroaders, the most interesting of all their trains.

It is the way freight that is pictured at the top and bottom of the preceding pages. It is the train that trundles along, picking up an empty car at this siding, dropping a full one at the next. In many cases, it will wind up with the locomotive in the center and cars fore and aft. At some convenient point, it will reshuffle the cars properly.

The way freight ducks off the main iron every time a scheduled train approaches. Its engineer and the conductor know the schedule of all trains on the division. They frequently check by phone with the dispatcher to check

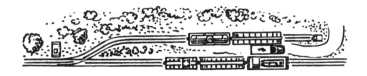

any late trains or any special trains. By this means, too, they receive orders en route. Since they know all trains and their approximate positions at all times, they are able to make sidings and clear block signals for through trains— at least, a really competent crew can do it.

A short line—usually considered as any road under 100 miles long—operates between two cities or small towns. Such roads are fast disappearing, either giving way to truck lines or being absorbed by large roads.

In many cases, there is only one train daily, and a combination baggage-passenger car at the end may serve as a caboose as well.

Many short lines serve a particular industry and may use special cars. A line serving a small iron-ore mine, for instance, or one serving a steel mill will use heavier cars than are usually found. A steel mill's line would have ladle cars for handling molten metal and slag.

Sometimes the short lines make connections between two major roads that are only about twenty to fifty miles distant at some point. In that case, they will usually advertise connections for both freight and passengers. Frequently such a road is owned by one or more of the industries it serves.

Railroads Run "By the Book"

Railroads are run by the book—the rule book. A schedule alone is not enough for a railroad, for one of the most certain things is that something will happen to any schedule. Trains will be late for many reasons. Rock slides and washouts will tie up tracks, trains, and schedules. Derailments and wrecks occur. Bridges catch fire. Special trains, such as circus trains, the President's train, or troop trains are run through. Anything can happen—and will happen if you wait long enough.

This means that there must be a method for coping with contingencies of this sort. The rule book is the answer.

In making up the rule book, railroads make use of a fabrication (even as modelers do). They assume that all trains run either North or South—regardless of what their actual route may be; or, on other lines, all trains are designated East or West. There are only two designations, and so a train which runs between two points on an East-West line may be called a Northbound train.

The reason for two designations seems to be so that the trains can be numbered, odd numbers running in one direction, even numbers in the other. This same method can be applied to model trains.

But first, back to the rule book. The thing which concerns us here is the rights of trains. In meets—as railroaders call the passing of trains in opposite directions—the train with the higher class has the right of way. When two trains meet and class is the same, one of the two directions is given the superior right.

In the event of emergencies, higher class trains have the right of way. This means that should a wreck occur, the dispatcher will work to get all first-class trains moving.

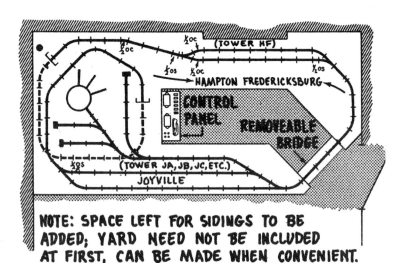

NOTE: SPACE LEFT FOR SIDINGS TO BE ADDED; YARD NEED NOT BE INCLUDED AT FIRST, CAN BE MADE WHEN CONVENIENT.

When they are all en route, second-class trains will move. And so down to fifth-class trains, which are considered last.

A night's operations on a model railroad can be handled in either of two ways. The first is easier by far, and is recommended, at least at first. It is program operation.

A workable program on the road opposite would be something like this:

No. 37 (passenger) leaves Joyville for Hampton
No. 442 (fast freight) is made up by switcher
No. 420 (slow freight) leaves Joyville for
    Fredericksburg
No. 420 takes siding at tower HF
No. 37 passes tower HF
No. 442 is delivered to siding at JA, picks up
    road engine
No. 37 passes tower JA
No. 442 leaves Joyville (JA) for Fredericksburg
No. 37 stops at Hampton
No. 420 leaves tower HF
No. 442 arrives tower HF, takes siding
No. 37 leaves Hampton for Joyville
No. 420 arrives tower JB
No. 442 arrives tower JB
No. 37 arrives tower JB, continues
No. 442 leaves tower JB
No. 37 arrives tower HF
No. 442 arrives Fredericksburg
No. 37 leaves tower HF for Joyville
No. 442 moves to classification yards
No. 37 arrives Joyville
No. 420 leaves tower JB
No. 420 arrives Fredericksburg
No. 420 moves to classification yards

Confusing? Not if you picture the layout at all times and if you constantly keep in mind that Joyville and towers JA, JB, and JC and so on are the same physical spot, and that Hampton and Fredericksburg are the same spot, depending on how they are approached, North or South. Tower HF is also at Hampton.

Trace the operation out. It is real, and the fictional changes of name and designation give trains time to pile up mileage while running several times around the layout.

The sample, of course, is on a very simple layout, a simple loop. The same principles, though, can be applied to a more complicated road.

Once the program has been worked out and tried, variations can be worked. An extra, running on train orders which supersede both class and direction, may be inserted. By trial and error, a program that has variety, reality, and interest can be arranged. It can be one that will give the operator problems in keeping time to the minimum.

Time? Why, of course—once you start running your program with an eye on the clock, you soon have time-table operation.

Run through the program three or four times and check the time carefully, preferably using a clock with a second hand. Set your timetable up in railroad-like fashion, showing arrival and departure time at each tower and siding, not just at passenger stations. Include passenger and freight trains—then you have a railroad-like operation.

At a station or terminal, you can add an imaginary junction with a large road. Here you can have large numbers of trains, and arrange your timetable so that you make the best connections for your passengers and your freight shippers.

If you can run well, get your operations right, who knows? Maybe new business will flock in, and you'll have to add trackage to take care of them. The operations are the heart of the road—and most of the fun, too.

LOCOMOTIVES

CHAPTER EIGHT

I N THEIR TIME, locomotives have inspired poetry, symphonic and jazz music, folksongs, and a host of books and sections of books. Their power, dominance, and rugged beauty make them the most fascinating part of model railroading. This chapter will explain real and model locomotives; for more detailed information, check any encyclopaedia.

Diesel Locomotives

Despite the moaning of old-time railroaders (who cry like a wounded doe when a high-stepping Pacific is scrapped for a noisy, foul-smelling oil burner) the Diesel is fast replacing the steam engine. It will probably confine

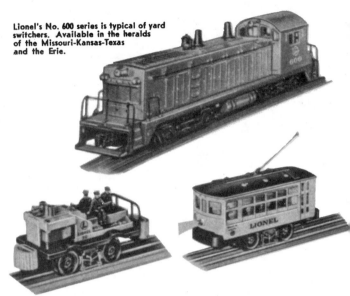

Lionel's No. 600 series is typical of yard switchers. Available in the heralds of the Missouri-Kansas-Texas and the Erie.

Although not classed as locomotives, these two motorized units are highly popular with model fans. Left is the Lionel Gang Car—right the Trolley. Both reverse direction when end buffers strike an object like a bumper.

electrics to those lines which are already powered.

In twenty-seven years, the Diesel has come to the front in railroading. However justified the regret of the old-timers—and it is certainly true that no Diesel ever had the appeal of a clean, swift engine whose every valve was laid bare as she ran past—they are here for good.

Most Diesels are actually Diesel-electric. The Diesel engines drive electric generators. The current from these drives electric motors that are geared directly to the wheels. This is done for efficiency, but it also results in an unusually smooth pulling effort and ease of reversing.

Diesels are economical in operation. Their fuel consumption is low, so that they can travel much greater runs without refueling. In general, Diesels fall into about five common types. Switchers are of two different types—yard switchers and road switchers for mainline switching and commuter service. There are high-power freights, high-power passengers, and there are dual-purpose Diesels that will handle either type of haul.

On page 99 are shown Lionel models of various types of

Diesels. At the top is the GM F3 Santa Fe twin-motored double-A unit. Twin-motored A-B combination can be purchased with the colors and insignia of the Denver & Rio Grande. A similar one-motored combination is offered with the colorful markings of the New Haven. Another twin-motored hauler is the 2400 horsepower Fairbanks-Morse "Trainmaster" used by the Virginian Railway Company.

The GM Electro-Motive Division's Type GP-7 (general purpose) engine can be had with the markings of the Wabash and a later type GP-9 in the fire engine red of the Minneapolis & St. Louis.

Santa Fe Diesel double-A units.

Denver & Rio Grande A and B units.

Fairbanks-Morse Diesel.

GP-7 (General purpose) Diesel.

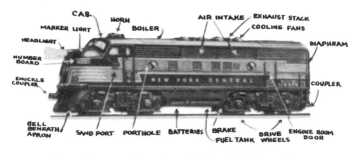

CAB
HORN
MARKER LIGHT   BOILER
HEADLIGHT
NUMBER BOARD
KNUCKLE COUPLER
AIR INTAKE   EXHAUST STACK
COOLING FANS
DIAPHRAM
COUPLER
BELL BENEATH APRON   SAND PORT   PORTHOLE   BATTERIES   BRAKE   DRIVE WHEELS   ENGINE ROOM DOOR
FUEL TANK

Shown above are the major parts of a diesel locomotive.

From a model-railroad point of view, Diesels offer one advantage similar to those offered to real railroads: they eliminate the need for large, involved engine yards. Since they run in either direction, they do not need a turntable or a wye—and they require little in the way of servicing.

A later chapter tells how to make a Diesel yard, and it also stresses why you should eventually have an entire engine yard. At first it may be advantageous to omit the fully detailed steam-locomotive yards.

The GM GP9 looks a lot like the GP7 but has the characteristic dynamic brake "blisters."

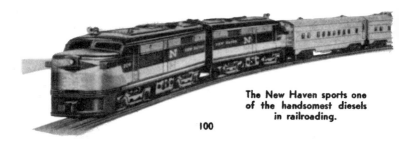

The New Haven sports one of the handsomest diesels in railroading.

A vast improvement over a steam locomotive cab, is the cab of a Diesel. Engineers are not roasted in the summer. Visibility is much better and they are comfortable in the winter. Cabs are heated, and controls are more convenient. These engines, in addition to the "Independent" brake (engine only) and "train" brake, have the "Dynamic" brake, which is a device whereby the motors act as brakes when going down long grades.

Many Diesels are equipped with a steam-boiler used to heat passenger cars and are equally at home either tooling along long strings of freight cars or high-balling a line of gleaming passenger streamliners. They can be double, triple or even quadruple-headed, depending on the power requirements of the moment and will run just as happily with either No. 1 or No. 2 end forward.

The Diesels' real claims to superiority over the steam locomotives lie in their ability to travel farther without refueling and their cheaper maintenance. The saving in maintenance involves not only shop repair but track repair. There is no evidence that a Diesel can outrun a steam locomotive over a given distance—but to achieve the speed of the Diesel the steam engine has a tendency to "kink" the tracks. The alternating movement of the driving gear of a steam locomotive results in a rolling motion, called "nosing," similar to the rocking motion of a pacing horse. At high speeds this produces rail "kinks." The axle-driven power of the Diesels does not produce this effect.

The savings in shop maintenance are illustrated in the picture below. When a steam engine comes in for check, it remains in the roundhouse while boilers, driving gear and everything else are inspected. As far as the railroad is concerned, the locomotive is "out of business" for a considerable period of time. When the Diesel is brought into shop they merely remove the top (like lifting the lid off a teakettle) and replace the Diesel motor or generator— the whole process can take place in four or five hours.

The refueling advantage of the Diesel is obvious to all railroaders, for in the railroading business time is of the essence.

Here is the interior of a Diesel Locomotive Shop.

Photo courtesy of Electro-Motive

Photo courtesy Lackawanna R.R.

This Lackawanna double A Diesel is the 1500 H.P. "G.E." type, used for either passenger or freight.

The Road Switcher is so called because it is used for yard work as well as short runs on the main line. These Diesels are often used in tandem like the passenger "A" units.

Here's the Diesel "yard bird" with plenty of pulling power and a catlike ability to stop and start fast. These switchers are available in model form.

The big "growler"—a GM A-B-A combination hauling a long streamliner along New York Central's Hudson River line.

Photos courtesy of New York Central R.R.

PASSENGER TYPES		
CLASSIFICATION	**WHEEL ARRANGEMENT**	**TYPE STYLE**
ATLANTIC		4-4-2
PACIFIC		4-6-2
HUDSON		4-6-4
NORTHERN		4-8-4
FREIGHT TYPES		
COLUMBIA		2-4-2
PRAIRIE		2-6-2
BERKSHIRE		2-8-4
SANTA FE		2-10-2
SWITCHER TYPES		
SWITCHER		0-4-0
SWITCHER		0-6-0
SWITCHER		0-8-0

Steam Locomotives

A steam locomotive is basically a simple machine consisting of two parts. First, a firebox and boiler that generates steam, and second, the "engine." The engine has cylinders in which steam pressure pushes pistons and driving rods to turn the wheels.

Of course, by the time all of the safety devices, automatic feeds, and reversing units are added, the complete locomotive is pretty complex. Also, today's locomotives are made to perform different jobs.

There are three main types of locomotives: freight, passenger, and switch engines. The diagram above shows a number of the most common engines. They are classified by wheel arrangement from front to rear. Thus, a locomotive with a two-wheel pilot truck (pony wheels), six driving wheels, and a two-wheel trailing truck is a 2-6-2. It is also called a Prairie type. If the trailing truck is omitted, it is called a Mogul, or a 2-6-0. Leave off the pilot

Lionel's famous 0-4-0 switcher is a powerful steam yard goat.

A 4-6-4 for heavy passenger and freight hauling.

Another 4-6-4 loco with a feedwater heater at the head end.

The Berkshire 2-8-4 is perfect for passenger or freight use.

This is the Pennsy RR's 20-wheel turbine which has internal driving gears.

A typically beautiful 4-6-4 model locomotive in a real-as-life setting. Like most Lionel locomotives, it is equipped with Magne-Traction.

truck as well, and it becomes an 0-6-0 switcher.

Today, quite a few locomotives are dual-purpose. They will haul passengers at a fast clip, or they can knuckle down and walk off with a string of freight cars. This makes it difficult to make a hard-and-fast rule about types.

However, it is usually true that dual-purpose locomotives have a four-wheel trailing truck to support the large firebox. With more than eight driving wheels, the locomotive will usually handle freight. A small locomotive with two or with no trailing wheels is usually a passenger loco.

Also, as a rule, freight locomotives have smaller drivers than passenger engines. This gives them much greater power, while large drivers deliver passenger speeds.

Switch engines have small wheels, and all of them are drivers. This enables them to make the sharp turns in passenger and freight yards. They have little speed; but as small as they are, they can trundle off a string of cars that would spin the drivers of much bigger engines. Their sizes range from 0-4-0 up to 0-10-0.

For extremely heavy freight loads—perhaps a string of loaded coal cars in mountainous country—articulated locos are used. These consist of an extremely long boiler and a vast firebox. Under the boiler are two sets of cylinders driving two sets of wheels. Looking at the side of one, you see the pilot truck in front, then the cylinder with a set of driving wheels, then another cylinder and another set of driv-

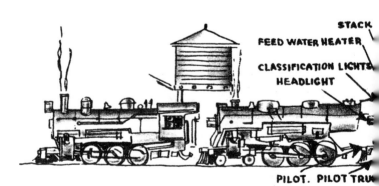

STACK

FEED WATER HEATER

CLASSIFICATION LIGHTS

HEADLIGHT

PILOT.   PILOT TRU

ing wheels, then a trailing truck. It is as if two locomotive frames had been put under one boiler.

These locomotives are so long that they must be hinged in the middle, and for this reason they are called "articulated." They are designated as 4-8-8-2 (Mallet—rhymes with ballet), 2-8-8-4 (Yellowstone), and several other classifications. Mallets vary somewhat in wheel arrangement, and the word is often used to mean all sorts of articulated steam locomotives.

Tenders vary a great deal. Those for short runs are usually small, while those for heavy freight work, which must carry a large supply of coal and water, are much larger. The trucks may have four or six wheels. Incidentally, the day of hand firing is almost completely gone; most engines have automatic stokers regulated by the fireman.

The locomotive below is marked so that you can recognize the major parts and their purpose.

Beginning at the front, there is the pilot (cowcatcher) and the pilot wheels. On the pilot beam is mounted the front coupler. Above is the smoke box, the front part of which is the smoke-box door. The cylinder is topped by the valve box, known as a steam chest. A valve rod leads to it; just behind are the valve hangers and the valve gear. From the cylinder comes a piston rod leading to a crosshead. This is attached to the main connecting rod. Along the wheels is the side rod.

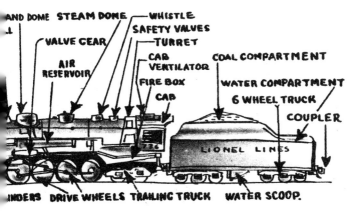

When you choose a steam locomotive look for accuracy in superstructure design as well as in movement of driving gear. Here are two
Lionel beauties—wonderful to watch in action.

On top of the boiler is the stack, and back of it is the
sand dome. A ton or more of sand can be stored here for
starts on icy tracks and emergency stops. The other dome
is a steam dome which houses the whistle controls and the
throttle valve. Also on top are the bell, the whistle and
safety valves.

Along the side of the boiler are the running boards, and
suspended from these are air drums. These hold high-
pressure air for the brakes. Also under the running boards
are the air pumps.

Just forward of the cab is the large section of the boiler
called the firebox. This contains the fire, the grates, and
the flue that takes the heat past the steam pipes. In here
is a superheater that heats the steam above boiling so that
it will retain its live-steam properties as it is used.

On the trucks of the pilot wheels and the trailing wheels
are small doors about six inches square. These are the
doors to the packing boxes, which contain oil-soaked packing that lubricates the journals.

On the tender of some models a small scoop can be seen
underneath the flooring. This is used to pick up water

while the train is running. The railroad has a long trough—up to half a mile long—with about a foot of water in it. When the tender is over the trough, the scoop is dropped into it. The water is forced up into the tender by the speed of the train. This method saves a stop that would take some time at a water tower or standpipe.

On page 105 are shown some of the Lionel locomotives that are modeled from drawings of real engines. Most of them will be recognizable, and they are all dual-purpose locomotives. They can be used for freight or passenger work. If possible, an engine with four-wheel leading truck should be used on commuter passenger runs. At most, it should haul a very light freight train, perhaps a peddler freight that pokes along from siding to siding, dropping a car here and there. Of course, it can actually pull a very long string of cars at a good fast rate. But if you have a choice of engines from your engine yard, pick something heavier to handle your long, fast, scheduled trips.

Notice also the steam turbine engine second from bottom. This is a model made for the Pennsylvania Railroad, and does not operate like the conventional locomotive. In this case, the steam that is generated turns a turbine that is geared to the axles. Since all this is internal, nothing shows on the outside except the steam tube leading to the turbine and the main side rod that drives the other wheels. This locomotive makes a different noise, too. There is no chugging sound; instead, there is a steady hissing.

The rest of the locomotives shown are types commonly seen, and all are powerful fast-stepping dual-purpose locos.

This is a 4-6-6-4 Mallet Articulated Locomotive used for hauling tremendous freight trains.

The magnificent "Hudson" 4-6-4 was first developed by the New York Central. Although, in a sense, a "high-wheeler" it was also a famous freight-hauler.

This big 4-8-4 has many names, one of them the "Niagara." Another dual-purpose engine, used for freight or passenger. This one is equipped with a pair of "ear-muff" smoke deflectors at the head end.

Next to the "Hudson," the hard-working 2-8-4 "Berkshire" shown here is one of most widely known steam locomotives in the country. Note the small diameter of the driving wheels.

Steam yard switchers come in all sizes and descriptions, depending on the type of work they have to do. Wheel combinations are usually 0-6-0 or 0-8-0, giving them maneuverability on short curves. Driving wheels are always small.

The No. 746 N&W "Niagara" Locomotive

This new addition to Lionel's stable of "iron horses" is a scale-detailed model of the Norfolk & Western's coal-burning, streamlined, 4-8-4, Class J passenger locomotive, designed and built in N&W's own Roanoke shops.

The Norfolk and Western services the coal country of the Virginias, Kentucky and Ohio, deriving 70 percent of its tonnage and 60 percent of its revenue from hauling coal, and is one of the last big and successful proponents of coal-burning steamers, not only for freight, but also for passenger service.

One of the most modern of all steam locomotives, this 250-ton, 16-wheel giant is also one of the few outstandingly successful efforts to streamline steam locomotives. Its bullet-nosed jacket follows the contour of the huge boiler, giving a powerful jet-black silhouette, which is relieved by a bold band of Tuscan red at the running board level.

Lionel's No. 746, together with its matching tender, is a strikingly successful adaptation of this powerful locomotive, constructed to operate on "0" and Super "0" track. It is driven by a well-proven, worm-geared electric motor. Its heavy, die-cast body and frame, together with an oversize Alnico magnet which provides it with Magne-Traction, combine to make No. 746 the most powerful steam-type locomotive in the Lionel line.

Electric Locomotives

The first electric locomotives were used in this country about 1901. Installation was expensive, and the movement lagged until 1902, when the New York legislature prohibited steam engines from entering the heart of New York City.

Both the Pennsylvania and the roads now known as the New York Central and the New York, New Haven and Hartford had to electrify. Eventually all of these lines were electrified for long distances; the Pennsy's GG-1's now reach all the way to Harrisburg, Pennsylvania.

The original electrics were boxlike engines, and since they had little need for the touches that lend charm to a steam locomotive, they remained this way until the Pennsylvania Railroad designed the GG-1. It is an articulated 4-6-0+0-6-4, and can be used on passenger or freight work. It is rated at 4,620 hp. which compares very favorably with the 6,000 hp. rating given to a three-unit Diesel.

These locomotives operate equally well in either direction, the only necessary effort being to move the engineer and to raise one pantograph and lower the other. In operating, the rearmost pantograph is always used, the reason for this being that should the pantograph foul in the overhead wires, it will not carry away the other. Thus, one is saved as a spare in case of need.

A miniature GG-1 made by Lionel faithfully duplicates the original and includes working pantographs. With a simple rewiring these can be used to carry the operating current for anyone who wants to make a complete catenary suspension. Ready made catenary components are available in most hobby shops.

A recent advance in electric locomotion has been the development of rectifier locomotives which utilize banks of mercury vapor rectifier tubes to convert the easily transmitted and controlled alternating current to the needs of powerful and efficient direct current traction motors.

Two types of rectifier locomotives modeled by Lionel and illustrated on this page include GE's new Type EL-C built for The Virginian Railway for heavy duty hauling across the Appalachians and the unusual dual-duty New Haven locomotive which negotiates the heavily travelled New York-New Haven run switching from 660-volt D.C. third rail power supply in New York City to 11,000-volt A.C. overhead lines outside the city limits.

Other types of electric trains include the multiple unit (MU) cars, familiar to thousands of commuters. These cars are each powered by their own trucks, and gather their current from their own third-rail shoes or pantographs. However, they are all controlled by one engineer.

Electric locomotives will retain their importance for many years to come, both in the East and in the Rockies,

where long tunnels make steam engines impractical. Their function is very real, but is probably limited to the present usage.

The major advancement in the department of electrified locomotion has been the recent in design, both interior and exterior, of the rolling stock. You probably have noticed in preceding pages how much the electric engines are being patterned after the new Diesel types. The illustrations on this page also show the transition. At the top is an earlier type "Box Cab," 0-6-0 switcher, equipped with pantograph for overhead catenary operation. Bottom picture shows one of the latest in MU trains, just put into service, with longer, roomier, air-conditioned coaches.

Electric power will probably be used in metropolitan and suburban service for a long time. It is clean, odorless and efficient.

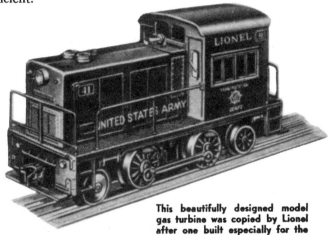

This beautifully designed model gas turbine was copied by Lionel after one built especially for the U.S. Army Transportation Corps.

Gas Turbines

One of the newest experiments in the field of railroad locomotion has been the development of the gas-turbine engine. The experiment was started by certain railroads and coal industries who believed that an efficient turbo-electric plant could be created that would burn coal as fuel.

Turbines like these were first tried out as stationary plants, built within the limits of locomotive dimensions. After tests it was the opinion of the engineers that a locomotive of this sort could be constructed that could use coal as fuel. A few of these locomotives are now in service, still in the experimental stage.

Many of these gas-turbines resemble the normal Diesels. They differ in the interior in that they include two 2000 H.P. turbine-generator sets with a central aisle between them. The usual wheel arrangement is four 4-wheel trucks. All axles are motored. They are geared to speeds of about 100 miles per hour.

Rail Cars

There is certainly nothing new about the rail car except the new types of locomotion and the new uses the railroads are making of them.

Practically everybody is familiar with the old interurban trolley car, which served the same relative purpose. Many people, however, do not remember that railroads used individual rail cars, powered by gasoline motors, for passenger transportation back in the days of the first World War.

Illustrated above is a Budd-built Rail Diesel Car (RDC for short) which are becoming increasingly popular on many railroads servicing suburban areas. Light, efficient and comfortable, self-powered RDC's carry suburbanites, baggage and mail beyond the terminals of catenary or third-rail systems. The illustrated RDC-1 carries about 80 passengers. Other models serve as combination passenger and baggage cars and there is even an RDC mail car. RDC's are operated singly or two or three coupled. Lionel makes both motorized and trail passengers and mail RDC's.

Model Locomotive Motors

No matter what the model locomotive pretends to be, it is usually powered by an electric motor (a very few are driven by live steam). Such a motor consists of an armature which revolves inside a field. The armature is a series of coils wound on a shaft; the field is magnetically induced by a permanent magnet or a series of coils on a soft-iron core.

The ends of the armature coils are soldered to the commutator. This is a ring which is split into several parts, and brushes made of copper-graphite ride against it. The wiring is in series, which means that after the current passes

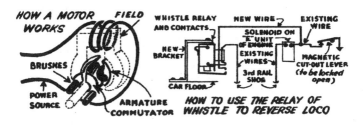

through the coils it goes to the field windings before completing its circuit.

The principle is as follows: One core of the armature is attracted to one side of the field the instant current is introduced. It is an electro-magnetic attraction, and the brushes are touching the commutator. As the coil nears the center of the magnetic field, that contact is broken. The attraction no longer exists, and that particular coil is free to be attracted by the opposite field.

Meanwhile, the coil that followed it in rotation was in turn attracted, and the attraction broken. This process continues until the current ceases.

On this type of motor, if the wires to the brushes are reversed, the motor rotates in the opposite direction. In each Lionel locomotive is an "E" unit which has the

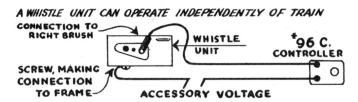

function of changing the wiring. Any interruption of the current actuates a small solenoid-and-pawl arrangement. This is rigged so that the unit changes from forward to neutral to reverse to neutral with successive interruptions of the current.

Locomotive Care and Maintenance

Locomotives and other model-railroad equipment are not toys, and they should not be given rough handling. They will stand considerable abuse, it is true; but they will last longer and work better if they are well treated.

Cleanliness is important to good functioning. Wipe your track regularly with a cloth dampened with cleaning fluid. Keep engines free from dust and dirt; do not wrap equipment in cloth that sheds lint.

Read your instruction manual carefully. Proper lubrication is imperative, otherwise sluggish operation will result. Never use too much oil. If oil gets into the electric motor and the "E" unit, they will function very poorly, or perhaps not at all. Oil and grease on driving wheels will kill the traction.

Oil according to the manual. Don't be afraid to disassemble parts of the locomotive where necessary, but do it gently. Never use force. Don't remove driving wheels; the axles can be bent and it will be extremely difficult to get the wheels on correctly.

When used sensibly and according to instructions, most model railroad equipment—certainly Lionel—is virtually indestructible, and it should last a lifetime.

PASSENGER TRAINS

CHAPTER NINE

PASSENGER TRAINS are a great problem to the railroads. With few exceptions, passenger revenue is a minor part of railroad income. Yet the railroads spend disproportionate sums of money and employ a large percentage of their personnel on passenger work. Even though contradictory, there is logic to this.

The government requires most railroads to maintain passenger trains, and even the one-train-a-day short lines have passenger service as a rule. Since they have to provide the service, the railroads try to do an efficient job of it. They have to have passenger agents and stations anyway, and they want them utilized as thoroughly as possible.

So we have a condition where the railroads spend time and money on a section of travel which often makes them lose money. In hopes of breaking even, they carry on heavy competition. Then, too, they know that they gain good

New Lionel Streamlined Pullmans are long, beautiful cars.

public relations from good passenger trains—and that is wise, even if it cannot be entered on the books.

Although there are many different kinds of passenger trains, they divide roughly into two groups: (1) local suburban runs up to about sixty miles; and (2) through Pullman and coach runs. These are not clear divisions, for they overlap in many cases.

A local train will consist only of coaches and one or two baggage cars. If there is any mail section, it will most likely be a part of the baggage car. There are no diners, Pullmans or observation cars.

The way these various types of trains are made up appear in six illustrations on page 123. The top train is a three-coach local, usually used for small way stops and generally known as an "accommodation" train. This same type too is widely used in "commuter" trains, especially in the New York and Chicago areas.

The second illustration is that of a train ordinarily

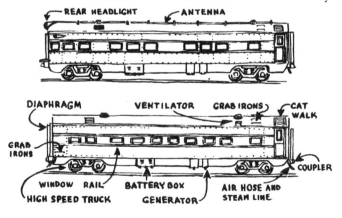

Vista Dome car is a model of the latest type.

used on a single division and usually consists of a baggage car, mail coach, a single large passenger coach and, because of a long run, a diner on the end.

The third train shown is more rarely seen and usually is a "Special." It has, probably, a day's run—few, but first class passengers. It consists of a coach, diner and an observation club car.

The fourth train down on the panel is frequently seen during the middle of the night, taking milk to the city. It consists of two milk cars, a baggage car and an accommodation coach. It's a real local, and stops at every station. Underneath it appears a three-coach combination with a single milk car on the rear. This train is deadheading a milk car back to country.

The sixth and last illustration is that of a combination accommodation and commuter train consisting of a baggage car, a mail car, a combination coach and a lounge, or club car on the rear. It carries mail, and second class passenger accommodations.

The most common order of cars in passenger trains is: locomotive, baggage car, mail car, coaches, diner, Pullmans, observation car. Occasionally a baggage car and one or two coaches will be at the rear, and these will usually be dropped at a branch to be picked up by another train or

Observation Lounge is car coupled to end of train.

engine. On short lines—100 miles or under—it is not unusual to find coaches coupled with freight cars in any convenient arrangement.

Some of the more common arrangements are shown
above and at the bottom of preceding pages.

Lionel coaches, Pullmans, and milk cars will run on "0"
and "027" track. Cars include Pullmans with the clerestory
roofs. These are not streamlined, and are modeled after the
older styles of Pullman cars.

There are also Pullmans of the streamlined variety with
smooth roofs, including an observation car with a boat-tail
end similar to ones seen on crack passenger trains.

Another series of cars is made, which are quite short
and can be used as commuter coaches. However, they do
not include an observation car.

For the milk car you can use the operating milk car
from which a man pops out and shoves cans onto a platform. In addition, you can get several similarly marked
cars which are non-operating.

In making up your passenger trains, try to follow rail-

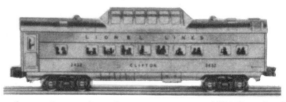

These shortened streamliners for narrower curves of "027" track include
the Vista-Dome pullman.

This line includes the pullmans "Elizabeth" and "Newark," and the
observation car "Summit."

road procedure as much as possible. Of course, ten- or fifteen-car trains will be out of the question. But many fast trains are run with only four coaches or Pullmans.

The trick to following railroad procedure comes in the operation. If possible, shift the cars about with a switch engine before delivering them to the terminal or the ready track. Have the engine back up to them at the last moment, then pull into the station and wait quite a while.

In running a fast train, remember that your engine can pull the cars at speeds far beyond scale, so even expresses should be throttled down. Remember, too, that there are reduced speed zones on any road.

A suburban local makes plenty of stops, and yours should too. Never let the speed work up very high, and make the runs seem shorter than for your through trains. This can be done by cutting the run short at some point.

A collector's item—Lionel 6-wheel pullmans, no longer in production, are excellent models of older type passenger cars.

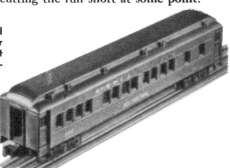

Photo, Courtesy New York Central R.R.
One of the new stream-lined New York Central baggage cars.

Photo, Courtesy New York Central R.R.
A shiny silver, "solid" roomette Pullman destined for the Middlewest.

Photo, Courtesy New York Central R.R.
One of the new New York Central diners. In standard grey colors.
(Below) A new stream-lined "tavern" lounge car on the Lackawanna Railro
Photo, Courtesy Delaware, Lackawanna and Western R.

FREIGHT TRAINS

I T IS ODD that most people are fascinated by the flashing streamliners of the railroads, but are little concerned with the freight trains. This can be accounted for only by lack of knowledge; for freight is by far the most interesting and exciting of railroad operations, real or model. It is not fascinating because it produces the most revenue for the roads, but rather because it produces the maximum in train movement.

Let us trace one movement by one car. A freight car of any type may be loaded for merchandise in New Haven, Conn., with material destined to Pittsburgh, Penna. It could travel by any one of many routes, but we will follow only one.

From the factory siding, a peddler freight picks up the loaded car by order, perhaps dropping an empty in its place. From there it is taken to a classification yard with other cars picked up by the way freight. It is then made up with any others in the yard headed the same way.

At Philadelphia, the New Haven train will be broken up and new trains will be formed. A through freight picks up the Pittsburgh cars and heads over the mountains, perhaps picking up and dropping cars on the way.

In Pittsburgh, the car will be dropped, probably at a hump, and made up into a small local freight and a peddler will deliver it to the consignee. Again the peddler may pick up a car that has already been emptied or loaded on the siding.

That is quite a bit of variety for one trip, quite unlike the routine of a passenger run.

Freight cars offer variety themselves, although coupler heights and other features have been standardized. Common types are gondolas, flat cars, hopper cars, tank cars, and house cars. Special cars are made for many purposes; and cabooses round out the list. All of the cars vary in size, shape, and features. Most variety is found in house cars,

Lionel's new operating box car is the "Pacemaker."

The green and yellow "Rutland" adds color to any train.

Lionel operating cranes are authentic models of real Bucyrus R.R. cranes. The wrecker caboose is a companion for crane.

among which are automobile cars, cattle cars, refrigerator cars, box cars, and other types.

Some idea of types will be found on the opposite page and on the following page, but these do not include such special cars as ladle cars which handle molten slag, ore cars, and others far too numerous to include in a general book.

Doors are highly varied on box cars, and range from the wide doors that admit automobiles to the narrow double doors of refrigerator cars. These "reefer" doors are always very thick for insulating purposes.

Many box cars and even more gondolas have ends which can be opened. The car can be run against a ramp at the tracks' end, and autos, trucks, or other vehicles run off. Also, lift-trucks can enter and pick up loads.

Wooden cars may be single- or double-sheathed, having one or two layers of siding. Most steel cars today have ribs on the inside and are double-sheathed.

Cars vary from 30' to 70' in length, and even then an occasional long bridge beam will have to be slung on two

A new type double dump car. Each half section can be unloaded separately. This Lionel model is remote control operated.

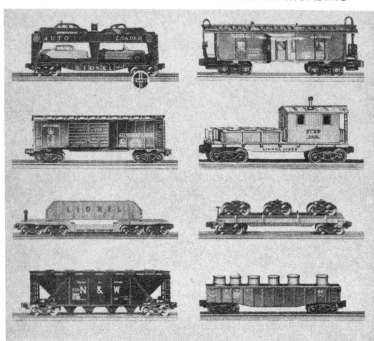

Above, left to right: Evans auto transport car, bay window caboose,
automobile car, work caboose, 16-wheel well car with girder, rail truck
car, covered hopper, and gondola. These are Lionel models.

cars and pivoted to make turns.

L. C. L. freight (less-than-carload-lots) are often handled
by a system of containers, four or five to a flat car or gondola. These can be swung off one at a time. This gives
the shipper nearly standard freight rates despite the small-
ness of his volume of business.

These loads can be taken off by the railroad's "big hook."
These cranes, which work with wrecking trains and work
trains, are necessary equipment of a big road. At strategic
points, a full wrecking train is ready for action on roads; for
in case of wrecks, traffic must be untangled as quickly
as possible. The wrecking trains, with their tool cars, bunk
cars, and tenders, make up the work trains, with such

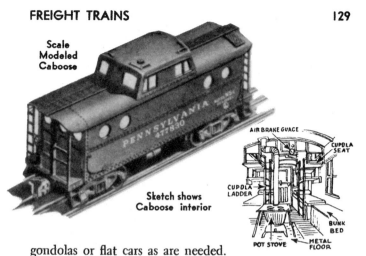

Scale Modeled Caboose

Sketch shows Caboose interior

AIR BRAKE GUAGE
CUPOLA SEAT
CUPOLA LADDER
BUNK BED
POT STOVE
METAL FLOOR

gondolas or flat cars as are needed.

Dump cars are possibly the most common of all specialty cars, since they save a great amount of time over other methods of unloading. (Hopper cars frequently have to be joggled by machinery or prodded by hand before loads flow out the small openings at the bottom.) As with gondolas and hoppers, dump cars haul almost any coarse material that is weather-resistant.

Tank cars are a very special grouping, and may haul anything from liquid oxygen to milk. Often they are contained within box cars and may be insulated. The variety of liquids required by industry seems endless, and so do the cars that haul them. The roughest breakdown seems to be by

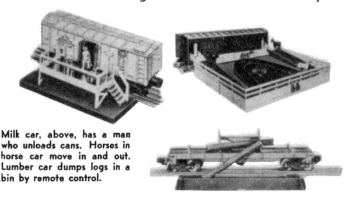

Milk car, above, has a man who unloads cans. Horses in horse car move in and out. Lumber car dumps logs in a bin by remote control.

domes, each dome covering a separate compartment. There may be as many as five domes to a car; but the most common type is the single-dome car. It frequently carries oil.

Lionel makes single- and double-dome cars, and these can be plausibly used to carry oil. The single-dome cars would pick up oil at the well and take it to the refinery; the double-dome cars would get gasoline and lubricating oil (or fuel oil) at the refinery and take it to its destination.

Missouri Pacific box car is scale-modeled.

Handling freight cars on a model railroad should parallel real railroad procedure. Through freights will arrive at your yard areas. There they must be broken down and reshuffled. Many cars will be picked up by a peddler freight, which may be pulled by your switch engine.

Before moving any cars, though, figure out where each one will go. The peddler, or way freight, will drop cars at one or another of your industries. It may pick up others. Once you have decided upon their destinations, just as a

Lionel's model of a 3-dome tank car.

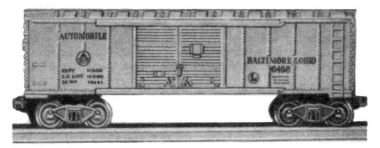

Authentic model of an automobile car—has 2 doors—
is blue with silver letters.

4 AUTOS CAN BE LOADED INTO A 40 ft AUTO-
- MOBILE CAR LIKE THIS. 60 ft CARS WILL HOLD 6.

dispatcher would, assemble them behind the engine by a
rule of thumb: "First on; first off." That is, cars nearest the
locomotive will be dropped off first. Cars picked up will
stay behind the locomotive.

This system will save one switching operation, since if
the last car was first off, the caboose would have to be un-
coupled, then picked up again.

All of this will take some time, and that is as it should
be. Efficient switching with a minimum number of moves
will save you time; on a real road it would also save money.

As was explained under Operations, this time spent in
handling freight can be used to give reality to the trips your

Model of an
up-to-date
flat car.

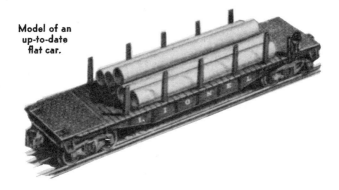

passenger equipment takes. For instance, an express is sent out and after some maneuvering is concealed by a tunnel or cut. Then, immediately, the switcher churns about the yard—which actually may consist of one or two sidings—and makes up a train, takes it out, and places the cars. When it is some distance off, it can be side-tracked to make

Another interesting Lionel box car.

way for the express which is only now returning from a grueling and fast trip.

Of such stuff is good model railroading made.

All of these cars should be carefully handled, of course. The operating cars should be used only as instructed—they can be damaged by mishandling. A drop or two of oil on the wheels—not too much—will save wear on cars and engines. A light oiling of the operating mechanisms will often help. Do not get oil in the solenoids that operate most cars, for it may impair or prevent action.

This will help you recognize parts of cars.

Single-dome tank car, usually used for oil and gas shipments to dealers in smaller towns.

A gondola of the 72-ton, fish-belly type used in shipment of coal, sand, gravel, and sometimes steel pipe.

50-ton flat car used in transportation of steel rails, pipe, poles, lumber and especially in wartime movement of Army guns and tanks.

90-ton hopper car, used by the large coal roads. The newest of these, in addition to the hopper dumps, have let-down sides for dumping by cranes.

Old-fashioned stock car used for shipment of sheep, cattle and hogs. Newer models are equipped with feed and drinking troughs.

A caboose with bay windows which trainmen praise for its advantages in overlooking their train while in motion.

YARD
BUILDINGS

THE SMALLEST railroad must have some sort of yard facilities for engine care. Where steam engines are used, a turn-around must be provided; and for any engine, service facilities must be available.

Yards should be small in the beginning. If your road has one or two locomotives, then yard requirements can be reduced. If there are many locomotives, you'll need one or two fair-sized yards. Build it up from the one or two key tracks, and don't be afraid to combine freight yards, passenger yards, and engine yards into one group first.

In the yard above, the full treatment is given locomotives, and the yard would handle half a dozen or more locomotives, though not all at one time. Even so, the yard uses few switches, and if one or more sidings are omitted, or if the stub track for loading coal were combined with another industrial track, the whole yard might be managed with two switches. As arranged here, it would take up a large amount of space.

Below is a smaller yard which uses an engine house. The profusion of switches is caused by the wye—which is used instead of a turntable, as above. The road was designed to fit into a very narrow space, perhaps the side of a hill; thus it takes very little running space from the track area. By combining these and other ideas, you should be able to work out a modest yard for yourself.

The Locomotive Transfer Table.

Roundhouse to Squarehouse

In model railroading, as well as in prototype, the famous old roundhouse-turntable combination, shown on the previous pages, is rapidly being supplanted by the transfer table and the "square" engine house.

Instead of the awkward old system of turning the engine into one of the "spokes" of the roundhouse, the transfer table merely slides the rail, with engine on it, to a parallel track, so that it can proceed to its proper stall for repair.

At shops using transfer tables, or in smaller engine yards which use a "wye" instead of a turntable as a turnabout point, as on page 135, rectangular-shaped "Squarehouses" are much more convenient and economical.

Engine houses are generally of two kinds: the maintenance type equipped to make extensive repairs and overhauling, and the "turnaround" type which does minor servicing and stores the engines until they are ready to go out on their next run. Each engine house contains one or more stalls with built-in pits, drop tables, cranes and other equipment to handle locomotive components. These stalls are normally 10 to 20 feet longer than the longest locomotive which they are expected to accommodate.

The transfer table, which was developed at the turn of

the century, but only lately came into general use, is also being utilized in freight yards as a means of facilitating the movement and distribution of cars.

To a model railroader, the compact, efficient operation of a transfer table is even more of a boon than it is to a real railroad. The Lionel model, shown on the preceding page, for instance, occupies just 17½ inches by 10 inches, although it can be built up to any desired width (not length) with additional track beds. It makes possible real railroading switching operations within a much smaller area than is needed by a turntable and its associated trackage.

Below are illustrated a few suggested layouts using single and double transfer tables. Note how they can be used to connect several parallel sidings without the use of expensive and space-consuming track switches.

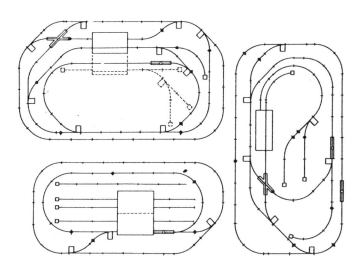

Track layouts showing use of Transfer Table.

"Tie-Jector" Car operates under its own power. Distributes ties at railside. Lionel No. 55.

No. 54 Track Ballast Tamper is a model of one of amazing new track-tending machines which have replaced the old work gangs.

Keeping the rails clean and oil-free is a big problem on a model railroad. Lionel's No. 3927 Track Cleaning Car does it easily with its detergent-soaked motorized sponge.

Yard Equipment for Maintenance

One of the most fascinating functions of real railroading is track maintenance. In fact, when it is done in populated areas, it draws as many entranced spectators as the erection of a new building.

Model railroaders are also finding this more and more interesting as part of operation of their roads, some to simulate maintenance, others actually hauling and maneuvering materials for new spurs or track repairs.

Miniature ties, rails, ballast, such as are described in Chapter 13, are loaded in the yards, hauled to location and carefully placed where needed. Logs for fence rails, canisters, small toolhouses—practically all of this lineside equipment can be loaded by crane in the yards and carried out into position in flat cars, gondolas and dump cars.

A great deal of new-type model equipment is now available for maintenance work.

One of the most interesting is the tie-unloading car (Lionel No. 55). This unusual car is self-propelled. As it travels along, the motor in the car automatically throws ties off on one side of the track. The sector of the track to receive the ties is controlled by track trips. The car is also equipped with a coupler and can tow a flat car with extra ties. For track-laying realism, an excellent companion car is the twin-dump car shown on page 127, which could be used to unload track ballast at railside.

Keeping the track ballast clean and properly tamped is the most important housekeeping chore a railroad has to do. The condition of the ballast determines the smoothness of the ride for the valued cash customer.

To pound the ballast under the track ties there is a model of a track tamper—another of a series of modern track tending machines that would break poor old John Henry's heart. Lionel's self-powered model runs along the track until it reaches the area where there is track work to be done. There it slows down automatically with tampers going until the job is done, then resumes normal speed.

Culvert Section Equipment

Because drainage is so vital to railroad right-of-ways, the handling and hauling of big pipe, or culvert sections is playing an increasingly important part in model train operations. The two accessories shown on the next page have been especially designed to meet this trend.

Lionel No. 342 is a replica of the loading platform of a manufacturer of the culvert sections. A typically realistic, overhead travelling crane picks up the sections one at a time from the platform, moves them over and deposits them in the awaiting gondola, which is so constructed that they automatically roll down into position. This complete, remote-controlled unit includes car and culvert sections.

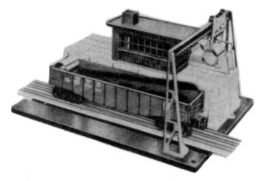

Culvert Loader takes pipes from platform —places them in gondola. Lionel No. 342.

At the other end of the line can be placed the Lionel No. 345 Unloading Station, which represents the railroad's receiving station, where culvert pipe is stored for future use. Here a magnetic overhead crane picks up the sections, one at a time, and transports them inside. This unit also includes car and culvert sections.

Either of these stations can be used individually but, of course, the ideal situation is to use them both, in combination.

This station unloads sections from flat car by overhead crane. Lionel No. 345.

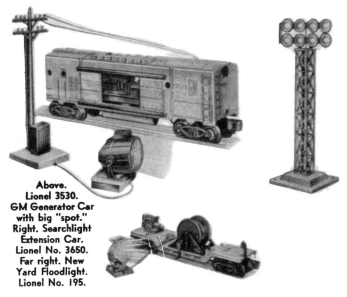

Above.
Lionel 3530.
GM Generator Car
with big "spot."
Right. Searchlight
Extension Car.
Lionel No. 3650.
Far right. New
Yard Floodlight.
Lionel No. 195.

Yard Equipment for Night Work

Any veteran model railroader can tell you that one of the big thrills of the game is operating in a partially darkened room, where you can get the full effect of headlights, flashing signals and maintenance lighting. Here are two pieces of equipment that deserve special mention.

The first is Lionel's replica of the GM Generator Car (Lionel No. 3530). This type of car is now used by railroads to furnish emergency electric power where needed. Exciting in action, when activated generator begins to hum, huge fan under roof rotates and powerful beam of searchlight, mounted on its own base, goes on.

The other unit is No. 3650 Lionel Searchlight Extension Car, which is ideal for night-time trackside work. Cable on reel in center of car feeds current to the big light, permitting it to be removed from the car and placed where most needed.

For the yard itself, there is the Lionel No. 195 Railroad Yard Floodlight, with a bank of eight lights.

Steam Plant and Pump House

The remaining buildings of an engine yard are quite simple. The added details, as always, make the difference between passable or amateurish models and expert models.

Make an effort to visit a complete yard area. Stop at the dispatcher's office and get permission to look around. Don't wander in without permission: you may get thrown out, and you might get yourself hurt. Most railroad men are exceedingly pleasant if approached pleasantly, and they will try to cooperate if they can. Some yards, especially electrified ones, are exceedingly dangerous—even so, you can wander around the perimeter with a notebook and check details.

A steam plant is a common sight and is used for power and other purposes. It is often joined to a pump house, which sends water through the lines to standpipes and towers.

Take the sizes for the brick building from the illustration. Use illustration board for the walls, bristol board for the trim on doors and windows. Make a shingle roof as shown at the right. In this case, the outside appurtenances are very important.

Make the coal-bin posts from balsa wood, ⅛" square, the sides from scribed illustration board. Coal may be simulated by a lump of plastic wood which is arranged in the proper shape over small wood scraps. Ground-up coal may be used (or Lionel's model coal) and pressed in while the plastic wood is soft. When dry, the heap is touched up with India ink or black paint, and the whole pile lightly shellacked.

Dowel forms all smoke pipes and vents. The boiler is made from a 1" dowel, 8" long. The swell to the firebox is made by wrapping strips of paper around the boiler in tapering fashion, then sheathing with light illustration board. The firebox domes, running boards, supports and so on, are made of bits of wood and illustration board, later painted appropriately. The boiler, of course, is a flat black.

As with most such models, this can be built on a ⅛" plywood piece, then installed and the edges disguised by the scenic materials described in Chapter 12. For this reason, it is all right, even desirable, to use odd-sized bases or irregularly cut pieces, since this tends to disguise the outline of the base. When installed, the building will be one to which frequent coal deliveries can be made, but more important, one that makes your yard come to life.

In painting this and other yard models, remember that smoke grays all colors and that the coal bin is black.

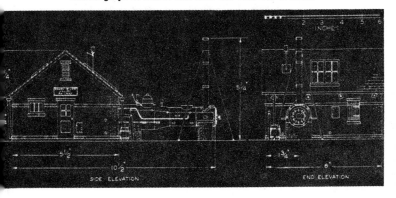

A Sandhouse

Railroads use sand in large quantities. The sand dome of a large locomotive will hold more than a ton of the stuff, and it is liberally used to grip the rails when starting and when making quick stops. When there is ice on the rails it will be used more often.

In yards, there will be a drying house to make the sand run freely, and a bin in which the sand is stored and unloaded into the locomotives. Start with the drying house, which is made from illustration board covered with clapboard (see chapter on Buildings).

Make the roof of illustration board with fine emery paper cemented onto it. This will imitate tar paper very realistically. Make the sand bin of illustration board and balsa, just as in the coal bin of the steam plant. The pile of sand is made by shellacking a cloth and shaping it so that, when dry, it takes the sand's shape. Add another coat of shellac and sprinkle liberally with sand. This can be done several times until the sand completely covers the cloth.

The bin supports are made of ¼" balsa wood, with strips added for bracing if desired. The bin is illustration board. The roof is shingle or tarpaper. The spout is 3/16"

The basic color for the sand house is flat gray. On sides nearest tracks, smoke will discolor the paint. For this, when the paint is dry, smear over lightly with a cotton or cloth swab, using a thin black paint. Blend tones to lighten at the top of the bin; and on the sides make it lighter, since they are farther from tracks.

dowel painted black, and with ingenuity it can be made to lower over the third rail of the track.

An Oil House

At some handy point in your yard, not too far from the roundhouse, an oil house should be placed. All of the wide variety of lubricating oils are kept here, isolated to prevent possible fires from spreading. More modern ones are made of brick or of cement block with a slate or metal roof, but this one is old, and is made of wood.

Make the walls of illustration board, the platform of wood and balsa posts. Make a barrel or two of dowel (or buy them) and place them about ready for refilling. A small "No Smoking" sign or two will help add reality. A small hand truck, made with two buttons and some wire, can be put by the door.

A Small Freight House

The small freight station above could serve a small community of half a dozen houses and one store. Or it could serve a couple of small industries. In either case, a cliff or some other scenic device might allow you to conceal the town, having it exist only in your imagination.

Walls and roof are illustration board and should be cut out with care. The upper sections can be brick paper cemented on the board, or bricks can be drawn. The concrete block base is easily made by using a basic gray color —then the joints are ruled in heavier gray. Don't make

The most carefully built small freight house will look unreal until some of the litter that is found near such a building is put in the right places. Make boxes from smoothly sanded wood that has been scribed for boards; these lines can be heavily penciled. A barrel, a pile of scrap wood, and a hand truck or two are things that will make the scene real.

them too smooth. Dimensions should be regular, but width of the lines should vary somewhat.

Around the bottom, a touch of umber color will look like the mud that normally splashes up on the foundation.

Make the small windows by cutting the trim from bristol board and cementing to heavy cellophane. The large door may be made the same way; traceline on which one side is glazed may be used.

The platform can be of thin wood, as shown, or it can be of illustration board. Either one should be scribed for planking, and a patch or two can be added to show where boxes have torn it up. Posts are balsa wood ¼" square. Steps are of balsa and illustration board.

Here's a portion of a compact diesel service yard—part of a huge new display at the Lionel New York showrooms—all set up to provide sand, fuel and water for several diesels. The towers are mounted on narrow platforms and can service parallel tracks. Dimensions for such a service platform are on page 155. In the background is the new Lionel flood-light for nighttime operations.

New Type Coaling Station

This amazing, new model railside accessory does all sorts of things by remote control. It tilts and unloads the car—then raises the bin to the overhead position. When a new car is moved into position, coal is emptied into it from overhead. Then bin is returned to railside position.

Rotating Radar Antenna

Reproduction of the type of radar antenna used for airport traffic control. Operated by "Vibrotor" mechanism which causes it to rotate continuously. Tower is 12" high.

As the handling of lumber constitutes an important part in yard activities, the two Lionel remote controlled operating accessories shown below are of special interest.

The No. 264 Fork-lift Platform utilizes the fork-lift truck, now a familiar sight in all rail yards, to pick up boards individually from the awaiting flatcar and place them in position on the loading platform. In the operation the truck backs up, turns around to drop the board and then returns to the car for another load. The platform set includes the extra-long flatcar and boards.

Other unit is the No. 464 railside Operating Lumber Mill. Logs are moved into the mill by conveyor belt, where they drop into a concealed bin. Dressed lumber comes out the other side, creating the impression that the rounded logs have been sawed into boards on passing through the mill. While in operation, mill gives out a real-life buzzing sound, just like a saw mill. The set includes logs and lumber.

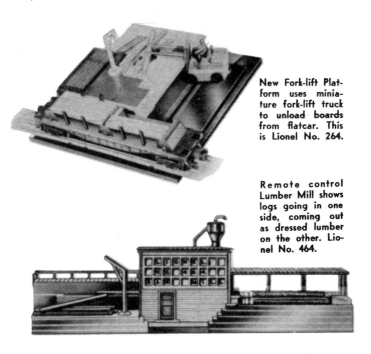

New Fork-lift Platform uses miniature fork-lift truck to unload boards from flatcar. This is Lionel No. 264.

Remote control Lumber Mill shows logs going in one side, coming out as dressed lumber on the other. Lionel No. 464.

A Handcar House

A handcar house makes good use of an odd-sized section of rail left over from some cutting and fitting on your trackwork. The house is quite simple, the main problem being the large doors. If you visualize these in layers, the first being the back, the second the heavy trim, the top layer the final trim, it is not so difficult. Use illustration board for the base layer, bristol board for the others. Cut all of them on a flat surface after carefully laying out with a sharp pencil.

If you wish, you can make a model of a handcar using the wheels from an old car truck. It might as well be a gasoline model, as these are most often used today. It is little more than a platform with a sort of bench along the center. This houses the gas engine and fuel, and provides

a seat for the men. With a bit of extra work, you can hinge the doors of the handcar house and really surprise visitors.

Water Towers and Standpipes

Locomotives consume a tremendous amount of water. Steam is used for heating as well as for power, and filling a single large tender may use a large part of a towerful of water.

On the opposite page you will see the Lionel operating

water tower. The touch of a remote control button will lower the water spout over the locomotive tender, then raise it again. When spotting this accesory on your layout, place it so that the spout drops directly over the center rail.

One tower is enough for a yard, but it will not supply all of your tracks. Therefore, you will want one or more standpipes such as the one at the bottom left of this page. Make them so they will pivot over the tracks. They are simply constructed from dowel and mounted in an illustration-board base. A bit of wire screen makes a grate at the bottom to allow for leaks.

Overpasses

Grading of model railroads lends to the excitement of operation. Shown below, at the right, is a series of graduated piers (or "bents") that you can buy, ready-made, to give you the overpasses you need. The Lionel No. 110 Trestle Set will accommodate any type of track.

The model layout scene shown on this page is, of course, an ideal one. It contains three separate and distinct railroading features. In the rear is the Diesel switcher, making up a train in the yards. The floodlight tower is for nighttime yard operations. "Making up" trains with remote control operating knuckle couplers is one of the most fascinating of all model train operations.

In the center of the picture is the main line, doubly guarded by the switch tower and the signal bridge. The observation car of the streamlined limited can be seen just passing under the signal bridge. This signal bridge, incidentally, is so designed that it can be equipped with additional targets and lights and can operate in either direction.

The passing train shown has just stopped at the station (right center) to deliver passengers and baggage.

In the foreground is a factory siding and a railside barrel loader. Wooden barrels placed on the lower platform ride up the slide-type ramp and roll off the upper platform into the car.

One of the most interesting features of constructing the smaller yard buildings is that you can give your imagination free rein. Railroads don't follow any set pattern for these structures as they do for stations, switch towers, etc. Tool sheds and workshops are individually designed to fill the particular needs of the section of track that they serve.

These auxiliary buildings can be constructed of all sorts of materials—scrap lumber, cigar boxes, cardboard, wood matches—even toothpicks. Paint will give them the worn appearance that most yard buildings have. Cut short chunks of wood to simulate tie piles. Long wood strips, painted black, will become spare rails.

The best way to plan your yard scenes is to visit a nearby railroad. It's fun to build a yard scene just like the one in your own neighborhood.

Diesel Shops and Yards

Most modelmakers will want to have a mixed group of engines. Few will want steam only; even fewer will want Diesel only. Except for storage, Diesel servicing is quite simple.

Storage will not become a problem until you have a number of engines or units, and if that problem arises, you can easily build a long, barnlike building with two or three storage tracks inside.

For servicing Diesels you will need fuel tanks, water supply outlets, and sand. Also, you will need facilities for washing and lubrication.

The simplest means, and the one used by the railroads, is a set of long platforms along a track. They should be long enough to service two A units at once.

In making the service platforms, use a long piece of illustration board 2" wide and scribe it crosswise for planks. It should be about 1¼" from the ground, and be supported so that maintenance crews can work under it. Support the outside edge with posts ⅛" or 3/16" square, which extend on up to support a railing and a frame for hose lines. These should be 3" apart.

Near the locomotive, have the posts run only to the bottom of the platform, and make them 6" apart. They can be backed up by a wooden strip under the platform which acts as bracing.

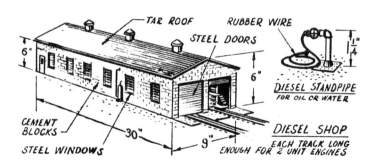

TAR ROOF   RUBBER WIRE   STEEL DOORS

6"

6"

DIESEL STANDPIPE
FOR OIL OR WATER

CEMENT BLOCKS   30"   9"

DIESEL SHOP
EACH TRACK LONG
ENOUGH FOR 2 UNIT ENGINES

STEEL WINDOWS

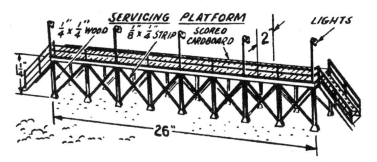

For hoses, use single-strand, rubber-covered wire. You may have one color for fuel and another for water. The latter is used for heating cars and cooling the Diesel engines. You will also want some tanks near by.

Tanks can be easily made from small cans—frozen-orange-juice cans are just small enough—or from sections of mailing tubes. In either case, plug the ends up and round them off with plastic wood. Sand the ends very smooth, shellac, and then use metallic paint. Supports are made of wood or illustration board. If wooden, they can be covered with brick paper. One system is to make high trestles so that the oil flows by gravity; these can be of balsa wood.

Put a few barrels under the platform, and with a bit of litter the model is finished. Painting should follow your road's color scheme, of course. Usually Diesel yards are considerably cleaner than steam yards. Thus, colors need not be smudged or darkened too much.

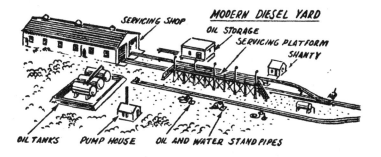

SCENERY

INTELLIGENT use of scenery will help the operation of your railroad. It is significant that nearly every major aspect of railroading goes back to operation—trackwork, buildings, and now scenery.

Scenery is the very last thing to be added to your road. If you are like most hobbyists, you will have put down your track and then rearranged it once or twice; your buildings will have been shifted from spot to spot. If your initial plans were good, track rearrangements were minor; if your buildings were on plywood bases, they were no trouble at all.

The scenery that is planned here is a permanent type, and it will not be easy or convenient to decide suddenly to run a line through a cliff. It can be done, of course, but it's easier if you get the road in shape first.

Although the railroad actually came first, the scenery should justify it—it should look as if the road came last. This means that when your track makes a sharp curve, there must be a cliff, a hill, or a river to justify the curve. A grade should lead into hilly or mountainous country. A lift bridge must have its river to justify its existence.

Also, we want to keep things within reality. We don't use a tunnel through a small hill; we use a cut. We don't bridge a creek with a model of the Hellgate bridge; we use a girder bridge. Where possible, we follow real railroad procedure in every respect.

If feasible, use your walls. Buy background scenes from the Skyline assortment, mount them on lath, then tack onto the walls. You cannot, on any model railroad, approximate a city, but if you are careful you can model the front of a few buildings, set them a few inches from the wall, and use a background scene to let the city stretch out for miles.

The same is true of countryside or suburban scenes. And here is the key trick of them all: Never let your background and your layout actually meet! Always allow a two- or three-inch gap between the table and the background. Disguise this fact by buildings on the edge of the layout, perhaps by a high level line running along a fill, by hills or mountains. By this means, the viewer has no way to judge the gap—there is no bridge for the eye—and he cannot tell whether the supposed distance between the layout and the scenic painting is five yards or five miles.

In addition to the materials shown here, you will need plaster, paper strips, wire screen, fine camel's-hair brushes, and perhaps a spatula.

If they do join, say by a road that winds through the layout and right onto the background scene, he will see the deception instantly. But if the road disappears over a hill, then reappears beyond, smaller and not so brightly painted, then he cannot judge the gap.

Hills and mountains are necessary to give variety and distance to the scene, to imply villages beyond them, to conceal trains for a moment or two. They are not difficult to build. There are a number of systems, one of which is pictured above.

One of the newest systems to bolster the art of scenic design is a development called "Celastic." It is a colloid-treated cotton fabric which produces the same effect as plaster but in much less time. Simple to use, this method requires less materials than other systems and you may find it affords many shortcuts in construction. Available in kit form, Celastic materials consist of a roll of the treated cloth, a can of softener, a roll of aluminum foil and a jar of patching compound. You will also need a container to hold the softener. Do not use a plastic container for the softener might soften that too.

Once you set up your Celastic materials, choose a section of your layout that is ready for scenicking. Then rough your outline into shape using chunks of wood, cardboard, paper or anything else you wish. Once this base is arranged, cover with aluminum foil those sections of the framework that are to be removed after the Celastic is applied. Aluminum foil prevents the Celastic from adhering to that material which you will be removing.

When the base is formed to your satisfaction, *tear* strips from the roll of cloth into pieces about 2 or 3″ wide by 12″ long. Tearing strips instead of cutting them produces a fine feather edge. Dip your strips into the tray of softener. In a few seconds, they will take on a jelly-like form which you then drape over the foil with one edge pressed firmly to the wooden sub-roadbed. If you miss any spots,

Realistic rock formations, great mountains, big embankments and rolling hills are easily made with Celastic.

simply cover with additional material. You can shape and work the surface for approximately fifteen minutes. After fifteen minutes, it will dry and adhere as though cemented to the wood. If it tends to dry too quickly while you're shaping, moisten it with softener. You can then remove contour material from underneath the shell and paint within a half hour if desired.

Extra details lend a realistic air to your layout and Celastic can also be used towards this end. Take an actual rock or boulder; cover it, first, with foil and then with softened Celastic. When the Celastic is dry, remove the hardened shell and fix it permanently to the desired position in your layout by using a few strips of moist Celastic. You thereby get an actual duplication of a real rock formation. You can also make trees a part of your scenery by wetting a strip of the fabric and wrapping it around the bottom of the tree and placing it in position. Small pebbles may also be imbedded and fixed. If you wish to incorporate ponds and streams with real water into your layout, you'll find Celastic excellent for the purpose. Just be sure to coat the bottom of the ponds with varnish or another waterproofing material. Remember too that water will have to be changed frequently to prevent it from becoming stagnant.

Celastic is easily painted and no priming is needed. Paint soaks in sufficiently to stick.

Here are a few incidental hints which you may find helpful when using Celastic. The softener has a tendency to evaporate quickly so when you're not going to be using it for a few hours, keep it tightly covered. It is also flammable so don't smoke near the solution and don't keep it near an open flame. However, the finished scenery is practically fireproof and no special precautions are necessary. Colloidal plastic that has stuck to your fingers can easily be removed by dipping your fingers in the softener and wiping them off immediately with an old rag. After giving Celastic a thorough try, you'll find it very practical to use. No elaborate preparations are necessary before working on the scenery; there are no materials to mix; no supports to build. Your finished job is ready for painting only minutes after application. Even though it is light, this material will not chip or crack. And because there are no forms to build, you can save valuable time which you can use to advantage with other stages of construction. The hardened shell will also take any type of paint readily and one coat is sufficient for covering.

Other Methods of Constructing Model Railroad Scenery

Light braces are cut from wood and tacked to crosspieces. On these is put a rough wire screen, a cheap ¼″ mesh variety. It is crumpled as it is applied. When it is punched into position, it is nailed. (Obviously, a canyon or a stream bed is made in the same way in a depressed area.)

With the proper shape achieved, and scenic effects planned, a coating of papier-mâché is applied with an old kitchen spatula. The papier-mâché is made from squares of newspaper torn about 1″ x 1″ and mixed into a wall sizing, plaster or glue solution until a thick mixture is obtained.

While the papier-mâché is still soft, any special scenic effects are inserted. Some thin, striated sandstone may be put in for a cliff, or pieces of cork bark will do equally well.

Here or there a tree may be added now if it would be harder to put in later. Some boulders may show through. If a roadway is planned, the guard rail might be put in now. Some of the buildings that are certain not to be changed may be placed and the base disguised completely.

A basic color—usually earth brown—may be added to the papier-mâché and it will save painting later.

All other systems are somewhat similar. Often simple plaster is used. An excellent method is to shape fairly heavy cloth over the frames and the screen, and then paint with cheap varnish, slapping the varnish on heavily.

When painting the mountains and landscapes, remember that there are no even colors in nature. Pour small quantities of paint into cheese glasses or other receptacles, and don't hesitate to mix them. Let earthy browns creep into your green grasses, let plenty of blue show up there. Allow grays to mix completely on roadways, blending into black in spots. Let earth on cliffs and cuts be darkened in spots. Just don't let it be a flat even color!

When the paint is wet, some sections can be dusted with dried coffee grounds, others with sawdust, still others

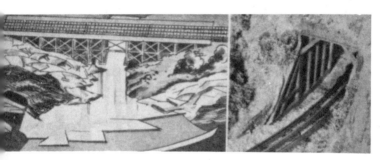

with green-dyed sawdust. These will lend texture and contrast to undusted areas. (Make the sawdust green by using dye and straining through a cloth.) Small pebbles may be used in spots.

If possible, don't use a mirror for your ponds. Get a piece of heavy gauge glass and paint the underside or a paper underlay with blues streaked with whites. A little experimenting will show you how to imitate water properly.

Although tunnel portals need not be put in while the plaster is wet, it is easiest then. A timber portal is easily made of ¼" balsa wood stained brown, and the plaster can then be molded around it. Concrete portals, consisting of illustration board scribed to show joints, are only a bit more difficult. Darken the tunnel portal where smoke would touch it; put some red streaks where reinforcing bars have rusted; let earth and rain stain it.

Jutting rocks are extremely interesting but are often neglected. They are just about the easiest of all things to model. Below are some rocks from Frank Ellison's Delta Lines right-of-way. Here a cut was blasted out of the side of a hill (Frank firmly believes) and since it is old, the earth has eroded, leaving the rocks exposed. Actually, they are small pieces of weatherbeaten wood inserted into plaster. They could be cork or actual stone. Notice how they run in layers, just as real rock does. That is the only trick, and an easy one if you will keep your eyes peeled for examples when you are outdoors.

Another Delta Lines scene on the next page shows Frank Ellison's deftness with trees and scenery. Notice the pebbles around, and the cut made by the railroad; see the artfulness with which the fence has been broken in places and not repaired.

The trees are made of wire. Short lengths (4" to 5") of light wire are gathered until they make the thickness of

Photo (r.) by Frank Ellison; courtesy of Model Railroader.

a tree trunk. One or two of them are then wrapped around the others until the tree is covered half way. The wires at the top are spread out in treelike fashion, maybe a few wires twisted a short distance to make heavier limbs. At the bottom, some wires are spread slightly to form a base which can be plastered.

The foliage is made by dipping the tree into shellac, then sprinkling green sawdust over it so that some sticks. Blossoms are tiny bits of cotton in this case. Small red berries could be attached by the gummy shellac. The trunk is coated with heavy paint or light plaster to hide the wires.

Lichen trees are just as easy, and will stand fairly close inspection. Norwegian lichen (rhymes with "That's a lie, Ken!") already treated to prevent drying out and dyed in various shades of green and brown is part of Lionel's No. 920 Landscaping Kit or can be bought separately. It can be glued to a suitable-size twig that has been shellacked or varnished as a preservative measure, and there is your tree. The twig can be inserted in a hole, and a bit of plaster will widen the base quite properly.

Photo (r.) by Frank Ellison; courtesy of Model Railroader.

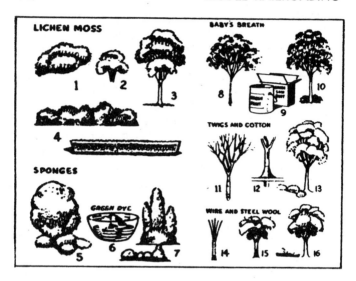

Don't make all trees in the same way. Incidentally, they can be bought from the Bert Welch Company or in most hobby shops; but if you use many, you will probably want to make some. You can get variety of appearance by making them in all the ways shown above; and even in an orchard, trees vary considerably in size and shape.

Lichen and different types of sponge dyed green will make hedges, bushes, and brush of all sorts. Use it, but sparingly, around buildings to break up the base line. It can hide switch machine fixtures, bolt heads, or bits of wood that stick through. It is excellent to break contours of hills.

Notice how the trees on Frank Ellison's layout, opposite, break up the horizon. And notice, too, how the hill avoids joining the background scene. Actually, the little cottage is only a few inches from the wall, but the adroit use of a small gap gives an illusion of distance.

When a layout has hills, it follows that there are streams. After all, the streams cut the hills down to size, and if the stream beds do not run under the railroad, they will wash it out too. Not all will use glass; most of the smaller ones will be only a tiny streak of blue with rocks peeping out at all available spots. Touches of white will show around rocks and over submerged ones.

You can route the streams under the track bed by a number of means, largely determined by their size. A small bed that carries water only during rains will have a culvert that is easily made of a section of mailing tube. It is painted a uniform gray and darkened at the bottom. A stone or concrete culvert will carry a steady small stream, and can be made of illustration board with heavy bristol board bent to form the inside arch. Mark the stones lightly in pencil, and with a fine camel's-hair brush use various grays and gray-browns to make individual stones.

Concrete is made just as the tunnel portal was made, but in this case, using browns, mark off some high-water marks.

The cribbing, opposite, left, is a common sight near tunnels and underpasses. It looks like concrete poured into a form, but actually it is illustration board with carefully cut bristol board applied to it. A fairly even gray paint, with only a few earth streaks would be enough coloring. In painting such a streak, figure out where the water would go and follow that. Actually, a note of disrepair is often

harder to achieve than a smooth job; but it looks far more real.

For larger streams, use a girder bridge. Such bridges require piers to support them. They can be handily made of illustration board. Coloring may be even, except for earth marks and a few rust streaks from the rails and girders. These rust streaks start out wide and dwindle down. Usually they peter out to nothing before reaching the bottom of the concrete.

Girder bridges may be either the through type, as on the next page, or they may be the deck type in which the girder is down and the track run on top with no guard rails. (The same thing is true of a truss bridge, but that is rarely practical on a model road.) If you do use a deck-type bridge, don't forget to paint out the lettering. You can re-letter it with your own road's name, although it takes a fine brush, a fine hand, and a fine eye to do a good job. Decalcomania letters can be used for this.

Girder bridges do not normally span a navigable stream, although they can be used to make sections of such a bridge. By placing one at each end and a truss bridge in the middle, a very reasonable and common bridge is made. In that case, piers must be placed in midstream, and by all means, don't forget the high-water marks made by flooded streams.

Small navigable streams may be spanned by the trestle bridge, while the rolling lift bridge or the horizontal lift bridge will cover somewhat large rivers. All told, it's a good bet that you can use several of the girder bridges but, unless your layout is quite large, only a limited number of the others.

In placing the larger bridge, try getting a couple of very straight sticks and whittling them into pilings. Don't use dowel, as it is too regular. Lash the sticks vertically, and put them as a guard to keep errant barges from knocking down your piers.

When planning scenery, remember that each and every feature implies industry. Rivers mean fish and gravel and sand and barge-loads of goods of all sorts. Build one or two refineries or a coaling station along the navigable stream and let visitors see just the corner of a barge sticking beyond the edge of a pier. The railroad services these industries, and the industries must be so located that it appears they are the reason the railroad exists.

Hills indicate coal and lumber and ore, not to mention

cement and gas and, often enough, oil. Make the scenery work overtime. First, it is adjusted to your trackage, so that routes are logical. Second, it justifies your industry. And third, it hides your trains when you like, and it implies that there is much more beyond the things seen.

Once you have established the general tone, work around to the smaller touches. Where will whistle signals be located? Where should cows graze? On what corner does a motorcycle cop hang out? All of these questions come last, for they will be dictated by the needs of the scene.

Probably the most common failing of modelmakers at the beginning—and it's an expensive failing—is to clutter the layout with a large number of trucks and people that crowd into the scene. Of course you will want a number of model items about the scene, but notice the sparing use of such things throughout this book.

Model-making becomes as good from what it leaves out as from what it includes. By all means have some people and some trucks and cars (also fireplugs, lampposts, and so on). But instead of buying quantity, get good ones. Most model stores keep supplies of these items, exactly to the right scale. A man should be about 1¼" to 1½" high, not more. A car should be about 1½" high, a large truck not more than 2" high. A number of companies make these, and while the price may seem rather high they are well

done. You won't need many. In the long run, they'll be better.

One thing you will want to dress up will be your grade crossings. Above are four possible arrangements, three of them operating. With careful placement, they will add a great deal to the scenes.

Scenery can make your road live. Remember: Don't start before you are ready; have all the materials at hand; make a careful plan for all work; let the road lead naturally into the background; and, lastly, don't overdo it.

LINESIDE EQUIPMENT

CHAPTER THIRTEEN

A N INTEGRAL part of the railroad scene is the equipment and material used along the right-of way. This does not refer to buildings of any size, but to the small items: phone poles, barrels, hand trucks, telephone boxes, small tanks, and all the other things that an observer can spot. These items add reality to your scene.

Telephone poles along part or all of your trackage will add to the picture. Try to avoid placing them where you will be working or reaching frequently, for it will take only a slight bump to knock them out of alignment.

Lionel poles, as used below, are convenient, and can be strung with simulated wires. One rule to follow religiously: Do not use wire to simulate wire! Hence, it follows that you will not actually carry power on your poles.

The reason for omitting wire is two-fold. Even with great care, the poles will be disturbed at times. And—the main reason—wire is difficult to string on poles without kinks. It will not hang normally or evenly.

WIRES, GUY WIRES, TRANSFORMERS ETC. MAKE TELEPHONE LINES MAKE INTERESTING MODELS

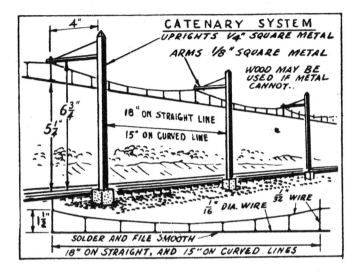

The best substitute is a medium-size black thread. It should not be particularly strong, and should hang in slight sags between poles. A simple half-hitch will hold it to the poles.

It is quite all right to have poles along a section of track, and then have them end abruptly. This often happens near towns and in very hilly sections. Just let the ends of the strings be drawn to the pole, run down it and into the ground where—presumably—they are carried in an underground cable.

The problem is very different if one wishes to make a catenary wiring, working or non-working. Here the wire which the pantograph touches must be rigid. The supporting catenary must be rigid too.

If one is made, poles and crossarms should be made of square wood trim available at lumber yards and some hardware stores. Use ¼″ or ⅜″ square trim for the poles,

MODEL RAILROADING

a slightly smaller size for the crossarms. Still smaller cross-arms at the top may carry telephone wires. The poles can be painted silver (or black) and mounted in a simulated concrete base made of illustration board cut to size and cemented.

The poles are placed four inches from the center rail of the track, and the height of the catenary should be taken from your locomotive dimensions. Poles are 18″ apart on straight sections, 12″ to 15″ on curves.

The catenary and supporting wires are made by solder-ing brass or steel rods of small diameter. A jig is made and used as a guide. The longest vertical supporting wire is 1½″ long, and the catenary dips in an even curve until it almost touches the trolley wire, then rises again. The rods should be nearly rigid, just flexible enough to be bent to the catenary curve. Avoid large amounts of solder, use just enough to hold. The wires can be painted flat black, with the trolley wire sanded if it is to be used as a power source.

The telltale (below, left) is a warning for men on top of box cars who might be hurt by bridges, tunnels, or

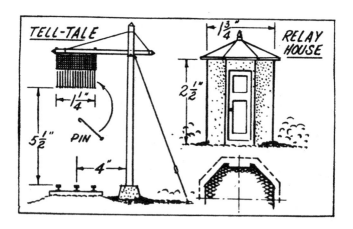

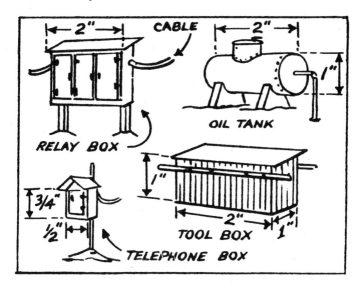

other overhead obstructions. The posts are simply made; the dangling string is a row of pins or is wire screen from which some crosswires have been removed. The height should be adjusted to fit your cars, but will have to be fairly high if a GG-1 is used, since the pantograph must clear it.

The small relay house at the bottom of the preceding page is octagonal, with each side made of a piece of illustration board ⅝″ wide by 2″ high. It should have a door as shown, and is painted concrete gray. The roof is flat black. The structure may have wires leading into it, so that its purpose is made clear. The wires, made of thread, can disappear into a cable entry in the ground a few yards from the relay house.

The equipment shown on these pages is mostly self-explanatory, and can be made from the dimensions given. The boxes above are made from illustration board. The tank and the gas cylinders are made from dowel. A few

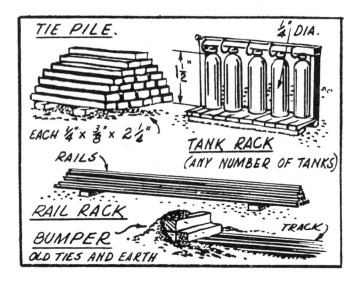

lengths of rail from old track from a hobby shop will make
stacks of rails. Some spare ties that are stained make the
bumper and the pile, as well as the rail supports.

The tank is for oil, and is usually found in yards, where
it has pipes leading to switches. It supplies torches to
thaw frozen switch mechanisms.

The gas cylinders hold oxygen and acetylene and are
used by welders and burners working near by, so they
should be near the shops. All have aluminum bases, while
the tops of some are painted blue (oxygen) and other
tops are painted orange (acetylene).

In both the relay box and the telephone box on p. 175,
the cables may lead to poles or they may go to underground conduit outlets made of small concrete squares
with a hole.

One point to remember about all of these items is that
they will come in for close inspection by visitors—small
things always do—and they should be made with care.

These details will be added work, but will lend atmosphere.

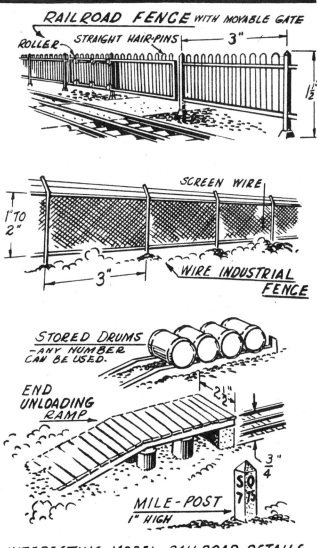

RAILROAD FENCE WITH MOVABLE GATE

ROLLER   STRAIGHT HAIR-PINS   3"   1½"

SCREEN WIRE

1" TO 2"

3"

WIRE INDUSTRIAL FENCE

STORED DRUMS —ANY NUMBER CAN BE USED.

END UNLOADING RAMP   2½"

3¾"

S.O 7 75

MILE-POST   1" HIGH

INTERESTING MODEL RAILROAD DETAILS

Of course, no one chapter can adequately cover all line-side equipment used by railroads. Nothing will substitute for a bit of observation on the modeler's part. Arm yourself with a small notebook and a few pencils, then go to a real railroad and walk beside it for a mile or two. You'll see many things you never noticed before, and you can sketch almost all of them. You can do it without practice or experience, because you don't care about the looks of the drawings—all you want is something from which to model. A few lines and a few of the major dimensions, and there you have it, enough to go on anyway.

The two fences opposite are not difficult to construct, but they do take time and patience. They are handy projects to work on "between times." Both can be made with a fine-tipped soldering iron, but they could be made with airplane glue. In the latter case, they will not be quite so sturdy.

The hairpin fence should be made on a jig to give even spacing. The pins are laid out and the long bars cemented or soldered to them. Then a number of the sections are cemented to the wooden posts or soldered to steel rods. By doing a section at a time and allowing post space between, very long rods can be used for the long members.

The industrial fence is easily made of screen cemented or soldered to brass or steel wires. The top wires, which are single-strand, may be thread or wire which is carefully drawn tight and attached. If kinks develop in wire, that section must be discarded and new wire inserted.

The drums and the mile post are easily made. The only trick to making the end-unloading ramp is to allow a space for the couplers of your cars to go under the platform so that the body is flush against the ramp. On model roads the platform works well with flat cars. In actual railroad practice, some box cars and some gondolas have ends that open or drop. This allows automobiles or trucks to be driven on or off and freight to be moved easily.

Almost anything can be built by a modelmaker who is willing to spend the time and effort. However, some things lend themselves to easy modeling; other things are more difficult. Naturally, companies making supplies for model railroaders tend to shy away from the easily duplicated items and stick to models which present a problem to even the experienced modeler.

Here are two items made by Lionel, which would take a great amount of time to build, or which involve work that is more finicking that most modelers care to tackle.

The airplane beacon on the left turns steadily, beaming red and green light from its fresnel-type lens. It is one of the few logical structures for the top of a mountain. It can, of course, also be near an airport. If you do build an airport keep it small and simple.

About the only other structure that suits the peak of a mountain (besides hunting lodges and firewatching towers) is the micro-wave relay tower illustrated at right.

Equipped with characteristic parabolic antennas and flashing airplane warning lights it can give an interesting modern touch to a quiet mountain landscape.

The floodlight tower and the small spotlights are common accessories in a yard of any sort. The streetlamps and platform lamps fit easily into street and station scenes. The billboard can sit beside a highway or along the railroad right-of-way.

In placing these and other small structures or lineside items, pay close attention to blending them into the scene. They should be visible, but not obtrusive. One way of making them seem part of the scene is to conceal the method of fixing them to the base. Full details of making shrubs and grass and earth will be found in the chapter on Scenery. Plan in advance to spend an extra few minutes making the lineside equipment look as though it had been in its present place a long time.

There will always be interest in your stations and terminals; to most people, these are their only direct acquaintance with the railroads. To railroad men, they are the beginning and end of their trips.

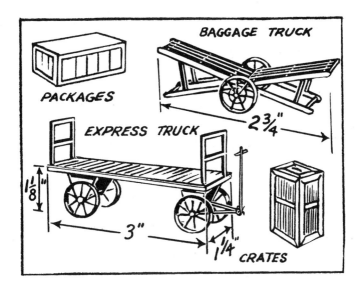

A few boxes and crates around your platforms will be of great additional interest. Baggage trucks can be purchased at hobby stores. Both English and American makes are sold. However, the models shown here were hand-made.

The frames and bodies of the trucks are simple, being made from illustration board which is shellacked and painted. The problem lies in the wheels, which are not so easily made and may be taken from dime-store toys.

Wheels can be fabricated from a thin bristol board strip, which is the rim, with toothpicks as spokes, and a tiny dowel section as the hub. If you do make them, use a jig and allow the cement to dry thoroughly before removing.

Boxes and crates may be made of a tiny block of wood with scribed bristol board cemented to them.

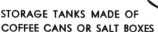

A COFFEE CAN WITH
A TOOTHPICK LADDER—
PRESTO! AN OIL STORAGE
TANK.

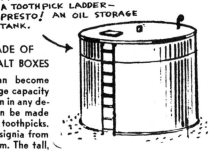

STORAGE TANKS MADE OF COFFEE CANS OR SALT BOXES

Empty coffee cans can become excellent replicas of large capacity storage tanks. Paint them in any desired color. Ladders can be made of wire or cemented toothpicks. Cut out oil company insignia from magazine ads for realism. The tall, vertical type tank can be similarly constructed from salt boxes.

WATER STANDPIPE IS
INSULATED WIRE CUT OFF
BX CABLE.
WHEEL WAS
TAKEN FROM
BROKEN TOY

$3\frac{1}{2}$"

STANDPIPE MADE OF INSULATED WIRE

This standpipe for feeding water to steam locomotive tenders is made of a section of BX cable. Wheel was taken off a broken toy. If so desired, it can be made to swivel and serve two parallel tracks. Base is a block of wood, scored to simulate planks.

A salt box or a juice can will make this horizontal tank. The pipe is just a piece of rubber-covered wire. Tanks like these are often used for snow-melting oil—used in burners to keep switches from freezing during cold weather.

SALT BOX OR
JUICE CAN MAKES A
HORIZONTAL TANK. PIPE
IS RUBBER-COVERED WIRE.

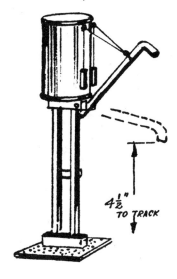

$4\frac{1}{2}''$
TO TRACK

SANDLOADER

This is a sandloader made from a frozen-fruit juice can, dowels and string. Can is mounted on two $\frac{1}{4}$ inch dowel pins. Spout is $\frac{1}{8}$ inch dowel pin. Weights can be sections cut from heavy nails. With care they can be adjusted to operate as actual counterweights.

ANOTHER CAN ON STILTS

DIESEL FUELING STATION

This little pump house was made from a block of wood, with dowel sticks forming the upright pipe and pivoted boom. A piece of metal can be used to counterweight the boom. Hose is rubber insulation stripped off of electric wire.

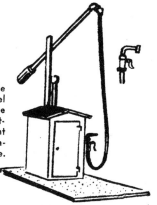

CLOTHES-HANGER WIRE
FOR THE POST AND HOSE-BOOM
RUBBER INSULATION FROM
ELECTRIC WIRE MAKES THE HOSE.

MULTI-OPERATOR RAILROAD

CHAPTER FOURTEEN

L ET'S FACE IT. It's a lot of fun to run a model train under any circumstances, but it's more fun when you have spectators. And when these spectators are youngsters, it isn't long before a number of them want to participate.

The same problem exists for the father who builds a layout for a couple of competitive children—a dispute is bound to arise as to "who's going to run the train?"

A neat answer to this situation is a two-operator railroad illustrated schematically below. Let's see how it works. Each of the circles represents a separate train circuit with its own transformer and control panel. (The transformers must be "phased" but more about that later.) The two cir-

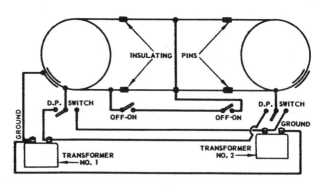

cuits are linked by connecting lines, each preferably long enough to hold a train. The connecting lines are insulated from both loops but are connected to one of them through two "off-on" switches connected in series.

Now, each operator has complete and independent control of his own train and switches, but moving a train from one circuit to the other requires cooperation and agreement since both "off-on" switches have to be "on" before any power can flow into the no-man's-land of the connecting lines. A similar agreement in regard to the double-throw switches will interchange the controls of the two circuits or throw the control of the entire system to either one of the two operators.

Of course, the two circuits need not be circular. An L-shaped corner layout, which can be built on a pair of 4 x 8 plywood sheets is illustrated below.

While the two-operator system has solved many a minor domestic impasse, it does not cover every model railroading contingency. A three-son father of our acquaintance has developed a king-sized U-shaped pike presided over by the oldest boy who has the option of delegating the operation

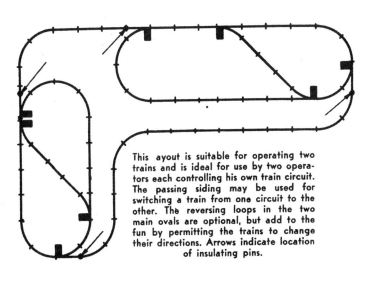

This layout is suitable for operating two trains and is ideal for use by two operators each controlling his own train circuit. The passing siding may be used for switching a train from one circuit to the other. The reversing loops in the two main ovals are optional, but add to the fun by permitting the trains to change their directions. Arrows indicate location of insulating pins.

of the freight yard and of the industrial branch, located along the sides of the U to his younger brothers, or assuming the control of the entire railroad empire himself. Unlike the two-operator system, this is far from being an equal partnership, but works out fine in this particular family situation.

Still another answer is a system which divides up the operational functions of the railroad and provides special duties for a number of individuals. Actually such a system creates a much more realistic realistic viewpoint of railroading, for the individual members must coordinate their operations, and may even, when the system becomes highly organized, have to use train orders. All the operators will then have turns at the different control stations.

The multi-operator railroad described here provides for four operators. If it is planned for children (7 to 12 years) it is best to set it up on a table about 2½ to 3 feet high. Individual stations should be placed far enough apart to permit freedom of movement.

Basically, this system consists of two separate but interlocking railroads and two train sets. The inner loop of track is controlled by one engineer and one dispatcher— the outer loop by another engineer and another dispatcher.

Engineer No. 1 (page 188) controls and has charge of the locomotive of the outer loop. He blows the whistle, starts, stops, reverses the engine, all according to signals.

All semaphores, block signals, switches, remote control tracks for uncoupling and operating cars of outer loop, are in charge of Dispatcher No. 1. The dispatcher also controls all uncoupling.

Functions of the inner loops are similarly broken down between Engineer No. 2 and Dispatcher No. 2.

Now for the fun! Switches and crossover lines permit No. 1 train to cross over into Dispatcher 2's division, and the No. 2 train into the No. 1 division.

Here's how this railroad works:

Let's assume that Track 1 is westbound and that trains

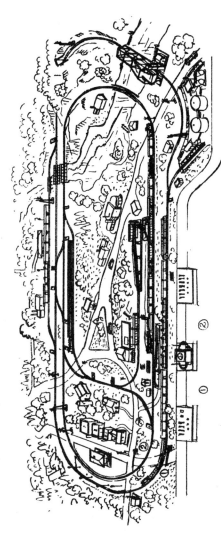

When Landscaping a Multi-Operator Road, Be Sure That Dispatchers Have Clear View of Their Divisions. It Is Also Vitally Necessary That Engineers' Views of Signals Are Not Blocked Off by Scenery.

Although the sketch above shows the center of the layout textured, the system is large enough so all control boards could be placed in the center. Operating portion can be made accessible through the use of a hinged section of table and track, permitting you to walk into the center rather than "climbing under." An interesting addition to a layout like this (or any one, as a matter of fact) is the model train version of

the "dead man's button." It consists merely of a door-bell-type circuit breaker between the transformer and the track lockon. This means that the train operator must keep the button depressed at all times while the train is running. In this case, such an arrangement could be used on both train controls. The "dead man's button" is an excellent device for use where young-sters might walk away, leaving trains running.

on it run counter-clockwise. Track 2 is then eastbound and trains on it run clockwise.

Engineer takes a passenger train out of the station, westbound, on Track 1. Watching all signals, he sees the red bull's eye of the 151 semaphore which warns him to stop for an open bridge. (See drawing on this page.) After crossing the bridge, yellow light on signal 153-A tells him to reduce speed to take the "A" siding. A yellow light on

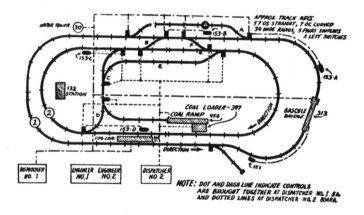

NOTE: DOT AND DASH LINE INDICATE CONTROLS ARE BROUGHT TOGETHER AT DISPATCHER NO.1 BD. AND DOTTED LINES AT DISPATCHER NO.2 BOARD.

signal 153-B means "slow" to take crossover "B" into the inner loop. Entering the inner loop, the train should be run through switches "C" and "D" to send it in the right direction, which is eastbound. If train is to be sent back to Track 1 in the right direction, it can be reversed by backing it through switches "D" and "C" out into siding "E," and from here back onto Track 1 via crossover "F."

Signals 153-C and 153-D are installed so that a train comes into them over "trailing points." If the switch is set against the train the signals give a red indication which is an "absolute stop" order for the engineer. He stops train and waits until the dispatcher clears the switch and gives him the "green indication."

When trains head into a switch with the choice of either route, a top green on the signal indicates normal speed for a straight passing, and the yellow light tells engineer to reduce speed to take the turn. Drawing below shows wiring of 153 signals.

This type of multiple-operator railway system is the closest approximation of real railroading there is, and, limited only by available space, it can be expanded to include six, eight and ten operators. It's a sample of the thrills in store for model railroaders.

MULTI-TRAIN RAILROADS

CHAPTER FIFTEEN

S OME INDICATION has already been given in the previous chapters how two or more trains can be operated on the same railroad. This seems a good spot to review some of the ways in which this can be done.

The first method, suggested in the chapter on Signaling and Interlocking, is to have two or more trains follow each other on the same track, like separate sections of the same

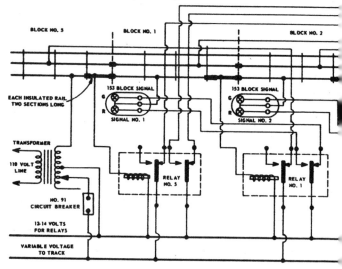

train. Since no two locomotives will run at exactly the same speed the faster moving one will eventually catch up with the slower one. To prevent rear-end collisions, the trackage is separated into several "blocks" insulated from each other by means of insulating pins or clips in the power rail. Power to each block is fed through a relay or a pressure switch so that the presence of a train within a block automatically disconnects power from the block directly in the back and halts the following train.

The advantage of such a system is that it looks like real railroading and that the track system need not be complicated. A simple oval, if long enough, can be used to run any number of trains. The disadvantage is that everything is automatic. The trains all run at the same speed, stop and start when they have to. All the operator can do is watch. A complete wiring diagram for a block system interlocked with a signal for each block is shown below.

A second method, described in the chapter on Multi-Operator Railroad, requires a separate and complete track loop for each train. Of course, such loops would usually be interconnected with crossovers but they are separate

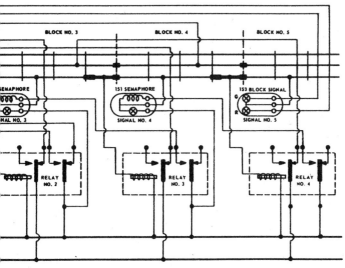

electrically so that each loop can be supplied with its own separately controlled voltage. On such a system the speed and direction of each train is independent of the other. The disadvantage is that a pike of this kind usually requires several relatively expensive switches for crossovers and a more complicated power supply which can consist either of separate, properly "phased", transformers or a transformer with several individually variable voltage circuits.

Phasing transformers means simply inserting their line cords into the wall outlet in such a way that the positive and negative peaks of their 60-cycle alternations coincide. Unless they do you will have a short circuit every time the rollers of a locomotive bridge an insulating track pin.

To make sure two transformers are in phase do this. Connect their ground posts together, set their output voltage at the same point, then touch the wires leading from the output posts together. If the transformers are out of phase you will get heavy spark, because the voltage difference between them will be twice the voltage of each one. To correct, reverse the line plug of one of the transformers.

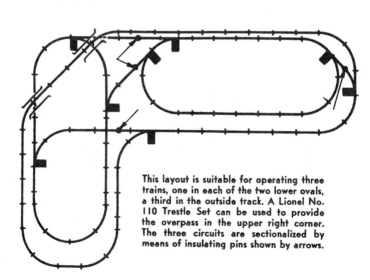

This layout is suitable for operating three trains, one in each of the two lower ovals, a third in the outside track. A Lionel No. 110 Trestle Set can be used to provide the overpass in the upper right corner. The three circuits are sectionalized by means of insulating pins shown by arrows.

MODEL BUILDINGS

CHAPTER SIXTEEN

THE NUMBER of model buildings on your layout will depend on its size and type, and your desire to make them. Their quality will depend on the time you spend, the accuracy of your observation, and your knowledge of a few principles and materials.

Skill was not mentioned. Like everything else in model railroading, skill comes with practice. Time and patience are the only requirements.

Proper tools and materials make the job easier. A good smooth cutting board is important. A steel straight-edge will be a great help—get a printer's 18″ or 24″ rule if possible. A square or triangle is required; get a 30°, 60°, 90° triangle and a 45° triangle if possible. Dividers and a compass will make your jobs easier.

Use some good cutting tool, which should be extremely sharp. A single-edge razor blade can be used but will become dull in a short while. Hobby knives with interchangeable blades, such as X-acto, are available in most hardware stores.

Model cement is a necessity—the sort used on airplanes is good.

A set of good oil paints and some good small brushes will be necessary in order to color models. Except for unusually fine work, it is most often the painting that distinguishes a professional-looking job from an amateurish one.

Skill is not required in painting, but observation and practice are essential. Look out of your window at a house. Perhaps most of the homes in your neighborhood are well painted, but unless a house has been painted in the past year, there will probably be a streak down the sides below each window. Other streaks will appear near the eaves. Bottoms of porch posts are usually splattered from rain. Notice the changes of light on a brick wall, on unpainted board. See and remember the torn tarpaper on a shed, a factory, a garage.

Don't forget that clean and pretty models look too new. Age them: they'll have more character and interest.

It is the small touches that make a good model, and a hardly noticeable sag in a roof can give interest to an otherwise dull model.

Give all railroad buildings a good coating of grime. Have some lampblack in your painting kit and mix it with the basic color of your buildings, or rub thin black paint over the color with a cotton swab. Figure where engines would stand belching smoke and how the wind would carry it. Blacken these sides more than others.

Signal Tower

In tackling model buildings you will need supplies. Among others, you will need a couple of sheets of one- and three-ply bristol board and several of illustration board. The first is a light cardboard suitable for trim on buildings, the second is a heavy board used for walls. They are better quality than ordinary cardboard, and will make more durable models. Both can be bought in artists' supply stores. Also get some dowel of various sizes, scraps of plywood for bases, cellophane for windows, and an assortment of small sizes of airplane balsa wood. Scrap molding is useful for interior braces.

To make the signal tower—a good addition to any pike —study the plan carefully. Use dividers to measure off any distances not given (set the dividers against the scale at the top of the drawing opposite).

Draw the sides on a section of illustration board, marking all windows and doors carefully. Do the same for the four roof sections, remembering that to get the slanting edge of the side you must measure the end, and vice versa.

Make three floors of illustration board (or thin plywood if desired) and allow for the thickness of the walls in measuring. These will fit inside the walls, and with interior wood bracing and cement will make a tight job.

All the trim is cut from three-ply bristol board. The stone corners, the coping on the wall, the roof trim, gutters, edge of chimney—all are made from the light board. The clapboard top of the building is made of 5/16″ strips of one-ply bristol board cemented one over the other.

Windows are cellophane cemented tightly inside the illustration board. Mullions and the other trim are cut from bristol board and cemented in place. Window frames are built up layer by layer; doors are similar.

For downspouts, use very thin dowel or the thin applicator sticks obtained from your druggist. The tank is thick dowel covered with bristol board, rivets pressed in the back with a clock gear. Steps are of illustration board and balsa.

Hobby stores have brick paper, but if you wish to make your own, check details on page 202.

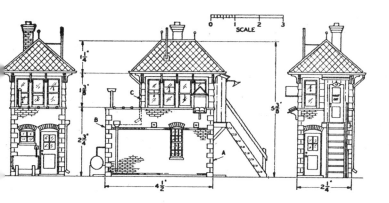

Gantry Crane

On the team track of many yards, gantry cranes are used to lift heavy loads to and from flat cars and gondolas. It is best to piece such a crane together from balsa wood or cigar-box wood and bristol board as a handsome, non-working model.

Dimensions and plans are simple enough if studied. These tips will help.

In making the overhead trusses, make a drawing on a

Above: Crane tracks must be off center so that loads may be swung from freight cars to trucks and then back again.

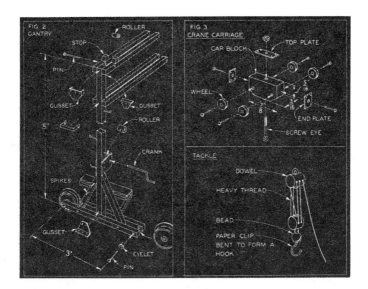

piece of illustration board or wood. Cut the sections carefully; sand with 00 sandpaper. Cement the joining areas and lay them over the drawing in their exact place. Use pins to hold them rigidly together until dry.

When joining the trusses to the uprights, small C-clamps are handy, but weights or rubber bands may be used.

Wheels should be obtained from a hobby store or an old and useless car.

The climbing rungs on the upright can be made from snipped-off staples (a useful item to have) or they can be fashioned from escutcheon pins that are filed to shape. These tiny nails are handy to have, and in this model and others could be used to help the cement hold the pieces.

For gantry rails, use two straight pieces from discarded track, and cement and nail to small ties. These can be purchased or made in a few moments from balsa wood.

Stain the model with a dark brown stain.

Section Gang's Camp

Actually, most section-gang camps are neat as a pin. But the camp shown here is more interesting because of its sloppy condition. It is the litter about it, the decrepitude of the buildings that gives it its charm.

Both buildings here are supposedly made from old box-car bodies hoisted over onto rough foundations. These were then enclosed with rough siding material.

Make the sides of the cars by carefully drawing each cutting line on illustration board. Before cutting, carefully measure off the width of the various boards and scribe lines into the cardboard. This is done with any instrument that is pointed but not too sharp. A filed nail will do. These small indentations will show up as cracks when the model is painted. Do the same for the coal shed and work box.

One roof may be made by carefully bending a piece of illustration board until it takes an angle. Before bending, score a deep line along the center.

The roof is then covered with fine emery cloth. A bit of lampblack brushed lightly onto it will give it tone variety and there you have roofing paper.

Shrubs will be discussed later under scenery, but don't neglect touches such as the shovel, clothes on the line, and ropes hanging from the side of the building.

A good rule to follow is: the closer the spectator, the more accurate the detail. If a structure is located at the closest edge of your layout, take pains with it. If it is far away, a mere suggestion of a ladder may be quite deceptive.

As with all of the buildings in this chapter, study the drawings; use your imagination and your ingenuity.

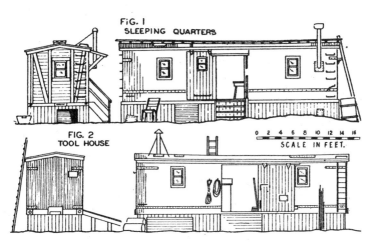

FIG. 1
SLEEPING QUARTERS

FIG. 2
TOOL HOUSE

SCALE IN FEET.

Making Your Walls Outstandingly Realistic

In a model building, the walls are the thing. Almost anyone can cut them properly; almost anyone can mount them in place. It is a good modelmaker who can give them surface texture and color that will fool the eye by completely imitating some other material.

Let us consider materials one by one:

Brick: Brick paper and stone paper can be furnished by a hobby store, either by mail or directly. It can be effectively used, but it has the disadvantage of sameness. The tone is the same whether in the foreground or background, whether near the tracks or far from them, whether on a new or old building. Good brickwork can be made.

Using illustration board, scribe lines ⅛″ apart, frequently breaking lines. Make vertical marks 7/16″ apart, usually staggered as in real brickwork. (This makes bricks actually about twice as big as scale bricks, but in order to be seen they cannot be reduced.) Paint the board quickly with a gray to which some lampblack has been added without thorough blending. When dry, the board is painted in the basic brick tone, a dull, rust red. Grays or blacks are wiped onto spots while the red is still wet, and browns may be added if the bricks are near earth.

If the paint was not slopped on, it will be seen that already the undercoating of "cement" gray peeps through at the dividing lines. When the wall is almost dry, use the scriber and draw it along the depressed lines just firmly enough to pick up any red; and the bricks are done.

Wood: Plain tongue-and-groove siding can be made by fine India ink lines on illustration board or by finely scribed lines which are darkened. Lines must be accurately parallel, but may vary in thickness. Clapboard is made with narrow strips of bristol board cemented from the bottom up in overlapping fashion. A very rough-hewn warped effect can be gotten by cutting lightly into bristol board and prying one layer away.

Lapboard is made by applying 1/16″ strips of bristol board to illustration board. They may be irregularly spaced, but should be vertical to cover the imaginary cracks between the vertical planks.

Shingle is made by cutting 5/16″ strips of bristol board, then cutting 3/16″ into the strip at 5/16″ intervals. These cuts show the divisions between shingles, and when applied, one on top of the other, they are very realistic.

Concrete: Illustration board tinted gray with oil paints, sprinkled with fine sand while wet, and scribed for any dividing blocks will give an excellent effect. Black is mixed heavily where smoke is present—as at the peak of a tunnel entrance. Brown may stain it where water carries earth down. Brownish-red stains will almost invariably mark concrete where reinforcing bars have rusted and water has spread discoloration.

Stone: Stone differs from brick in that the size usually varies with each stone; so must the scribed lines. Also, colors vary, so each stone should be touched up individually after a basic color has been laid down.

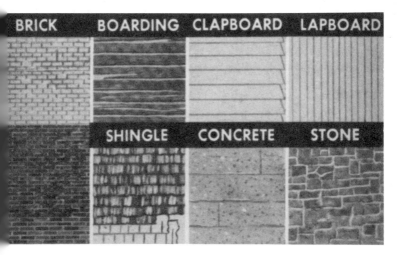

Highway Overpass

Bridges present a problem for the model railroader. It is possible to build a complete truss bridge to scale. But the modelmakers who tackle elaborate bridges either achieve a crude imitation, or they end up building beautiful bridges and do not have time for anything else.

The trick to bridgework on a model railroad is twofold: (1) wherever possible, buy the best commercially made bridge and work it into a plan; (2) when building your own bridge, keep it simple, keep it in the background, and —again—keep it simple.

For the wooden truss bridge shown here, use wood, ½″ thick, 5″ wide, and of a length suitable for the distance you wish to span. Be sure the wood is seasoned. This will form your roadway, and so should be painted with two or three coats until the grain has disappeared. Assuming a macadam surface, paint it a very dull black with some gray mixed in. Make a dingy narrow white stripe along the road 2″ from one side.

One inch from the other side, place a low guard rail made of ¼″ square strip placed on bristol board squares. This will be the pedestrian guard rail—the squares holding it up every 2½″. It should be stained a dark brown, nearly black.

The kingposts and trusses are made from ¼″ or ⅜″ square wood; the main columns of ⅜″ or ½″ wood. Each edge has a guard rail similar to the pedestrian guard rail.

The hand railing along the edge is built of wire which must be soldered while held with pins, the excess solder being filed off. Cement is not satisfactory for this, and perhaps the best advice, if soldering is difficult or impossible, is to make the railing of 1/16″ square wood strips.

Make a concrete abutment at each end of the bridge. This will be of illustration board tinted gray, scribed in large blocks ¾″ high by 1″ wide. With darker brownish-gray, make a few marks where rain has run off.

The main columns are set in small concrete bases that are made like the abutments, but they are colored in a darker, dirtier tone.

After the bridge is assembled and securely cemented and dried, check the paint job before installing it. See that the underside is smudged a dull black.

Carefully installed, it's a bridge to be proud of.

Railroads in the Atomic Age

A railroad lives, grows and changes with the times. New industries change railside scenery. New, strange cargoes require new cars and rolling stock. Our infant Atomic Age has already made its mark and the changes are quickly reflected in model railroading as well.

On these pages are a few scenes from Lionel's elaborate showroom railroad. Below a flatcar has just delivered an ICBM rocket to its launching site. Here again the model railroad has to take a few liberties. In real life a siding would not be nearly as close to the launching pad!

Radio-active atomic waste requires special disposal cars which take it in the thick-walled concrete containers to be permanently buried—flatcar and all—deep within a mountain. Lionel model of it, on next page, flashes a red warning signal automatically.

Not all products of the Atomic Age look as ominous, however. Before very long atomic power houses will be as common a sight along the country side as the coal and oil burners are today. Many such power houses are already under construction and special railroad cars have been devised to carry the huge components to the construction sites.

Below is a special Allis-Chalmers flat car designed to carry a huge heat exchanger used in atomic power installation.

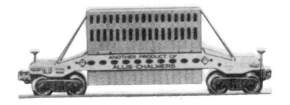

The station platform (above left) is sold with an extra piece of fencing so that two or more of them can be joined into a real long station.

Other structures commonly associated with passenger stations are newsdealer's booths, several kinds of which are available—with built-in horns and whistles and with animated figures.

Watchmen's shanties and traffic gates mark many grade crossings throughout the United States. Others are guarded by flashing signals. All of these can be obtained and put in place, since your roads will inevitably cross tracks at places other than bridges and underpasses. Their landscaping will be covered in the next chapter.

Above is an amusing animated newsstand. At right a section gang car, reaching a grade crossing has just set the "banjo" signal to work.

Ice Storage Plant

Railroads face a problem in keeping refrigerator cars iced and keeping passenger cooling systems and drinking water tanks filled. Usually they provide small storage buildings for ice in the car yards; often these are put together from one or two box-car bodies, as shown below.

Make the car bodies just as you did in the section-gang camp (p. 200). Use office staples for ladder rungs on the car, and heavy dowel to support the platform. The small cooling tower is built up of layers of heavy illustration board. This can be cut on a sharp bevel, and when painted will resemble the small refrigeration towers commonly seen. The stack on the rearmost square section of building is a ½″ dowel.

The section of building added to the cars is easily made of scored cardboard. It can be neater than the others, since it presumably is new.

Color the model, using a railroad bed. Smudge it liberally, using a cotton swab and thin black paint. Piers may be concrete splashed with mud; the stack should be dull black.

Model Concrete Plant

Industrial structures of all types lend character and purpose to your railroad. A concrete plant such as this one justifies the use of gondolas, box cars and covered hopper cars (see chapter on Freight Trains). Your switch engine can be kept busy supplying the plant.

The structure looks complicated, but it is actually a combination of simple parts. All walls are scored to represent wood siding except the open space "A." This gap is the large hopper inside the structure, and is braced by angle irons made of bristol board. To bend these, score a ¼" strip down the center and bend on that line. Score heavily, but don't cut through. On the underside of one flange, punch lightly to represent rivets.

Windows in the structure would normally have a heavy coating of white dust on them. Use flat white paint and an almost dry brush on the cellophane. It is almost impossible even to see through them.

The endless-belt conveyor on the building is a dummy,

and is made from a strip of thin bristol board with tiny buckets cut from wood. On the side nearest the railroad is a covered conveyor. Hopper cars drop their material in a bin under the tracks, and the covered conveyor lifts them to the top.

A dime-store cement truck can be used with this model. The yard conveyor shown is a dime-store plastic model painted to fit the scene. When in a store look for other figures, trucks, and cars. You'll find plenty of them of just the right size. In painting, remember that the side of a building closest to the tracks will be the dirtiest.

Meat Processing Plant

In most cases when making a building, lay your track in the best manner, then fit the building between sidings or alongside the track. Don't forget, of course, that one siding can serve more than one building.

The meat processing plant shown can have its dimensions altered to suit the space available. This is especially true of the stockpen. Naturally, this can be used with the Lionel stock cars, and the Lionel stockpen can be used here or can be put at the other end of the layout. Then the cars could be shuttled back and forth.

As a guide, these dimensions are given: length, 9¼"; width, 6½"; height from base to ridgepole, 7¾". Make the doors 1¾" high by ¾" wide. Windows are 1¼" high by ¾" wide. On the side shown, allow one full inch at each end, then place a ¾" wide window. Allow ⅞" between windows. Other dimensions may be judged from these.

Notice that the far side is not shown. This happens be-

Photos by Frank Ellison; courtesy of Model Railroader.

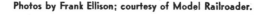

cause the building was made by Frank C. Ellison of New
Orleans on his cellar, round-the-room layout. A visitor can-
not see the rear, which is only a few inches from the wall.
Frank Ellison, considered by many to be the unsurpassed
expert in this field,[1] rarely finishes all four sides of a model.
This is one advantage of a layout against the wall.

This building can be the reason your cattle cars and
refrigerator cars are used on your layout.

[1] Ellison's articles appear regularly in *Model Railroader*. Many of the ideas
here and elsewhere are directly derived from correspondence and his writings.

To get the most activity from your
cattle cars, make a cattle corral
as shown here. Using Lionel stock
cars, you can then put the Lionel
corral at the opposite end of your
layout. This will give you a good
reason for shunting your cars back
and forth, which should be done by
your switcher while shunting cars.

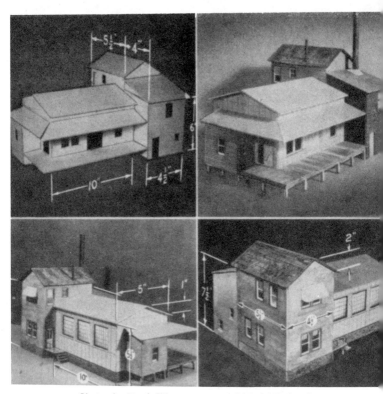

Photos by Frank Ellison; courtesy of Model Railroader.

Small Parts Factory

Small industries lend themselves especially well to model railroading. Large plants would overshadow the trains. One such small plant is shown here. It makes small parts for heavy industry and receives daily shipments of material in box cars, gondolas, or flat cars. It ships products the same way.

As in all of these buildings which "just growed," make one section at a time, simulating the different materials. In some cases they should be painted separately if there is a wide variation in age. Even if newly painted, don't forget that wood and metal do not look alike when painted.

This building, another one of Frank Ellison's, shows the care with which he simulates brick or builds window frames and similar trim. Attention to the small details is what keeps your models from looking like decorated boxes.

Most of these buildings can be lighted if that is desired. Be careful not to overdo it, but leave some parts dark, some dim, some bright. If lighted, don't omit window shades; do include some interior details.

In making buildings, join with cement very carefully and use some means of holding the joints together for a time. Weights or rubber bands are good methods, but where that is not possible, use pins.

Use the size of a door—1¾″ high by ¾″ wide—to get the other dimensions of the building. Adjust the size to the space you have. Using a door as a gauge of size can be done with real buildings. Doors are about 7′ x 3′, rooms are about 10′ high. On the day when you can look at a structure near your home and decide to model it, you will have come a long way. When your friends can recognize the local scene—then you are a modelmaker!

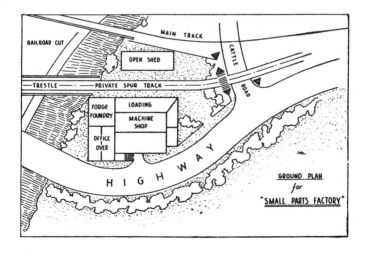

Oil Storage Depot

Tank cars are most often used for oil, although they carry many other products; with a working oil well on your layout (see p. 208) the cars fit in well. The chances are that the smallest refinery is too big for your layout, but there is a small oil yard on Frank Ellison's layout that would serve as a good design for a small space.

The yard consists of two tanks, an office, a small pumping shack, a fence, and some barrels made from dowel. The fence is made from wire window screen carefully cut to size, painted with aluminum paint, and soldered or tied with fine wire to posts made from coat-hanger wire.

Photos by Frank Ellison; courtesy of Model Railroader.

The office and loading platform are very simple. Make the loading hoses from lengths of solder, since it is flexible but will hold its shape well. Make the tanks of cardboard cereal boxes or from tin cans. Make the outside tank sheathing of bristol board. On the reverse side punch out rivets with a rounded nail on soft wood, or use a gear from a clock and roll it along. Several of these gears will give you different sizes. Paint with aluminum and smudge with cotton and very thin black paint.

Make the shack as usual, then carefully attach the ribs to the sides. These will be 1/16″ wide and must be carefully applied to look like the ribs of a galvanized metal shack. The unloading tubes may be made from solder or wire.

One of the tricks of model railroaders is to use a piece of plywood or beaver board as a base for a model building. They can work on their bench or in the kitchen and complete the model before installing it. In most cases, this saves time and effort. When set in place, bits of scenery and plaster will hide the edges of the board.

In the picture opposite, notice the small guard rail along the highway. This is made very simply and can be duplicated in a few moments. Use a few small sticks (about ¼″ diameter) for posts, and bristol board or string for the rails. One building tip: don't use wire to make model wire or cable. Use string. It hangs naturally and is easy to work with, while wire invariably kinks. The ladder on the tanks can be made with heavy wire sides. Sections of toothpick can be glued to them. Make it on a board and leave it until thoroughly dry. Wait until you're ready to put the model in place before applying the ladder. Remember: it is a delicate bit of model work.

Modern Factory

While most of your buildings should have a weathered appearance that lends character to them and to your road, a modern plant will fit in. It will serve as contrast.

A factory similar to the one that appears here is made by Skyline Manufacturing Co. Many other buildings can be bought in kit form at hobby stores. For the most part, they are well made, and while some are harder to build than others, all can be made by any hobbyist.

If you do use kits, it is a good idea to add a wing or a shed to alter them slightly, otherwise they will look exactly like the one on the next fellow's road. Repainting the signs with fine camel's hair brushes and good paint is another possibility.

The model shown here was made for the Lionel layout in New York. On a new building, commercial brick paper is a handy thing and looks quite good. Make the windows by ruling black India ink lines on sheets of celluloid before cementing them in position.

The tank is made of stained balsa wood parts, a heavy dowel for the pipe, and a can covered with illustration board. Wooden tanks usually show vertical boards and

should have wires wrapped around as reinforcement. The wires are closer together at the bottom, wider at the top.

Overall dimensions of this model are: length, 18"; width, 10"; height to roof edge, 5". The clerestory windows at the top will rise about an inch, making total height 6".

A feature often found on new buildings is a metal roll-type door. It may also be seen as an improvement on older buildings. These doors are not difficult to make. Use illustration board as backing. Get some heavy lead foil or aluminum foil. Press indentations with a straightedge, using a soft backing. Then cement them together.

Model of a House Under Construction

A model of an unfinished house will create a lot of interest. Such a model may be carried to a more or less completed stage. The ground around the house should be rough, with even mounds of earth. You will notice that in the background appear the familiar automatic signal and, across the tracks, the base of a water tower, or tank. The placement of these has been described earlier.

These models are built of real scale building material obtainable in model railroad shops, and are most readily adaptable to 2″ x 4″, 2″ x 6″, or 2″ x 8″ scales, which will turn out to be about 1/16″ x ⅛″ to 1/16″ x 3/16″ in actual size, and fit readily into any shape community formation.

Foundations can be built from cardboard covered with red brick building paper which is also obtainable in most model train shops. Note that the method of construction on these "to-be-left-uncompleted" buildings follows that used by contractors in real construction work. A few odds and ends in the way of pieces of scantling, unused boards and "blocks" of the miniature brickboard left lying around on the premises as real builders leave them, add a lifelike appearance to the scene.

These pieces of "scrap" material may be cemented or glued into fixed positions once the best arrangement to effect "character" has been decided upon. It has been found that a very effective design may be laid out at little or no expense, beyond the time spent in tinkering away at your hobby. In these unfinished structures it seems that there is no call for the installation of model windows, or even frames, as the buildings appear more real without them.

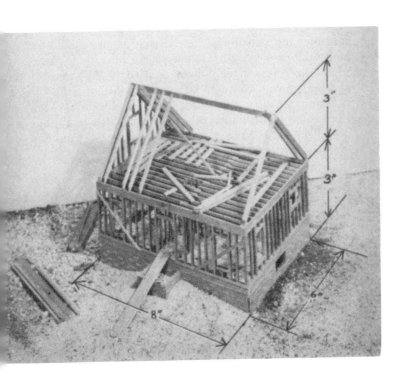

Two Small Suburban Homes

In some spots on your layout you will want to build a
house or two to quarter the dwellers of your landscape. It
is possible to buy Skyline or other home-building kits, but
you can easily duplicate these or even your own house.

Enough dimensions are given on the photographs to let
you infer the remaining ones. Usually homes should be
built with care, since few homeowners allow their places
to run down very much. Of course, if you build a number
of them, one or two might be somewhat dilapidated.

In any case, do not make the finish too glossy and clean.
Even a new home is a flat color, and in a matter of months
it will show slight variations in tone where the wind and
rain have weathered it.

As always, a few homelike touches help. A tiny and recognizable wash hanging on a thread-like line will amuse anyone who sees it. More important, it lends reality to the scene. The same thing applies to a stack of cordwood or any other of the numberless things around homes.

It is wise to be careful about the scale of the things you put in a home or factory yard. One thing that is not in scale will make the whole scene look poorly done.

If you choose to light the houses, partition them so that only one or two rooms light up. You'll be surprised how easy that is and how much it helps appearances.

You can get model plans in many of the home-making magazines, and full dimensions are usually given. If you use these plans, it is wise to cut the dimensions down so as to reduce the height slightly, and the width and length quite a bit. They will look much better.

A Small Barn

Rural settings will be thoroughly covered under Scenery, but probably you will want some farmland or a suggestion of it. That should include some buildings.

The barn was made by Lawrence Gieringer, builder of Roadside America near Hamburg, Pa. (route 22 north of Harrisburg). It was made with a plaster base simulating cement over large stones. The sides are made of strips cemented on cardboard or plywood, and simulate random-width boarding. Tin roof is illustration board with ridges added.

Small Café

Originality is the hallmark of the model railroader, so when Fritz Schumacher made a Western town he built the Silver Dollar Café. To give it a fresh twist, he planted a real silver dollar right over the door. This makes the model unusually expensive, but then, he can always get his money back if he needs it.

A rough emery paper can be used to simulate the tarred roof of the café. Lettering can be done on artists' board with India ink, then the signs can be cemented on. When lettering of this kind is done, make horizontal guide lines, then lightly pencil the letters. Then make the fine letters, lifting the pen at the end of each stroke.

A Community Church

Throughout this chapter on buildings, the emphasis has been on small versions. This is because a building that is too high will tower over everything and dominate the layout. Like all general rules of the sort, it can be violated, but only at times and with discretion. Keep tall buildings or very large ones at a minimum unless you have a spectacularly large layout.

Even though the church shown here is small, it still is 13" to the steeple top. At the ridgepole it is 7" high, at eaves 4" high; length is 16", width is 9".

Build the steeple with great attention to detail, for it will be under close scrutiny. Windows should be set in, and you can simulate stained-glass windows by touching tiny dots of different paints onto the rough side of celluloid. With lights behind them, the effect is good. Experiment a bit before applying them.

Don't omit the announcement board on the front lawn.

Use imagination and ingenuity on your models. Try new materials. Maybe you can make a model chimney that is closer to the real thing than has ever been done. Look for uses for common materials—spools, pipe cleaners, sawdust, and salt. But now, on to landscaping and scenery.

Models on the Green Hill and Atlantic

Meet Walt Hill, wearing engineer's cap, model builder of the Green Hill and Atlantic Railroad of Madison, N. J., with headquarters in the cellar of a home. The "Brass Hat" and General Superintendent has dropped all dignity to operate the turntable.

The G. H. & A. is an 0-gauge model railroad, and has 1,100 feet of track. It is equipped to operate six trains at once. It has well-coordinated freight yards, a freight station, steam service yards for eight locomotives, a Diesel house for an A & B passenger engine, and a yard switcher.

It has 20 passenger and 70 freight cars, and its electric equipment is two multiple-unit trains, one engine. A gas-electric car does the railroad's light passenger work. A water tower, a signal tower and five passenger stations dot its orbit. There are three bridges, one wood, one concrete and one painted to resemble steel. Several tunnels grace its mountainous aspects. Its tracks vary from 39" to 54" above the floor. The scenery is of asbestos and plaster of Paris, based on an old window screen. Plenty of turpentine was added to the oil paint to dull the "shine."

The turntable has a four-foot disc of ¼" plywood fastened to the vertical shaft on which it pivots as the disc is turned.

PLAN OF THE GREEN HILL AND ATLANTIC R.R.

6-loop track layout uses 1,100 ft. of track and operates 6 trains at once, requiring 6 people to keep it running. (1) Painted Scenery background conceals furnace, (2) Waterfalls, (3) River, (4) Concrete Arch Bridge, (5) Section Camp, (6) Tower, (7) Steel Girder Bridge, (8) Tower, (9) Diesel Shop & Yard, (10) Movable Bridge, (11) Station, (12) 2-Level Steel Arch Bridge, (13) Interlocking Tower, (14) Yard Office, (15) 8-Track Freight Yard, (16) Controls (Main), (17) Sand Tower, (18) Coal Tipple, (19) Water Tower, (20) Turntable, (21) 5-Stall Roundhouse, (22) Steam Plant, (23) Pond, (24) Coal Mine, (25) Passenger Terminal, (26) Tower, (27) Brush Factory, (28) "Stone Gulch" Station, (29) Freight Station, (30) Roundhouse Controls, (31) Secondary Control Board, (32) Station.

227

S HOWN BELOW is No. 5344 Hudson type locomotive just about ready to roll off the turntable in readiness to be coaled. The roundhouse operator's shanty, like all the buildings on this set, are made of illustration board on a wooden frame with bristol board trim. The shanty is painted red with white trim and black roof. The awning is red and white stripe.

An innovation, inasmuch as almost all railroaders are "nuts about flowers," is the flower box which is filled with artificial buds bought from the local 5-and-10. The whole arrangement seems so cozy that one almost expects "a fussy little old man" to step out the shanty door and warn away intruders. The chimney is ⅛″ dowel and the handrail is made with ⅛″ square uprights and $\frac{1}{16}$″ rails.

One of the most impressive things about the whole model is the attention paid to small details and the care taken in working them out. In viewing the entire picture, one is readily aware of how these depict an atmosphere of realism.

This coaling station in the steam locomotive service yards is shown with only one chute down loading up an old 10-wheeler. The station is 17″ high, 13″ long and 8½″ wide. The tower shack in the rear houses the motor drive and upper wheels for the endless chain of buckets hauling up the coal from the storage pits.

In the rear may be seen part of the companion water tank with a section of its ladder. In operation, as shown above, the coal is quickly fed into the tenders of the loco-motive in a direct stream. A second locomotive, turned around, could be coaled at the same time.

The machinery on the tower overhanging the roof is reached by a tortuous stairway in the rear. The heavy, vertical framework of the station is ¼″ square-sawed pine. The boxlike structurework under the timbers is of illustration board scored to resemble heavy boards. The roof is of heavy paper ¾″ wide and painted black to look like tar paper. The building is painted dark gray. After the paint was dried, it was dusted with dry lamp black with a dry brush. Sprinkled lamp black around the base adds to the appearance of coal dust as it would have settled through long use.

IT WOULD take a hardy soul indeed to mount this plank-stepped, rather intricate zigzag stairway leading to the shanty atop the coaling station. This cabin is called the "Drive House," and is where all the machinery used to operate the coal conveyor is housed.

The treads of the stairway are $\frac{1}{32}$" x $\frac{3}{16}$" pine or balsa wood. The supports under the treads are $\frac{1}{16}$" x $\frac{1}{4}$", and the handrails are $\frac{1}{16}$" square. The photo above shows the $\frac{1}{4}$" square timbers of the building, and the illustration board to which everything is glued. The doors and ladder in the lower corner are to service the chain bucket mechanism. This photo was taken before the building was painted.

S HOWN BELOW is the photograph of a "through suburban" two-level, typical New England station with three
platforms. It represents an imposing brick structure with
a scenic background, with an unusual "portico" over the
tracks. At left center can be seen a caboose at a spur end
and a miniature parking lot.

The upper platform level leads to the upper floor of the
station, and then downstairs inside the building, to the
lower level. There are outside stairs at each end. Inside the
building is also an underpass to the other platform, across
the tracks, which has a shelter from the weather.

The building is 13″ long, 6½″ wide, and 10″ high. It
is covered with red brick paper, with white trim. The roof
is green, streaked with brown to resemble copper.

THE PHOTOGRAPH above is the replica of a modern factory
building, with the office wing and administration building on the right. It has a special spur leading in from the
railroad, so that a car may be "spotted" to expedite ship-
ping. This is in conformity with the movement, "Ship by
Rail," inaugurated by the leading railroads several years
ago. The factory building is of red brick; the smokestack,
in reality, a small water pipe covered with red brick paper.

Below, the bridge is a double-deck imitation "steel" arch
structure, painted an aluminum shade to resemble its
real counterpart. It is built of wood on the outside surfaces, while the gussets, plates and small angle beams are
made from bristol board. It is 46″ long, 7¼″ wide and
15¼″ high.

"STONE GULCH," shown here, is a lonely way station at which only local passenger trains stop. The
station is of brick which conforms to that used in the highway bridge-underpass in the background. The telephone
poles are ¼″ dowels, and as tall as any model constructor
chooses. They are painted dark brown and black. The insulators are white beads fastened with small pins, or glued
on. The stonework is made by cutting illustration board
¼″ wide and in various lengths from ⅜″ to 1″ long. They
should be glued to a back of illustration board which
has been stiffened by wood framing. Paint all over with

two coats of light gray to represent mortar between the
stones.

From a paint store buy a tube of black, a tube of white
and one of burnt umber (ground in linseed oil). Squeeze
about one inch of each onto a small board which you may
use as a palette. With a brush about ⅛″ wide apply the
color to a stone. Use plenty of white and brown, not too
much on the black. The paint will be sticky and will dry
slowly. It will build up to look like rough stone, as the
rough texture appears the best. Clean the brush in turpentine often while painting.

THE BLACK DIAMOND COAL COMPANY tipple and loading tracks shown below are typical of most of those served by the railroads of the Eastern mining districts. The main structure itself is built over the entrance to the mine, and underground tracks or hoists deliver the freshly-mined coal directly into the tipple. It is then "dumped" directly into the "hoppers," or "gondolas," used by every railroad.

Usually, in making a model tipple, the structure is painted light and dark shades of brown and dusted generously with dry lamp black to resemble the "real thing." The supports are ¼″ timbers. The roads are cut from orange crates. This material is cheap and readily available. The fence posts are ⅛″ dowels stuck into holes at the edge of the roads. The trees are golden rod. Pick it in the Fall when it is dry. Spray it with several shades of green show-card paint to which some glue has been added. The cement block cellar wall is painted with "Grotto Blue" Bondex to represent the sky.

Here is shown a typical makeup model switchyard with its "Green Ball Express" trains (perishable goods) being made up ready for the take-off on either side of a slow freight hauling coal, and just pulling out with only its caboose and a few coal cars in sight.

MODEL
INDUSTRIES
FOR YOUR
MODEL RAILROAD

THERE IS REAL FUN in owning a model railroad. But the first step is in acquiring a model locomotive, trackage, equipment, etc., and then gradually adding piece by piece until you have the system complete—switchyards, terminals, classification yards, towns, villages, industrial buildings and a varied number of assorted cars, coaches, engines and scenic effects to make up a little railroad empire of your own.

Petroleum and Railroads

Each particular type of car has a use all its own. Take tank cars, for instance: They are one of the most interesting types on any railroad. They serve the vast petroleum industries, carrying crude oil from the oilfields to refineries, and in turn, from the refineries to tank storage fields, to big industrial plants, to wholesale merchants in almost every city and, in some cases, directly to individual consumers who have pooled their interests to lower costs.

Each phase of this system of distribution is a vivid illustration of modern life, and modern life could not go on,

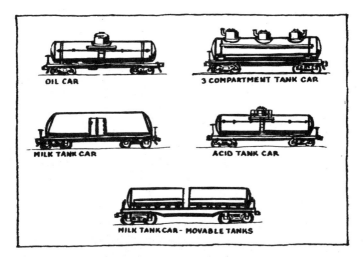

OIL CAR

3 COMPARTMENT TANK CAR

MILK TANK CAR

ACID TANK CAR

MILK TANK CAR - MOVABLE TANKS

as it does, were it not for the vast network of rail lines which cross and criss-cross our wonderful land.

Tank Cars to Box Cars

Tank cars are also used in various other industries, such as in the transporting of great quantities of milk, chemicals and acids, and even in some arid communities the carrying of water. In some localities it is not uncommon to see great trains composed of 100 cars or more each, all tankers. Many, what the railroaders themselves call "solid tank trains," start out daily on regular schedule from the various oil fields in the great Southwest, headed for Kansas City, St. Louis, Chicago and similar large cities where big refineries are located.

Modern tank cars of newer design and capacities, are usually aluminum-covered, thus eliminating the great hazard of bygone years when it was not uncommon to see an oil tanker explode and catch fire from the intense heat of the sun.

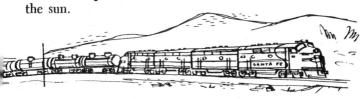

Oil Derrick

The model oil field shown below consists of producing wells out of which flow oil and natural gas under their own force. This is called a natural flow and marks the heaviest and least costly production of all. All of these wells gradually lose their nature-provided propulsion forces, however, and derrick engines and pumps must be installed. Most of these are operated with so-called "walking beams," which may be seen at the base of the derricks.

In the left lower background of the picture is shown a series of field storage tanks into which the oil is pumped prior to being siphoned out by a different set of suction pumps to tank cars on a siding such as is shown in the upper left background.

Trained employees keep a constant watch on these oil fields, and the moment the natural propulsion (gas pressure) forces begin to weaken, the walking beam pumps, now usually operated with "donkey" Diesel engines, are placed into operation so as to drain each well of its last drop of usable fluid.

The first known oil well in the country — called "Drake's Folly."

Crude Oil Farm

One of the most interesting oil structures for your model railroad system would be a reproduction of the first oil well experimental stations brought to public notice by a man named Drake at Titusville, Pennsylvania, in 1859. Shown above, in miniature, it was a rude clapboard affair with the pumped oil spouted into empty barrels which were carried away four barrels to a horse-drawn wagon.

This first producing well was called "Drake's Folly," the populace at that time having little faith in the so-called "new-fangled" oil lamps for which the crude oil was first used. Later it took the place of whale-oil, lubrication fats, etc., and was the basis of many such great fortunes as the one created by the late John D. Rockefeller.

Nowadays, instead of a single, ill-constructed pumping station, as shown, the country is dotted with great crude oil "farms," where hundreds of vast storage tanks receive the gushing crude oil to hold until it is graded and classified to various forms of refining and distribution to often far-off manufacturing plants.

Gasoline, naphtha, kerosene, lubricating oils and even

plastics and cosmetics are now manufactured from the various grades of crude oil and the residue after refining.

To reproduce such a crude oil farm you need only a few empty coffee cans for tanks. These may be partly submerged in artificial soil to resemble sunken tanks, and a miniature ladder can be constructed from a few toothpicks, a dab of glue, and a bit of rubber-covered wire and dowels used to imitate connecting pipelines.

The various buildings on the farm may be made of thin wood or cardboard, windows may be painted in, and smaller storage tanks may be made from sawed-off bits of dowel.

FIELD PUMP HOUSE

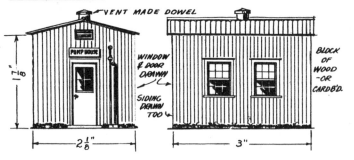

VENT MADE DOWEL

PUMP HOUSE

WINDOW & DOOR DRAWN

SIDING DRAWN TOO

BLOCK OF WOOD —OR CARDB'D.

$1\frac{7}{8}$"

$2\frac{1}{8}$"

3"

These pipelines are made of dowel sticks cut to proper length and supported by wood blocks. When multiple lines are used (as in tank farm on p. 240) pipelines feeding individual tanks are painted different colors.

aluminized or painted black and sprinkled with fine sand to give a real earthy and natural look.

All "pipelines" may be simulated by lengths of wood dowel sticks which may also be painted to correspond with the dowels. Pumphouses, as illustrated, may be built out of cardboard and striped with gray paint to resemble corrugated iron siding.

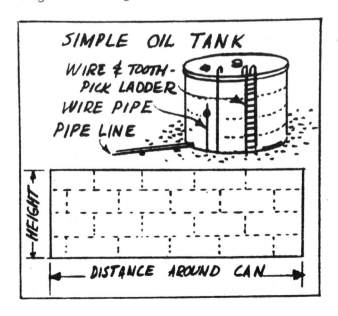

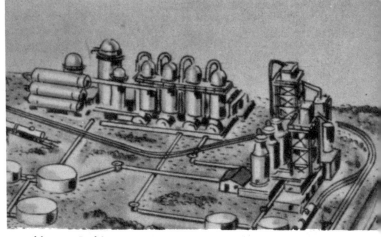

How to Build an Oil Refinery

The erection of a model oil refinery for use as an adjunct to your model railroad system is comparatively easy, as shown by the diagram above and its reduction to a measuremental basis on the following page. Again the simple process of sawing off pieces of dowel wood, and the rounding of tops with an ordinary pocket knife will give the appearance of the real thing after being arrayed as shown with the horizontal and partly-submerged tanks and the connecting pipelines of rubber-coated wire and dowels.

The painting of these pieces has a large part to do with the actual appearance of your set after it has been finished. Refinery colors of tanks and shafts are usually of a silvery tint, the production of which has been described in an earlier chapter.

Most of the buildings, as many or as few as are desired, may be constructed of bits of cardboard, or of buff-colored brick board which can be purchased in most any model store. Other buildings may be built of corrugated cardboard painted any color desired. All pipeline connections are built of rubber-coated wire and wood dowel sticks. They can be painted aluminum color and a few may be colored as real ones often are to make tracing pipelines easier.

Other similar lines may be carried off to a considerable distance to simulate connections with your crude oil, or products farms. A railing built of toothpicks with small upright posts of wood, all painted, can be built around the tower platforms illustrated on page 242. Fine drills may be used to make the holes for hand rails.

Side tracks may be built up to any position wanted at the refinery, so that your tank cars may be "spotted" for loading as on any real railroad.

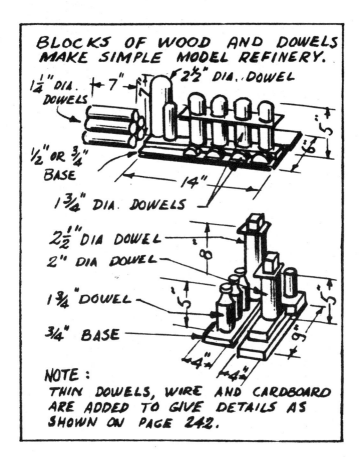

The Bulk Storage Depot

The model bulk storage depot shown above is an interesting unit to make, and adds additional reality to any model railroad set. The buildings and equipment may be made neat and attractive to the eye, or else in the case of those who like to think of railroading in the past, when effects were not so glamorous as they are today, they may be treated with dry lamp black to give the atmosphere of long and hard usage.

A tank car on the spur siding in the background is spotted for loading into the two horizontal tanks with the ladders and cross-walks pictured. The pumping station and the general sales office for on-the-spot deliveries to large trailer tanks, and a loading trailer, appear in the foreground.

The trailer tanks and auto engine cab can be purchased in many five-and-ten stores and the remainder of the equipment may be manufactured at home by the use of balsa sticks and toothpicks for ladders and support posts, and for

the handrails and catwalk across the tops of the two
horizontal tanks. All that is needed is a little glue and a
little ingenuity and patience to build this unit one of the
most effective in your model community.

Building the Oil Loading Rack for the Bulk Storage Depot

On page 245 are shown drawings for the oil loading
rack. The roof can be shaped from cardboard and the
concrete base is a block of wood. The assembly of pipes is
effective and simple if drawn on a solid cardboard strip.
The loading pipe (shown above side view and measuring
3⅛″ long) is drawn on both sides of the cardboard and
cut out as black outline shows. Notice on the side view of
depot the five wide black vertical lines. These are slots to
cut out. The five loading pipes that you will make are
slipped into these slots. See dotted lines on end view of

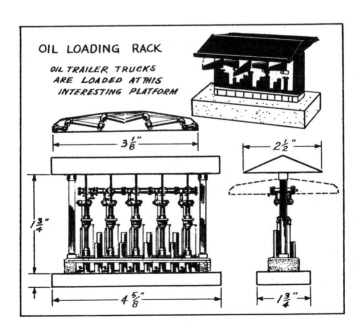

depot. Perspective sketch in upper right corner of picture shows all five loading pipes—three are up and two are down.

Tractor Trailer Oil Truck

Here on page 246, inserted as a pattern," appears a sketch of a tank tractor and trailer which may be bent and

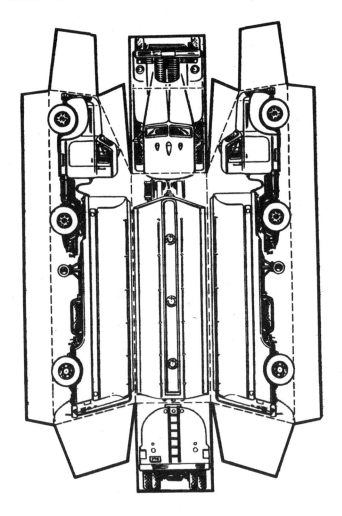

glued together to give the effect of a real truck; this, of course, in event your favorite five-and-ten was unable to supply you. Painted a "fire wagon" red, this cutout will make an effective standout on your model set.

Building A Service Station

Below appears a drawing of a modern gasoline station such as is used and practically made standard by most of the big gasoline companies with stations in cities and towns throughout the United States. It is far more attractive than most community gas stations, and with a little care and ingenuity can be duplicated without trouble.

The station itself is built of cardboard. Drawings and dimensions appear on the following page. Make each side up complete and then assemble the walls and roof. The roof looks best when painted a dark gray, and the light-toned walls with a light shade of ivory. The dark walls are painted dark blue to contrast with the ivory walls. Side-walks are concrete gray color. The pump island is concrete gray and the pumps themselves are bright yellow.

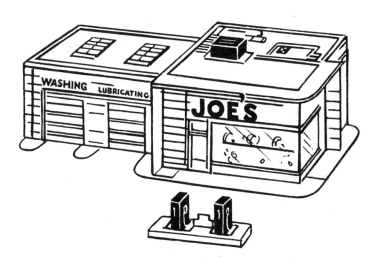

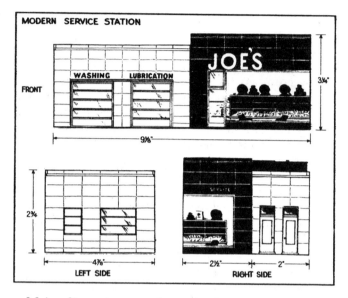

MODERN SERVICE STATION

FRONT

WASHING   LUBRICATION

JOE'S

3¼"

9⅛"

2¾"

4⅞"

LEFT SIDE

2½"   2"

RIGHT SIDE

SERVICE

Major dimensions are shown in drawing above:

A thin wood base or thick cardboard for the "sidewalk" base will facilitate building this model. Lay out the sides, cut them out and draw and paint all details on before assembling. Thin wood strips inside the corners will strengthen the model. This will make a colorful model.

The gasoline pumps for above Service Station. Make two. Lay out on thin cardboard that is easily bent. Layout at right can be followed. Fold on dotted lines and paste flaps underneath.

SERVICE PUMPS

$\frac{3}{8}$"

1"

Up to this point attention has been drawn only to the handling of petroleum products in tankers. But oil products are by no means the only ones which ride in tank cars. There are acid cars, or chemical cars, that have special linings inside, depending on the cargo they carry. You can usually tell an acid car by its single dome with an iron-railed guard built around it.

Another single-domer is the asphalt car. These are equipped with heater coils inside so the cargo can be kept at a constant temperature. The entire cargo might be ruined were it allowed to freeze. Railroads have to be very careful in handling such shipments and every effort is devoted to seeing to it that there are no mistakes.

Many tankers are broken up inside to form compartments which can be unloaded at different points along a waytrain's (peddler train's) route. You can always tell the number of compartments inside by counting the domes on top of the tank. Each dome is a sort of loading and unloading hatch for the compartment underneath it. Some large cars may have as many as six compartments.

Milk tankers come in all different types and styles. Some have big, long, glass-lined tanks that extend the full length of the car. Others are really just flat cars, carrying two separate removable tanks. When they arrive at their destination, the consignee just pulls up a trailer truck next to the spur and the removable tanks slide right off onto the truck. Other smaller removable tanks rest on the car sidewise and can be slid off the tail end onto the body of the smaller auto truck.

Perhaps I have used the word "tanker" rather loosely. But to me, any car that carries a liquid, or a semi-liquid product, is a tanker. Anyway, now you've got a fair idea of how many kinds there are, to what uses they are put, and what you, as a model railroader, will have to contend with, if you decide to go all out in emulation of the real thing.

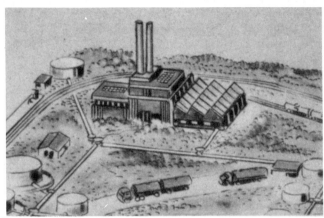

Synthetic Rubber Factory

One of the newest big users of the various types of tank cars is the series of large synthetic rubber plants scattered around the country, erected during the emergency period of World War II, when it seemed that Japan and Germany were just about to shut off our importation of live rubber from the Far East and Malayan countries.

For a time it seemed that our quest for a rubber substitute was hopeless, but as we always do, the leading scientists attached to our great industrial plants, such as Goodyear, Fisk, U. S. Rubber and many smaller manufacturers of tires, got together and really went to work.

What they came up with was not only a workable substitute for real rubber, but a product that, in everyday use on heavy trucks and resiliency parts equipment, turned out to be better than the real thing. The industry developed by leaps and bounds and soon our manufacture of synthetic rubber became so great that we were able to keep our own mobile warfare vehicles moving, and also to provide our Allies, especially Russia, with the necessary rubberized equipment to keep their vast armies moving.

Most of our great synthetic rubber plants were located in the Southwest, near to the principal source of supply of petroleum products without which the modern synthetic rubber tire, and foam rubber products for auto seats, mattress filling, raincoats, shelter tents and any number of military necessities could not be made.

Many great military leaders have often remarked since our rousing defeat of Naziism and Japanese Fascism, that we might have lost the war had it not been for our "rubber," and the splendid efforts of the petroleum industries and our incomparable railroads that kept the synthetic rubber products ever moving toward our widely scattered war fronts.

In the drawing on page 250 is shown the complete plete representation of a synthetic rubber factory, with its various railroad spurs, storage tanks and giant single and double trailer trucks, its various pipelines and conduits, and the giant, twin-stacked factory with its loading sheds, tank cars and other equipment drawn down to scale size. All these can be easily duplicated by following previously given instructions in this book. The model plant itself for instance, can be made of wood blocks with painted doors and windows, or even, using paper brick board, to resemble a brick-walled structure.

Below appears a rear view of the same factory shown on previous page with a model box car in the siding next to the roofed loading platform.

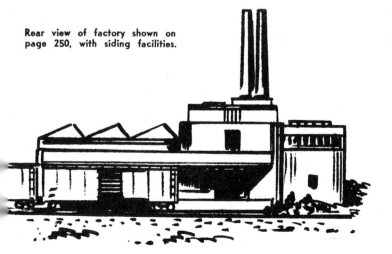

Rear view of factory shown on page 250, with siding facilities.

Pharmaceutical Plant

Another interesting model manufacturing plant for your model railroad layout would be a pharmaceutical factory with its various vast expanses of railroad trackage, spurs, loading and unloading sheds, administration building, widely-separated mixing sheds and chemical kilns and even a modern athletic field for use of its employees when off duty.

Pharmaceutical manufacture is one of the biggest industries in the country and a large user of petroleum and

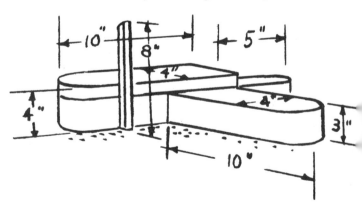

other natural products. The plant shown on p. 252 can all be made from the usual materials described in the construction of similar buildings earlier in this book.

Almost every type of car used in railroading falls into the category of those used daily by these large plants, and model railroad devotees may work up some most intricate and intriguing trains by switching them around.

The dimensional drawing at the bottom of page 252 shows the measurements of the main building in the upper drawing. It has been found to be a popular size that will fit in with almost any ordinary model railroad set.

Here, on page 253, is shown another combination which may be worked up in connection with your pharmaceutical plant: note the waxworks, the asphalt diversion building, the coke works, the synthetic rubber works in the background. Sketches shown here are quick impressions with little detail. All sorts of empty boxes or cartons may be used for these.

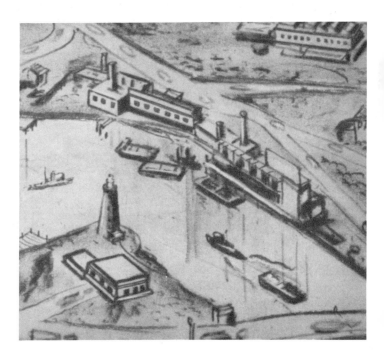

Super Market

Here, taken from the pamphlet, "Petroleum and Your Future," is shown a modern super market in which everything from a can of canary seed to a pair of rubber boots, a pack of playing cards or a tailored-to-measure suit can be bought, a place where you can get a haircut or a permanent wave, buy a pack of cigarettes or get a prescription filled, without moving your car from a comfortably-large parking space, or walking more than a few feet.

These new super markets are really little cities in themselves. They are becoming more and more prevalent in various parts of the country, and in many almost any article imaginable can be bought. Such a model is quick and easy to build for your railroad.

To Your Homes

Naturally, such institutions have to have vast yardage space and storage room. They maintain their own trucking fleets and each of the individual stores making up the super shopping community has a store design all its own. All of these buildings are easily constructed, as explained earlier in this book, with the exception of the plate-glass fronted buildings shown here.

Non-inflammable plastics, transparent, of course, may be used in the constructing of these stores with the ordinary, paper, cardboard, wooden blocks, etc., fastened together with a good quality glue. The transparent plastics may be bent to fit any shape desired.

Don't fail to note the collection of large factory buildings which appear in the background, and it might add to the looks of your model railroad community set to build a miniature park with artificial trees, and imitation pond.

Such is our modern world. Who knows what will come next? At any rate we seem to be riding "tall in the saddle now." Take, for instance, this model village shown below which lives from the shelves of the modern super market described on the last page. Our *railroads* especially, our modern trucking facilities, and our great petroleum industry make all this possible.

Plasticville houses, barns, garages, etc., are available in most 10c stores and toy stores. These are quickly "snapped" together and just as readily taken apart. Shown are the variety of models available.

Here is shown a model community scene such as has been described in the preceding pages. Note the vast industrial area in the dim background, the hovering tanks and derrick crane structures and, of course, the model Lionel train already made up and ready to highball.

MODELS FOR YOUR "GREEN BALL" EXPRESS

M AKE WAY for the "Green Ball" Express, boys! She's all
made up with about 100 cars, most of them on roller
bearings, and she's a'rarin' to go. On the head end is a great
dual-purpose Diesel engine, maybe two, making her a
double-header, and she'll do up to about 90 miles an hour
on her transcontinental trip carrying perishables.

Years ago they used to call the Green Ball a "manifest"
train. It was a swanky run even in those days, but since the
new, center-thrusted Diesel all but shoved the good old
"iron horse" onto the shorter, slower runs, the new "speed
merchants" rank right up with the ritzy streamliners.

For almost 30 years now the first little 300-horsepower switcher model Diesel has been trying to supersede the ancient iron horse. And it seems that the latter is doomed to languish and, perhaps, even die. The Diesels, in that little more than a quarter century, have taken on more and more of the railroads' work.

They have a distinct advantage. They can run a lot further without refueling, and run at high speeds without damaging the costly roadbeds. The old locomotives had a heavy downthrust at high speed that put dents in even the heaviest rails.

A farm scene on a model railroad. Background hills are painted on back wall. Scale livestock purchased in a hobby shop.

Another thing is, that to modern farming communities, such as the one shown on page 258, the Diesel is a real "glamour girl." She wears gay colors, on the Green Ball as well as on the "big name" streamliners, and who is there that doesn't like glamour?

Every road has a different pattern for painting its Diesels. Some even change the painting design to differentiate between those pulling the streamliners and those hauling the Green Ball. Some are gaudy; some are so loud they almost scream; but all of them "hit the ball" and, to me, recall the good old days when the old woodburner locomotives had red wheel spokes, brass fittings, a beautiful picture of a Tiger

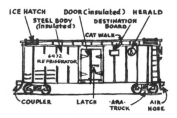

Link-Belt car icer travels on its own track; re-ices 1,400 cars a day.

painted on the tender, and an American flag in the diamond-studded smokestack.

Refrigerator cars, or reefers as they are commonly called, are carrying more railroad tonnage every day. In addition to meats, dairy products, farm produce, and similar perishable stuffs, these cars are now whizzing cross-country loaded with quick-frozen foods. Cargoes of these refrigerated cars are very delicate and the railroads handle them as they would a new-born baby.

All along the route on the long hauls, every road maintains an icing station at intervals. All reefers should be re-iced every 24 hours. Usually the ice is loaded through roof hatches in chunks weighing about 30 to 40 pounds. In the

MILK DELIVERY
DEPOT

case of quick-frozen foods, bunkers also receive about 30%
salt, to produce lower temperatures.

In the smaller station this re-icing is done by manual
labor. But in many of the larger ones it is all done by
machines. Endless belts, automatic shut-off chutes and
many similar devices are used in the process. The main re-
icer itself is a sort of rolling tower that moves along a platform on its own tracks, like a military tank. The big chunks
of ice are fed by conveyor belt up to the tower where a
grinder breaks them to bits of the proper size. Then the
tower feeds the broken ice into the car hatches through
the hanging, long chutes.

Refrigerated cars must have space at the bottom and
top for the circulation of cold air. Some of the newer ones,

Canning plant in rural area where produce is brought for processing.
The railroad delivers finished product to warehouses in the city.

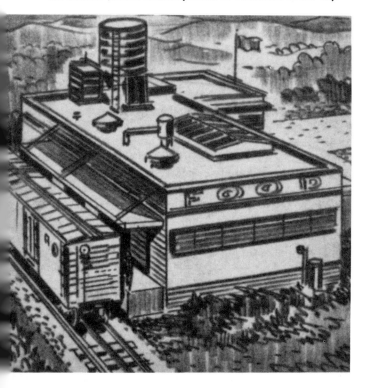

Another view of canning plant shown on page 261, shows truck platform with trailers loading to go to market.

are equipped with fans to promote more circulation and the interior of the cars heavily insulated.

Believe it or not, reefers can get too cold. In the case of potatoes or bananas, both of which require a steady temperature of about 40° to ship to best advantage, sometimes it is necessary to install heaters to reduce the arctic grip of the freezers. This usually happens when such shipments as potatoes and bananas are passing over the Great Divide. Usually charcoal heaters are placed in the icing bunkers to raise the temperatures until the cars are over the mountains and once again in "normal" temperatures.

Most cars are iced and left empty for about twelve hours before they are actually loaded. This is called "pre-cooling," and just before they are loaded with perishables they are iced again.

On page 260 appears an illustration of a typical re-icing station, and at the bottom of the page is shown a shipment of milk being loaded into one of a train of reefers. On page 261 is shown a typical food storage plant with reefer cars drawn up for loading. On the following page is another picture showing the other side of the same loading station.

Many modern reefers get along without icing stations altogether. Like household refrigerators they have their own refrigerating systems. Above is an accurate Lionel model of one such mechanical reefer used by Railway Express. Cars like this get preferential treatment, sometimes being the only freight car on a passenger train.

The illustration on page 259 shows the section of a "reefer" car—a refrigerated car used for perishables—at a freight station platform awaiting unloading. Most of the nation's foodstuff rides at some time or other in the reefer.

But, getting back to our narrative: Sometimes the Green Ball is made up entirely of cattle cars. Railroaders call it a "solid" cattle train. She too gets a green light on a clear track all the way, as livestock is considered as delicate a cargo as perishable foodstuffs.

Cattle cars have to be thoroughly inspected before loading, for an exposed nail or a broken board might seriously injure some of the animals. They have to be thoroughly cleaned too at the end of each trip, and a fresh bed of straw or sand must be spread over the floor before the stock is driven in. According to regulations, written up by the Goverment, about a bale and a half of hay is used in normal weather, and more if the weather is extremely cold.

The reason stock trains are given the "green eye" all the way, is because these Green Ball trains are run exactly on

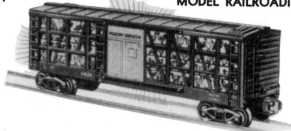

Live turkeys travel from Texas ranches to Eastern markets in special triple deckers.

Here's a model of the double-deck cattle car, used for pigs, sheep, goats. Doors open manually.

a finely-drawn schedule, so as to reach specified railside pens where the animals can be unloaded for exercise, feeding and watering, not less than once every 36 hours. Usually, to be on the safe side, and to keep the animals from "worrying" off poundage, they are given this break religiously every 24 hours. The railroads are just as thoughtful of the animal's comforts as is the Federal Government.

While the animals are out exercising, etc., station attendants rapidly clean out the cars and install new beddings of hay in place of that already dirtied. In hot weather usually the floor of the car is cooled off with a strong-pressured water hose before the hay bedding is put in.

Cars carrying cows, mules or horses have only one deck. Sheep and hogs are usually transported in two-deckers, and poultry, separately penned in crates, will occupy three or more decks in a specially partitioned car.

Other cars which are carried by the Green Ball include large, clean box cars hauling grain. These are fitted with special doors, built inside the regular side sliding doors, and are leak-proof to prevent the grain from filtering out. Automobile cars too usually ride the Green Ball.

As you can see, it is no easy task for the railroads to keep the important "Green Balls" moving without interfering with the scheduling of passenger trains and regular freight.

You model railroaders will have a lot of fun dispatching your own "Green Balls" and keeping the main line clear.

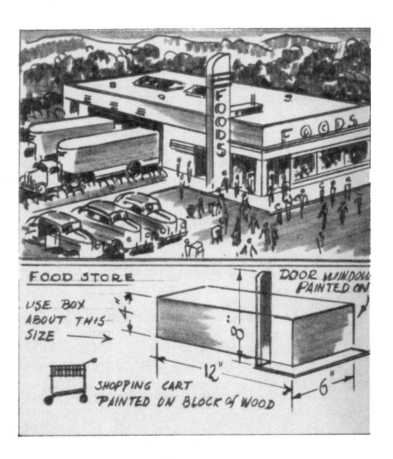

FOOD STORE

USE BOX ABOUT THIS SIZE ——→

DOOR WINDOW PAINTED ON

12"

6"

SHOPPING CART PAINTED ON BLOCK of WOOD

A BRISK HISTORY
OF
AMERICAN RAILROADS

CHAPTER EIGHTEEN

CREATING the railroad empires of the U. S. was a job for many men over many years. There are some great names in the roster. But perhaps one of the cagiest men of railroading was Horatio Allen, civil engineer of the Charleston and Hamburg Railroad. In designing the first road specifically made for steam locomotives and passenger traffic, he said: "There is no reason to expect any material improvement in the breed of horses, while the man is not living who knows what the breed of locomotives will place at our command."

It was a far-sighted remark for 1829. Scattered throughout the young United States were railroads, all horse-drawn. A few used gravity as the main propelling power, letting the weight of the load take stone downhill to canals or roads. But in the main they used horses, for in 1829 there was still no very practical locomotive as we know it.

But it was coming.

The horse drawn cars made their mark, though. Even today the caretaker of a locomotive is called a hostler. A roster of locomotives is often called a stable, and there are many other items handed down through generations of railroad men.

Years earlier, some unsung men in England had realized that their wagons pulled easier if they laid boards in the wagon ruts. Since boards wore out quickly, they put strap-iron on them. This wore the wheels, so iron wheels were used. And then their horses could pull up to fifteen times as much load as before.

And it is from those wagon wheels, incidentally, that we get our present gauge of 4'8½". That was the spread of the wagon wheels in Britain. The Britons took that measurement from Roman war chariots. And today in ancient Babylonian excavations, cart tracks are found— you've guessed it! They measure 4'8½". From what untold source it came, no one knows, but we live with it constantly.

Honors are widely scattered in adding up the "firsts" in railroading in the U. S. John Stevens received a charter from New Jersey in 1815, but a rough tramway had been in use in Boston in 1795. The first locomotive in the Western Hemisphere was run over tracks of the Delaware and Hudson. The Charleston and Hamburg, mentioned above, quickly attained a length of 135 miles, then the longest in the world.

But apparently the closest thing to a railroad as we know it was the Baltimore and Ohio. Americans had heard wondrous tales of George Stephenson's *Rocket* and other locomotives in England. Peter Cooper, an inventive fellow, built the *Tom Thumb* out of rifle barrels and other materials at hand; on August 28, 1830, it ran for 13 miles along the B. and O. pushing a car with 24 passengers at four miles an hour.

B. and O. officials then offered prizes for a practical locomotive, and in 1831, a watchmaker named Phineas Davis produced an engine which he called the *York*, but which railroad men immediately termed the "grasshopper." The *Traveller* which he built later was still in service in 1893.

The *De Witt Clinton* in New York State and the *Best Friend* in Charleston came soon after, and the race for better transportation was on.

In 1835, the B. and O. carried nearly 100,000 passengers over its 70-mile route. Locomotives were still hazardous affairs, not designed for the terrain or the problems, and local opposition from canals and turnpikes forced the roads to develop routes as best they could. Roadbeds were rarely straight, and generally looked as if a tipsy surveyor had lost his bearings and simply followed fenceposts, arriving at his destination only by accident.

To aid in negotiating the abrupt turns so common then, a four-wheel swiveling truck was added to the front of the locomotives. It piloted the engine around the curves, and is still called a pilot truck today.

Cattle and other obstructions were also common, and the "cowcatcher" was introduced to sweep the tracks clear. Now it is usually called the pilot.

Headlights were a thing that came slowly, and the first one was a bonfire built on a sand base on a flat car. The flatcar was pushed ahead of the locomotive. Soon, though, reflectors and oil lamps came into use.

It was out of such necessities that inventions came. As the roads grew, they created new problems. As the problems arose, ingenious men concentrated on them. Many of the problems were solved independently by several men at the same time.

The railroads grew geographically as they grew mechanically. In 1840 there were 2,800 miles of railroad; in 1870 there were 54,000 miles; in 1900 there were 193,000 miles; and in 1930 about 250,000 miles of railroad.

As the roads grew geographically, they also grew in corporate size. Mergers were made, and the resulting bigger roads gobbled up the little ones. It was a natural thing and

THE FIRST RAILROAD TUNNEL IN THE UNITED STATES WAS CONSTRUCTED NEAR JOHNSTOWN, PA., IN 1833.

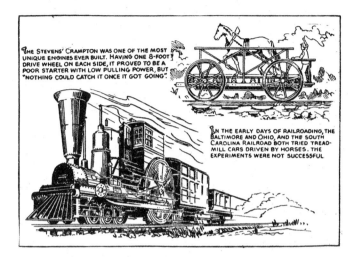

THE STEVENS' CRAMPTON WAS ONE OF THE MOST UNIQUE ENGINES EVER BUILT. HAVING ONE 8-FOOT DRIVE WHEEL ON EACH SIDE, IT PROVED TO BE A POOR STARTER WITH LOW PULLING POWER, BUT "NOTHING COULD CATCH IT ONCE IT GOT GOING".

IN THE EARLY DAYS OF RAILROADING, THE BALTIMORE AND OHIO, AND THE SOUTH CAROLINA RAILROAD BOTH TRIED TREAD-MILL CARS DRIVEN BY HORSES. THE EXPERIMENTS WERE NOT SUCCESSFUL

a good one in most ways. Such growth is graphically shown by the New York, New Haven and Hartford—made from an aggregation of about 200 once-separate properties.

The biggest moment in railroad history in the U. S. was in 1869 when the Union Pacific met the Central Pacific to form a line across the continent. The joining of the roads was flashed across the country by telegraph, and the excitement of the people was at a pitch hard to imagine today. Lindbergh's flight was comparable; but in truth, we are not likely to see such a day until we hear the flash that a rocket has landed safely on the Moon and that inter-planetary travel is practical.

All this scurrying about on rails meant more and more demands on the designers. Much earlier, the Campbell engine had added extra drivers on each side. These were coupled by rods to the powered drivers, and traction was increased greatly. Bigger and bigger locomotives were going faster and faster.

And more and more men were being killed, too. Rarely did boilers blow up any more, but cars were still held together by link-and-pin couplers. An unwary brakeman caught between two cars would be crushed as a locomotive pushed them together—it happened many times.

Trains were difficult to stop, too. Locomotive traction was not high, and cars could push one along for hundreds of yards, even for miles on a downgrade. Brakemen braved all kinds of weather to walk along icy car tops turning down brakes by hand. Then they went back and loosed them. (This method is still used in Britain.)

A number—a very large number—of men were killed in wrecks from lack of brakes or by slipping from the cars on a bad night.

Eventually, the American Railway Association working with the Master Car Builders Association developed the standard coupler in use today. No longer is a man required to step between the cars each time a coupling is made or unmade. And if he is between the cars and a slight movement takes place he will not be crushed.

Many men, George Westinghouse among them, worked to get a practical brake for trains. The Westinghouse brake is still in use; it has been highly developed, of course. It is an air brake, working on compressed air built up by the locomotive. The principle is that the air pressure holds the brakes loose, a release of pressure tightens them. Thus, when error occurs or a train parts, the brakes are applied automatically. Of course, some means are given to release the brakes by hand if desired, otherwise a defective car could not be taken to the shop.

The growth of the roads and their increasing traffic has inspired a joke known to most railroaders.

It seems that at an investigation, a farmer was asked to

THE CHICAGO-NORTHWESTERN RAILWAY IS THE ONLY RAILROAD IN AMERICA THAT RUNS ON THE LEFT SIDE AND HAS A LEFT-HAND DRIVE! THIS IS EXPLAINED BY THE FACT THAT ENGLISH ENGINEERS, WHOSE TRAINS ALWAYS RUN TO THE LEFT, DESIGNED THE ROAD.

explain his actions on a certain day. He said: "I was plowin' in the west forty, and stopped at the end of the furrow fer a minute. I looked down at the railroad, and there on the single track was the west-bound express tearing along like a hound dog after rabbits. I looked back of me, along the curve, and there was the east-bound freight charging down the grade like Betsy heading for the barn with a load of hay at night."

"And what did you do then?" asked the inquirers.

"Not a thing—I just thought to myself, 'What a hell of a way to run a railroad!'"

And it was a hell of a way to run a railroad. A lot of good railroad men were killed in just that way—by what railroad men call "cornfield meets." Despite their bitter humor, and because of the loss of crew and passenger lives and the damage to property, railroads set to work.

Electrical systems fast began to displace the hand signals and train orders used for so long. Automatic block signals came in, and the Union Switch and Signal Company developed device after device to take the human element out of railroading.

On many roads today, a locomotive cannot pass a red signal without tripping a device which will stop it if the engineer does not respond in ten seconds. The red signal is the railroad man's end-all—he cannot pass it. And the signals are so arranged that all of the thousands of things which can (and do) go wrong give a red signal. A short

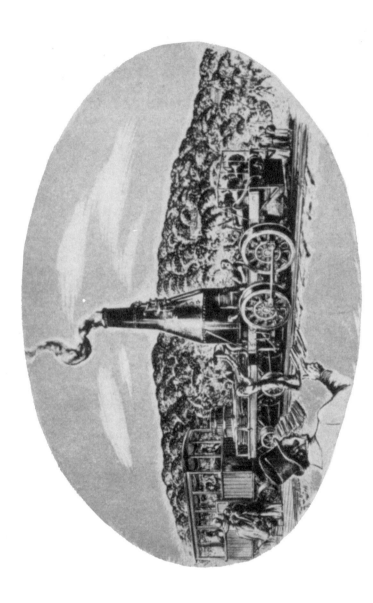

19th Century Locomotives

Nearly everyone who has gone to school has heard of or seen the famous DeWitt Clinton train. Let's look at some others, not so well-known, but which were in themselves important milestones of railroading.

The "Best Friend of Charleston" was the first train to operate on a regularly-scheduled passenger timetable. The locomotive of the "Best Friend" had a vertical boiler. Cylinders were ahead on top of the frame. They drove the rear wheels, which were connected with the front wheels by external side-rods. The "tender" carried cordwood and a barrel of water.

This train made a trial run on November 2, 1830, hauling four loaded cars at the amazing speed of 21 miles per hour.

Proud owner of this new engine was the Charleston and Hamburg Railroad, later known as the South Carolina Railroad.

Built at the West Point Foundry, New York, the "Best Friend" was the victim of a serious mishap. A "back-woods" fireman, disturbed by the noise of steam from the safety valve, held it down. The ensuing explosion resulted in his death and serious injuries to the engineer.

The Pioneer

The old wood-burner, usually of the American-type wheel combination, was the steam engine that welded this country together over the "golden spike." In those days the pilot was known as a "cow-catcher" and for good reason. Straying livestock were an imminent danger, not only to the cattle, but to the locomotive itself. A large, healthy heifer could easily derail a transcontinental express if it weren't for the long, pointed, shovel-shaped apparatus at the front of the engine.

Firing was hazardous, too. The "ash-cats" pitched big chunks of wood into the firebox door, from a swaying platform, and a "near-miss" could result in a ricochet that might mean a broken leg. Woodburners consumed fuel quickly which made frequent stops necessary for replenishing wood and water.

In the era of the woodburner, locomotives became a sort of personal property of the engineers who operated them. Each was individually named. It is reported that often the brass fittings and the paint jobs comprised as much as 20 per cent of the total cost of the locomotive.

The early "hoggers" who sometimes earned the munificent wage of sixty dollars a month would save from their own pockets for cast-silver bells and unusual painted artwork on the stacks.

The Record-Breaking "999"

When Engineer Charles Hogan first drove locomotive No. 999, fully loaded, from New York to East Buffalo at an incredible mile-a-minute speed, New York papers broke out in a rash of extra editions. This occurred on September 14, 1891.

Two years later, Charles Hogan took the New York Central Empire State Express over a measured mile between Syracuse and Buffalo and was clocked at 112.5 miles per hour. When this feat was announced in the papers, most people refused to believe it.

Naturally, "999" was an exhibition piece for the Central and was carefully conditioned by the locomotive shops. An American 4-4-0, she had immense driving wheels for speed—the wheels measuring over seven feet in diameter.

However, she showed the way to high-speed railroading and today, although out to pasture, gets periodic free rides to railroading exhibitions as a symbol of the railroads' progress.

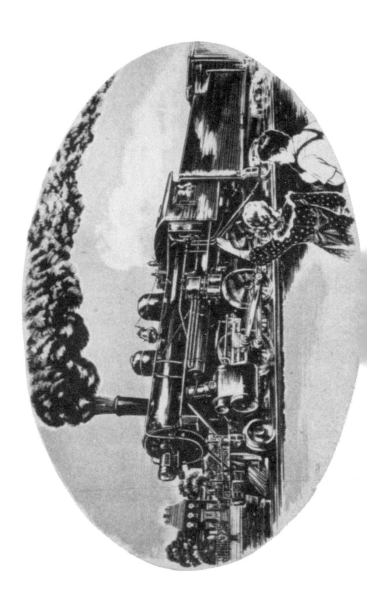

The "Great Mogul"

We haven't any idea who conceived the idea of naming a certain wheel-type locomotive the "Mogul." The dictionary tells us that the word describes a Mongolian Emperor, who reigned for many years. Surely, the Mogul steam locomotive ruled the high iron for many years as a freight hauler, supplanting the faithful American.

The Mogul came into prominence shortly after the Civil War. Although it used the same number of wheels as the American, it increased the number of driving wheels, becoming a 2-6-0. Driving wheels were smaller in diameter than those of the American, furnishing greater traction and power.

Original Moguls were equipped with diamond-shaped stacks and oil lamps. As they graduated into the 20th Century they acquired new-fangled equipment such as knuckle couplers, air brakes, electrical headlights and Stevenson valve gear.

The name of this locomotive contributed a new word to American slang. Your father will tell you that "Big Mogul" was applied to any person of great importance. To the general public the name came to mean any large locomotive, of any wheel combination, either passenger or freight.

circuit, a damaged relay, a defective switch—all give a red light. A false red is commonplace; a false green is unheard of.

In spite of this, of course, accidents do happen. In 1949 one passenger death resulted from railroad operations. 1950 opened with a horrible crash on the Long Island Rail Road when an engineer ran through a red signal and crashed head-on, killing thirty-some people. Accidents can happen no matter what devices are used, but railroads are still the safest method of transportation, by far. That was due to the strenuous efforts by the men of railroading.

And what of the future?

In the 1870's it was thought that railroading had reached its peak—there was nothing more to be done. That is not the attitude today.

Coal-hauling roads are experimenting constantly with superior types of coal-burning locomotives. They blow powdered coal into gas turbines and see what they can get in the way of power. They build steam turbines. They work steadily, not for size, but for efficiency.

The Diesel is not the end product either. A small gas turbine can produce the power of large Diesel motors, although today it takes a large plant to service the turbine.

Unquestionably, motive power will increase in efficiency and will achieve lower relative costs.

Then, too, there have been big advances in freight yard handling and the idle time of cars is constantly being pared down. Vast humps onto which a long string of cars is pushed and allowed to coast down the other side—these can automatically separate out a tremendous number of cars in a short period.

Terminal operations have been smoothed and speeded and advances will continue.

More safety measures will be introduced, and proven safety devices will enjoy wider use.

Labor—the men who make the trains move—will become more adept and better adjusted (and this is a continuing thing despite temporary labor troubles).

Will the airlines or highway transports take away business? Yes, they will take some, but not much more than they have already taken, not percentagewise anyway.

Speed is a splendid thing, but after a few times, most people agree that there are some drawbacks to air travel (one of which is that if there is a bad storm, you may suddenly find yourself in Boston or Kansas City instead of in the place that was your intended destination). It is hardly practical to leave Pittsburgh after a day's work and fly to Chicago for a conference next morning—you simply need a hotel room. A compartment will cost about the same, probably less, and you arrive fresh and ready for work.

The airlines have a service to sell, certainly, but not one that displaces the railroads.

Highway transport, too, has something to sell, but in many ways it cannot compete with the railroads. Although there is bitter rivalry, the trucking companies and bus lines have actually aided the railroads in some respects. By servicing smaller communities, trucks and buses have enabled railroads to eliminate marginal operations. This elimination, streamlining if you prefer, has left the railroads in a healthy position where they can concentrate on their more efficient routes.

Yes, the railroads will be around for a while yet.

Almost every railroad fan in America is acquainted with the ballads and stories of the two most legendary wrecks in ra lroad history, "The Wreck of No. 97" and "Casey Jones' Last Ride." Down through the years, these stories have taken on various dramatic highlights and shapes, depending on who was doing the narrating. In fact, they have been so misquoted and distorted that there are many people who now think the "Wreck of No. 97" and "Casey Jones' Last Ride" are one and the same. In order to clarify any misunderstandings and, at the same time, bring the correct versions of these two historic but tragic events to new railroad fans everywhere, here are the real facts as told to reliable persons by people who actually witnessed the accidents.

One warm Indian Summer day, Sept. 27, 1903, No. 97 hurtled over a trestle in Danville, Ill., and fell 75 feet to the rocks below. At 3:25 A.M., on April 29, 1900, just outside of Vaughan, Miss., Casey Jones—refusing to leave his throttle—smashed into the last car of a freight train that had not been completely shuttled off the main line onto a siding.

Six men were killed and ten injured when No. 97 went over the side. One man, Casey Jones, went to his eternal reward when the Cannonball Express hit the freight in the dead of night.

E. H. Chappell of Danville, witnessed the wreck of No. 97 from his home which commanded a perfect view of the trestle. It was noon when he saw No. 97, making an unusual noise, roar into sight. The train, running abnormally fast, hit the trestle. The engine, two mail cars, a baggage car and an express car plunged into the abyss with a roar of splintering wood and rending steel. Although all eyewitnesses agree that No. 97 was going faster than usual, the official reason for the wreck was given as a broken flange and not excessive speed.

The fireman on Casey Jones' last ride, Sim T. Webb, is still alive to tell how Casey cried out just before the crash, "Jump, Sim, jump." Mr. Webb says, "We had just finished our regular run into Memphis on No. 382 but we took over the Cannonball because its engineer was sick. We were about an hour and a half late. But with Jones at the throttle, the Cannonball began to make up time. Roaring into Vaughan, 200 miles south of Memphis, the Cannonball was on schedule. But the freight loomed on the main line just ahead and Jones knew he would never stop in time. Fireman Webb, obeying his chief's last command, jumped and saved his life as the Cannonball plowed into the rear of the freight. Casey Jones, so named because he hailed from Cayce, Ill., died that night but his name will live on as the greatest legend in the colorful history of railroading.

MODEL RAILROADING
AS A CIVIC PROJECT

**CHAPTER
NINETEEN**

No book on model railroading can be complete without a story of the amazing operation of the Police Athletic League of Rochester, N. Y.

The originator of the "Model Train Heaven" is Captain Henry Jensen, now Director of Rochester's Youth League. Captain Jensen conceived the idea while attending the FBI

Stools and control switches for multiple operation

National Police Academy. Part of the study of crime fight-
ing involved solving problems of capture, which were laid
out on miniature landscaped layouts. He decided that
something similar to this would provide an excellent way
to teach youngsters how to think straight and plan carefully. The obvious was a model railway system.

On his return from the Academy, Captain Jensen pre-
sented his idea and received enthusiastic support of the
city manager, council and all city departments.

The next step was a consultation with representatives
of the model railroad clubs of the city. They advised him
that "0" gauge, 3-rail operation would be the most satisfactory for the complicated train setup he had in mind.

It was also decided that the train "Heaven" would be

divided into four separate sections, or dioramas, one for each season of the year.

The project was started in February, 1950. Basic framework of the layout platforms was built by members of the Department of Public Works. Local model railroad clubs and a hobby shop owner laid the track and did the wiring. Members of the Rochester Art Club contributed their time for painting scenic backgrounds and landscaping. Local industries contributed. Everybody pitched in.

Grand Entrance

Entrance to the "Heaven," shown on page 283, is a full-size replica of the rear platform of a New York Central observation car. Marker lights and "Empire State" insignia are real, contributed by the railroad. Simulated car side is painted with real coach enamel. A painter from the New York Central shops applied the official lettering to the side of the car.

Summer in Rochester

As you enter, first on the left is the summer scene, which tips you off to the system of multiple operation used throughout. The counter in front of the entire L-shaped layout is equipped with switches and control panels, the transformers being in the center of the L. The counter is lined with stools to accommodate the many operators necessary to work the layout. No single individual can run this complicated setup. Engineers in the center only operate trains. Switching, uncoupling, activating of operating cars is done by dispatchers and brakemen along the line. Train orders are of first importance.

Background of this diorama, beautifully executed by the Art Club, is the city of Rochester itself, outlining most of the principal buildings. Another feature of this layout is a scale reproduction of a pier, alongside of which is probably

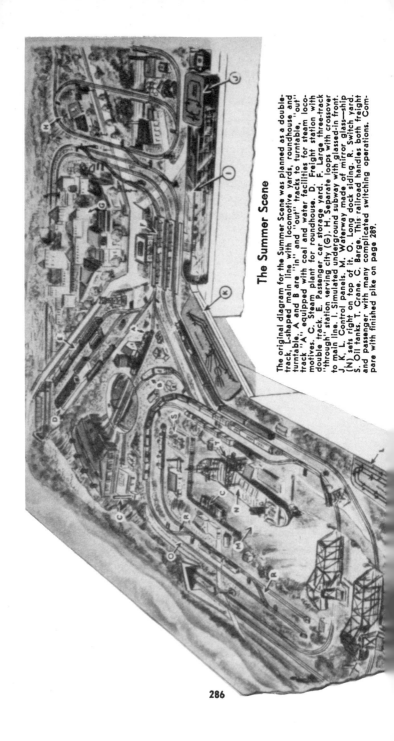

The Summer Scene

The original diagram for the Summer Scene was planned as a double-track, L-shaped main line with locomotive yards, roundhouse and turntable. A and B are "in" and "out" tracks to turntable. "out" track "A" equipped with coal and water facilities for steam locomotives. C. Steam plant for roundhouse. D. Freight station with double track. E. Passenger car storage yard. F. Large three-track "through" station serving city (G). H. Separate loops with crossover to main line. I. Simulated underground subway with glassed-in front. J, K, L. Control panels. M. Waterway made of mirror glass—ship (N) sets right on top of it. O. Long dock siding. R. Switch yard. S. Oil tanks. T. Crane. C. Barge. This railroad handles both freight and passenger with many complicated switching operations. Compare with finished pike on page 289.

the largest cargo ship ever included in a railroad pike. In-
clusion of this ship was a problem, but P.A.L. experts
solved it by following blueprints of the smallest cargo ship
of this type they could find, and came out with an "0"
gauge model built to the scale length of 385 feet.

A Photographic Record

The facilities of the Police Department's photographic
section made it possible to take "work-in-progress" pictures of the building of the layouts. Some of these inter-
mediate pictures will be interesting to model builders as a
guide to set construction.

Page 288 shows the initial groundwork for the Summer
Scene, with part of the trackage laid down. The "L"-shaped
platform was so re-inforced that subsequent pictures were
taken by a heavy man standing right in the center of the
layout. Remember this yourself. Although you do not need
to use grade one plywood or other sheet materials, the
foundation underneiath must be solid. Inexpensive, or
knotty materials are just as effective, because they will be
covered by texturing anyway, but re-inforcing of these materials is of double importance, as it prevents warping.

The next step in the layout shown is the erection of
wood forms, such as ramps, station platforms. The remaining track layout and basic wiring should follow.

In the center of the Summer Scene is a "through" station and locomotive yard. Here, too, is the turntable, with
an "in track" and "out track."

Turntables are usually the finishing touch for any big
table layout—there are instructions for building one on
page 136 of this book. The P.A.L.'s turntable is electrically
operated, but it could also have been arranged to operate
by a crank at the edge of the table.

The original sketch for the Summer Scene (page 286)
shows how plans have to be readapted to meet existing conditions. When P.A.L. decided to divide its space into four

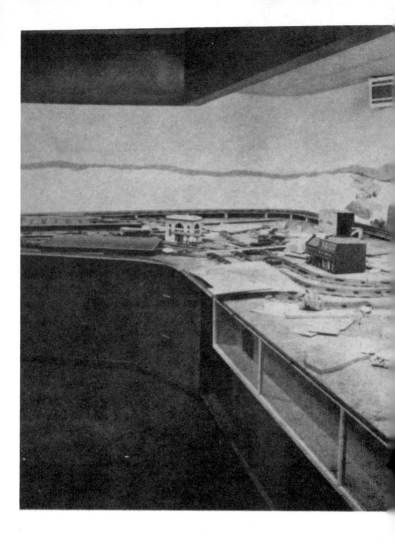

This shows the Summer Scene in the early stages of construction. Although two of the larger buildings are in place, tracks are only partially laid. In the background appears a grade, temporarily braced, in the "testing" stage. In the foreground, hanging below the table, is the cabinet which is to be "glassed in" to exhibit an underground subway line. Background is in place, but only roughed in. Long, dark object immediately to the left of the station building is foundation for the central control board which will house the transformers.

An Unusual Classification Yard

The "Rochester" yards are neat in appearance and fascinating in operation. Backed up by a painted panorama of the city itself, these classification spurs take up a good fourth of the entire Summer Scene. At the
lower part of the picture can be seen the controls and the toggle
switches that operate the individual spurs. Each spur ends on a bumper,
and has at least one remote control track section. Ground texturing is the
usual "scrubble" found in switchyards and can be duplicated with ordinary sand and/or gravel.

This is the heart of the Summer Scene. Transformer controls for trains can be seen on the far left. In the background is the waterfront section, containing the big sea-going ship. At right is the electrically-operated turntable and the roundhouse.

rooms, sizes of each scene had to be reduced. Most interesting variation from the original sketch was the substitution of the involved switchyard in the right hand corner of the layout. The addition of all these spurs, with switches and remote control sections, provided more individual operations for more members of the club. Each spur, with its switch and uncoupling track, can be cut off by a toggle switch, so that train operators at the transformers, who are operating more than one locomotive in the yard, do not interfere with each other.

The Rochester Summer Scene can operate nine different trains at the same time. Locomotives used are both Diesel and steam.

Waterfront scenes such as the one included in this layout really "spark" a model pike and are desirable if there is room for them. The boats are much easier to build than you'd think, for they do not require the building care or materials used by model boat builders. Layout boats can sit flat on a mirrored surface, and thus eliminate the necessity of rounded hulls. Since they need not be waterproof, they can be constructed of light materials. Hulls and superstructure are merely cardboard, formed around wood frameworks. Windows and ports are painted on the sides. Booms and spars can be made of any available material—dowels or even heavy, rolled paper.

Autumn Scene

The Rochester "Fall Scene" has its own complete personality, over and above the coloring of the backgrounds. Backgrounds and texturing, of course, achieve the autumn atmosphere with shades of brown, ochre, yellow and red mixed in with the natural greens.

This diorama lays more emphasis on grades and elevations. On the right hand end is an overpassing track that crosses over two others—the lower tracks leading clear out of the room and back again via tunnels. Background of this

Fall Scene

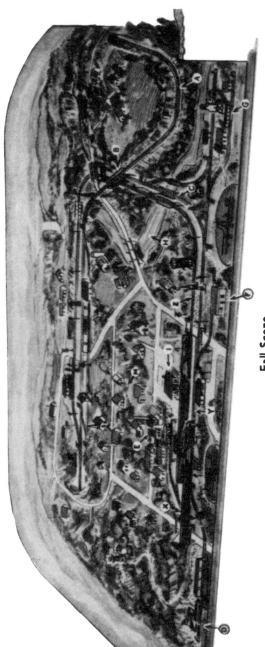

This original diorama was called the "Village," and featured a number of crossovers on the right side, which were retained in the final layout. Track A rises up and passes over double track main line at B. Track C is actually track A after it has emerged from the tunnel. In the foreground are a number of industrial plants and sidings. D. Coal yard. E. Meat packing plant. F. Small factory. G. Another coal yard. River H. is a winding one and passes under tracks several times. I. Passenger station for residential district (M). In reality, this layout is a big figure 8, but it uses an overpass at B rather than a crossover. Passenger train X has two routes to follow. Continuing on track Y, it climbs the grade on track A and passes over itself at B. Alternate route is track Z, which is a plain loop. Compare this diorama with pictures of finished job.

end of the layout naturally shows mountains and the actual built-up hillsides blend into it imperceptibly.

The contributing members of the Rochester Art Club can well testify how a minor error in over-all planning will make scenic work difficult. Their services were not solicited until platforms had been finished and tracks laid. Picture on page 295 is evidence of the difficulties under which the painting was done.

Artists at work need the whole run of the layout for their paints and other materials. And they'll tell you that they'd much prefer to paint standing up on the floor, before the table platform is completed, rather than crawling around on a half-finished setup.

Let us use their experience in our own building. Remove all trains and accessories from the layout while coloring and texturing is done. Cover all tracks so that paint and other texturing materials are not spattered over them. This is particularly important in the case of switches, where sand or sawdust could seriously affect operation.

The Outdoor Theatre

One of the most spectacular elements of this diorama has no connection with railroading at all. It is an outdoor drive-in theatre, complete with scale cars, and even a projection house.

The movie screen appears to be right into the side of a hill, and is flanked by strata rock formation made of plaster, modelled into horizontal layers while still wet.

Our guide steps over to the counter, picks up the whole mountain and tunes in the dials of a television set! Yes, the screen of the outdoor theatre is actually that of a small television set, and when the lightly constructed mounain is removed, it can be tuned in to show a real movie in the miniature theatre.

Slightly back of the theatre is a simulated airport, with a rotating air beacon. Although the flat surface of the platform is not large enough for landing fields, the background painting picks up the idea and gives the illusion of a large field.

There are other interesting details here for the model railroader. Pictures show the realistic handling of roadbeds. This was done by using a foundation of heavy, gray-and-white mottled asbestos board. The board was cut in long strips to follow track lines, and was beveled on the sides, giving an excellent reproduction of ballasted track. Extra wooden ties were inserted between the regular ties of the three-rail track, for added realism.

Another feature of this particular layout is the excellent job done on highway crossings over tracks. No special tricks are used—just a little more than ordinary care.

Locomotives for this diorama are steam only.

Winter at the Mines

Although it is always difficult to keep visitors moving around to the various rooms of the Rochester project, it is at the Winter Scene that they linger longest.

This room is a magnificent job of planning, landscaping, lighting and overcoming obstacles. The entire background panorama is made up of snow-covered mountains. The center of the layout itself consists of deep ravines and gullies, similarly snow-covered. This mountainous treatment made it necessary to build all of the railroad right-of-way on platforms raised above the main table.

In planning the basic foundation of the Winter Scene, the architects of this venture even made ingenious use of its disadvantages. An ugly pole in the center of the room, became a handsome mountain crag (see pages 301 and 303). A big hydro-electric plant set in the deepest ravine really disguises a center well for servicing of tracks and equipment.

Mountains, and much of the other landscaping were made with a material called "Celastex," but the same effect could also be produced with papier-mâché made of torn-up newspapers, soaked in a solution of wall sizing and spread over a wire framework.

Painting of background was brown and ochre, streaked with white and sprinkled with artificial snow. We all know how many different materials are being used these days for

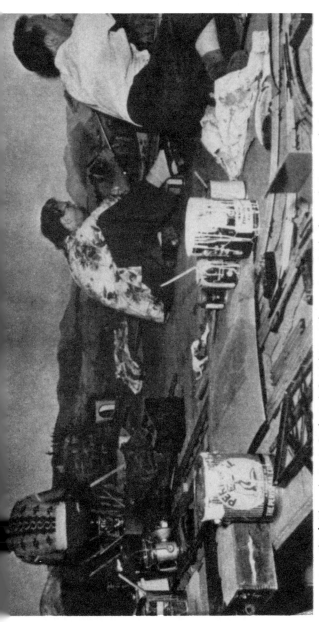

This (with apologies to Rochester's P.A.L.) is not the way to paint backgrounds. In error, platforms were finished and track laid before the artists could work. As a result, "stooping and squinting," was necessary. Much credit is due members of the Rochester Art Club for a swell job, under difficult circumstances.

The double tracks running under the trestle bridge run clear out of the room housing the Fall Scene. Track on which the passenger train is running will double back in a figure 8 and cross the bridge where the freight train appears.

The "removable mountain" in the upper center of the picture conceals a Television set that shows real movies to the occupants of the scale automobiles facing it. Small white house inside the fence is a "projection room." Tunnel entrance at the right is made of the same asbestos board as trackbeds, sprinkled with sand and shellacked.

imitation snow, but Rochester has come up with one a little out of the ordinary. Theirs is a white, flaky substance used usually for waxing dance floors, which, under light, creates the impression of wet, gleaming snow.

The lighting features of the Winter Scene are the attraction for spectators. In an effort to create a night atmosphere, a number of experiments were made. Officer Gerald Deprez, who is the technical mastermind of the complete exhibit, came up with several solutions. With a combination of fluorescent tubes, shaded by dark blue glass shields, he accomplished a wonderful reproduction of night light. Stars, house windows, the windowpanes of the electric plant were treated with luminous paint.

As a result, when the switch is pulled, the stars come out, the plant comes to life, lights twinkle in the cottages and the church of the little mining town at the left, and the whole scene is covered with a solf glow.

Just to add an extra fillip to the whole lighting plan, the creators will also show you the layout under daytime conditions. A large orange spotlight has been placed in a high corner of the room, shielded from the observer. This spot creates the impression of late afternoon sunlight, which casts shadows over all the miniature equipment.

Emphasis on Electricity

Lighting is not the only operating feature in which the emphasis is on electricity. All locomotives on this layout are Pennsylvania GG-1's. Although actually operated by third rail, the main lines of the Winter Scene have dummy overhead catenary systems throughout. The main industrial factory, as before-mentioned, is a replica of a hydroelectric plant.

The other large structure in this scene is a fine model of mining coal loader, astride the tracks. From it a mining tunnel runs into the side of the mountain. Name on the side indicates that this is the property of the Palville Mining Corporation, a subsidiary of the Rochester P.A.L. The mining section of the layout is equipped with several coal loading accessories, and plenty of hopper cars.

Winter Scene

Final Winter Scene at Rochester was not as deep as the plan shown here but still gave the illusion of distance through the unusual handling of background and lighting effects. A. Dam which provides power for hydro-electric plant (B), down in the ravine. C. Simulated rapids below power plant. D. High tension power lines carry high voltage electricity to a distant city. E. Airline beacon. F. Tipple delivers coal to railroad sidings. G. Lumber mill handles logs floated down the river and includes a log conveyor at railside. H. Car storage siding. I. Coal receiving yard. Long passing siding is partially concealed under mountain. The P.A.L. intends to make another crossing of the river directly in front of the center control board, thus completing an entire outside loop. Compare this diagram with pictures of finished Winter Scene.

This diorama works its waterways to the hilt. The river which is dammed up to operate the electric plant runs down to branch into another which is used to float logs from the timber country in background down to the lumber mill. The lower part of the Rochester rapids is filled with floating logs, even to the "jams." The mill, of course, is a wonderful spot to locate operating log conveyors and operating lumber cars. Outgoing gondolas and stake cars can also carry simulated "cut lumber" as well as logs.

The Winter Scene reminds us that night scenes lend a great deal of enchantment to railroading, whether or not the ground is covered with snow. In a dark or dimly lit room, rails glisten, headlights stand out, and accessory lights show to the best advantage.

Spring in the Country

The last scene we visit depicts all the freshness of Spring in the country, and is laid out, trackwise, on the basis of bringing farm produce to the market. Background and texturing are colored in greens, yellows, whites, and the bright Diesel locomotives and freight cars make it altogether a brilliant spectacle. Flat spaces in the scenery show newly plowed fields, and fields showing green sprouts. Tiny cattle are in abundance.

Passenger trains wind through the layout, stopping at quiet country stations. Freight trains are predominantly cattle cars, milk cars, and refrigerator cars which bring products of the farm into the stockyards and dairy plants.

Background of the Spring Scene was painted by students of the Rochester Institute of Technology. It features mountains, rolling farmlands that blend down into the table texturing with scarcely a noticeable break.

Another innovation was introduced here by the PAL planning board, an idea for constructing a complete one-piece background without any unsightly seams. The entire scene painting, measuring about 20 feet across the back and 6 feet on the ends, is done on a single piece of light linoleum, over a backing of 3/16″ wallboard.

Although the pictures shown on these pages only indi-

Track building for the Winter Scene was especially important as creation of river-beds and gullies made it necessary to raise all trackage above table level.

A picture of this mining scene cannot do justice to the realism of this section when viewed under proper lighting conditions. The stars shine bright and houses light up in "Palville" when overhead fluorescents are turned on.

It's hard to believe, but this layout conceals an unsightly pole. The mountain peak just to the right of the coal loader, and toward the rear, covers it. The line of waiting cars indicates that coal and lumber are the predominating cargoes handled in this Winter Scene. Lights on small lamp-posts are painted with luminous paint so that they "come out" when the set is illuminated. In the background may be seen the little houses of the mining town that is adjacent to the Palville Mining Corp., shown on page 302.

cate room for about five operators, this layout is now being expanded, like the others, to accommodate many more members. The Spring Scene uses only Diesel locomotives.

The Spring Scene is typical of the P.A.L.'s insistence on giving each diorama a complete and separate personality. The country Springtime feeling pervades throughout. The "produce to market" theme was followed through logically by texturing of newly ploughed fields and the background illusion of a plunging stream. Industrial structures are all entirely in keeping with landscaping and the type of trains used. Even the small passenger stations fit in with the country atmosphere. The final touch, artistically, was the choice of Diesel locomotives for this layout. Their bright colors blend in perfectly with exciting coloring of the background and the landscape.

Operation PAL

The Rochester PAL's scheme for participation of members is as well-planned as the layout itself. And, according to its staff, it is just as subject to experiment and change as the original layouts were. At the present writing, here is the way the plan works.

Youngsters are organized into groups of 64 for an evening's participation. These groups are then divided into four sections of 16 each, one section for each of the dioramas. As mentioned before, each child will have a certain function to perform on his particular diorama. These young operators will then rotate, under direction of a monitor, so that each has an opportunity to operate every one of the controls. When all of them have had their chances to complete the operating circuit, the whole group is moved on to the next diorama, where the layout, the locomotives, the entire scene is completely new. There is never a dull moment in this rotating routine—everybody has a lot of fun and the scene is always changing.

The Rochester exhibit has become a showplace for civic-minded organizations who come from far and wide to see it. These include Parent-Teacher groups, YMCA's, other

Police Athletics Associations and many others. In fact, Patrolman Gerald Deprez, who is "master-of-ceremonies," was in danger of shouting himself hoarse explaining things until he was able to install a public address system, which could be plugged into each diorama for the purpose of describing the setup to visiting adults.

Jerry says the kids are "nuts" about the operation, but must be carefully directed by the volunteer adult monitors to prevent crack-ups. This is particularly true in the Autumn diorama, which includes the "drive-in" television feature. Television devotees often forget to pull switches on time, leading to disastrous railroading crises. Therefore, the television has to be shut off during intricate railroading maneuvers.

Another Civic Project—The Train Race

Train races are not by any means new. For many years they have been organized by YMCA's and men's clubs, to bring large groups of boys together for some good, competitive fun. One organization has been operating these races for nearly twenty years and reports that only a few years ago it abandoned the train classification of the old Standard (2⅛ inch) gauge locomotives because there were too few entrants.

Planning and operation of these contests require a lot of work, a lot of patience—and a good knowledge of electric trains. There must be a somewhat complicated classification of locomotive groups, in order to make the race fair to all. There must also be a classification of age groups of boys. Finally, because the contests are usually limited to one day, competitive classes must be moved along quickly and smoothly so that all of the entrants get a chance to race their locomotives.

Races are ordinarily held at the first of the year, before "Christmas" trains are stored in the attic. Entry blanks are mailed, giving time and place and the various classifications. When these are returned the organizers get some idea of the number of contestants and the types of locomotives to be entered.

Spring Scene

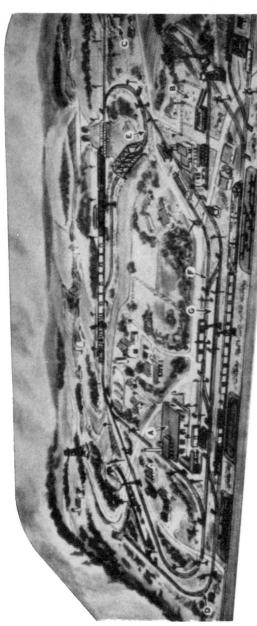

In its finished form, the Rochester Spring Scene adheres closer to the original plan than the other three, as can be seen here. A "produce to market" project, it emphasizes farmland scenery, and its freight trains contain a number of operating milk and cattle cars. Logically the buildings include a milk processing plant at A, and a stockyard at B. Dirt roads and a winding river add to the country atmosphere. Scene was originally planned, also, to include a stone quarry (C). The track arrangement provides for two or three trains to run on the same track, by sectionalizing. Track D has a reversing loop inside the mountain. Track E can reverse trains in the other direction. Side tracks F can be approached by a train running in either direction. Platform G is a local passenger stop.

In keeping with its rural atmosphere, the Spring Scene has plenty of switches and sidings to permit freights to wait for through passengers, or for local passengers to bypass freight manifests. There are two "disappearing" tunnels. The one shown is matched by another which is off to the left of the picture. Buildings on this layout are particularly well done.

307

HERALDS
OF THE REAL RAILROADS

The use of the word "Heralds" describing the insignia of railroads presumably comes from the heraldry involved in the "coats-of-arms" of knights of long ago. Whatever the case, the rolling stock of the great roads of America carries its "Heralds" just as proudly as did any knight in armor. Here are some of them. They are an integral part of the grand history of American railroading.

Grand Trunk
Western Railroad.

Union Pacific
Railroad.

Chicago, Rock Island and Pacific
Railroad.

New York Central
Railroad.

Southern Railway
System.

Chicago and
North Western
Railway.

Illinois Central
Railroad.

Missouri-Kansas-
Texas Railroad.

Texas and Pacific
Railway.

Erie Railroad.

Great Northern
Railway.

Northern Pacific
Railway.

Western Pacific
Railroad.

Pennsylvania
Railroad.

Baltimore and
Ohio Railroad.

Minneapolis and
St. Louis Railway.

Lehigh Valley
Railroad.

Minneapolis,
St. Paul and
Sault Sainte Marie
Railroad.

Wabash Railroad.

Atchison, Topeka
and Santa Fe
Railway.

Georgia Railroad.

Chicago and
Eastern Illinois
Railroad.

Gulf, Mobile and
Ohio Railroad.

St. Louis,
San Francisco
Railway.

CHAPTER
TWENTY

A TRIP ON
A TRAIN

L ET'S TAKE a leisurely trip on a train and look over some
of the unusual operations and equipment that most
people seldom see, but which are part of the life-blood of
railroading.

To make it really interesting, we'll start from the island
of Manhattan, New York City, and pick up some of the
marine equipment which railroads own and operate on
the waterways as an integral part of their systems.

We'll board a ferryboat at any of a number of ferry slips
which the railroads utilize to carry passengers or commuters over to the New Jersey shore. The boat we choose may
be any one of an entire fleet of ferries maintained by a
single railroad for passenger service.

Although our captain is technically a railroad employee, he is governed by rules and regulations of navigation laws and must have a "skipper's" license to operate in these waters. The "North," or Hudson River, which we must traverse, can be as crowded as Times Square on a Saturday night.

Our boat will undoubtedly be a double-decker, with room for passengers above and below, while the center section of the lower deck will be crowded with cars and trucks.

The trip across may take anywhere from five minutes to half an hour, depending on our embarkation point and destination. Waiting time at the slip will depend on the length of the ride, as most ferries operate in groups of four, one leaving the slip as an incoming one docks.

Our captain blows one long blast to give warning that he is on his way out. Then he begins to thread his way through the heavy traffic that may include ocean-going ships, tugboats and barges, coast-wise freighters and even pleasure boats.

As we move out into the river we get a glimpse of one of the most unusual boats in Marine service—the "Sea-train." It is built along the lines of a Great Lakes freighter, with the bridge forward and the funnel aft. Amidship are rows of railroad freight cars, several tiers deep. This is an ocean-going vessel, 480 feet long. We are told that this type

The ocean-going carrier of freight cars is an oddity in Marine architecture. Certain types of cargoes make it more efficient and economical to deliver the entire loaded car coast-wise to ports in the South.

Where bridges would be too costly, tugs and barges take over.

of ship plies weekly from New York to New Orleans and from New York to various Texas ports.

For certain kinds of cargo it is simpler and cheaper to transfer the whole freight car and its contents, rather than to unload it at the pier and then reload it into other cars at its destination.

The Car Float

A whistle from our ferry tells us that we are about to pass another water-borne piece of equipment. As we look over the port side we see a pair of car barges or "floats," escorted, "one at each elbow," by a railroad tugboat. Both tug and floats are an integral part of the railroad system, for the railroads have found that with a few tugs and a

Derricks move freight from ship to shore and shore to ship.

number of floats they can transport a complete train across this huge river, where a railroad bridge would be out of the question.

The barges, or "floats," which we see are not fully loaded, but we know that the larger ones may contain as many as 24 loaded freight cars. They are usually of steel construction and will run from 150 to 250 feet in length. They are equipped with two, three or even four tracks.

Car barges are loaded on specially-designed slips that insure good connections between the running rails of the road and those on the float. The switching engine that loads them pushes a lightweight flat car ahead of it so that it is not necessary for the locomotive to run out on the gangway.

Derricks and Cranes

As we near the Jersey shore we begin to notice the many towering cranes and derricks that line the waterfront. Wherever tracks meet the shoreline, these are a prime essential. They are of all varieties, in size, shape and operation, depending on the work they have to do. Some are equipped with huge slings for transferring cargo aboard ship. Others use big hooks which will pick up even a big locomotive and stow it aboard ship. Cranes with swinging booms are used to handle cargo that must be delivered to various sections of the ship's hold. Although most cranes and derricks are firmly anchored on shore, some operate from barges—these are usually of the "lobster-claw" variety, used principally for transferring "soft" cargo such as sand or coal.

Diesel Fueling Station

We pick up a train on the other side of the river and our next inspection stop is the fueling station of the big Diesels. It looks very much like a roadside gasoline station, with its long fueling hoses and pumps. Diesels, of course, need sand on the track for traction, so sand and water are replenished, too.

Boom cranes are the "handymen" of the water-front. They may be equipped with slings, "lobster-claws" or hooks. Some are mobilized by placing them on easily moved barges.

The big Diesel stops at an oil station.

While we are here we also take a peek into the Diesel shops and discover why maintenance of these locomotives is so much quicker and less expensive than steam engines. The tops of these Diesels are removable like the lid of a teakettle, and the motors can be lifted right out for servicing. While this is going on, the whole outer hood can be cleaned and the running gear checked.

In this same terminal are the great yards containing waiting passenger cars and we see the never-ending job of putting Pullmans and coaches back into the line again. Linen in dining cars and sleeping cars must be changed, ice placed in water coolers, seats brushed. Cars with faulty or even questionable gear have to be checked. We learn that those long lines of quietly standing cars mean a lot of work for the railroad man.

Car Washers

Comparatively new, and fascinating to watch are the

railroads' automatic car-washers. These ingenious machines can handle as many as 400 passenger cars daily.

As each car moves through the washing station, it will receive one complete bath of cleaning solution, and will be washed down with two clear rinses. The trains will run the cleaning "gauntlet" at two miles per hour, with approximately one minute spent on each car.

As the car enters the battery of machines, the roof, sides and windows will be attacked by 12 brushes, rotating as fast as 400 revolutions per minute, and each equipped with

A N. Y. Central Diesel gets its face washed while motor is checked.

There's work to be done in these standing cars.

spray holes permitting water or cleaning solution to assist in removing dirt.

The car's first contact is with a pair of roof brushes—mounted on overhead, retractable booms—which scrub while they spray. Then 10-foot, 6-inch brushes, mounted vertically, go to work on the sides while smaller brushes are used for the windows. All brushes and sprays are operated mechanically and are controlled by an operator from a booth mounted above the track.

Icing Platform

Farther out along the line we stop off to watch the operation of an icing station for "reefer" cars. The refrigerated car works on the same principle as the old-fashioned ice box—it is cooled by large bunkers inside both ends of the cars which are filled with wet ice. Refrigerated cargoes must have clearance both underneath and above to permit circulation of cool air and, of course, waybills for these cars specify when and where they must be re-iced.

Icing of "reefers" has become increasingly important

with the advent of quick-frozen foods. These foods require very low temperatures, which necessitate extra insulation of cars, and more frequent re-icing. To keep temperatures at a low level, some shippers specify a 30% solution of salt be added to the ice.

Icing platforms are built at car-top level to permit easy access to hatches on top of the cars.

Some of the larger icing stations are now being equipped with automatic icing machines. These "icers" resemble an overhead coal loader with an operating tower on top. This whole machine runs back and forth over the icing platform on its own tracks. Large chunks of ice are delivered by conveyor belt to the tower where a grinder breaks them up into proper size. Cracked ice is then fed into car hatches by means of long chutes. The proper amount of salt is also delivered into the hatches from the tower. This big automatic "iceman" can really service a lot of cars in a short time.

Modern machinery keeps streamliners sparkling.

Even in wintertime ice hatches must be filled.

Over the "Hump"

Our next stop is the much-talked-about "hump" classification yard, complete with car-retarders. The hump system of sorting freight cars by gravity instead of locomotive
power is not new by any means. It has been operated for
years with hand-thrown switches and brakemen riding the
cars and braking them with their clubs. Today, with the
car-retarder and electrically-operated switches, the yardmaster or towerman can control a vast switchyard, just as
you can control your own model train layout. The car-
retarder, invented by E. M. Wilcox of the New York Central, is actually a brake rail, cushioned by springs, set parallel to the running rail. Operated either electrically or pneu-
matically, it can be pushed against the flanges of the car
wheel at the will of the towerman, to stop the car wherever desired.

The Giant "Barney"

Now let's take a long railwise jump to the Great Lakes

at Toledo to watch the great "Barney" ore car dumper. We'll watch the well-known hopper car get its "come-up-pance." For many years, the hopper car has provided the solution for quick, efficient unloading through its hopper doors. Now we are to discover a situation where this handy railroad car is not fast or efficient enough.

Actually it is easy to see the reason for this new-type system of unloading into ore and coal boats of the Great Lakes kind. To use the "hopper" method of unloading would require a track right over the ship so that a car could drop its load into the hold from overhead. The "Barney" simplifies the problem by picking up the big hopper and emptying it into the ship like turning over a cup of sugar.

The "Barney" stands high at dockside, amidship of the

With electrically controlled switches and retarding brake rails the towerman can sort cars without a locomotive.

coal or ore boat to be loaded. Incoming cars are pushed up the hump by an electrically driven unit which operates out of the pit between the tracks. The full car is shoved up into what is known as the "cradle." When in position, car and cradle (weighing together more than 300 tons) are raised 25 feet and completely turned over. A giant retarder controls the load and eases it into a tremendous pan for distribution into the ship's hold.

As the coal is unloaded into the pan it is simultaneously "sluiced" with either water or "Wetsol" in any degree that the shipper specifies.

This great machine also has a very clever method of disposing of emptied cars. When the electrically-operated "Barney mule" pushes each new car into the cradle, the incoming car bumps the preceding empty over the hill into

This is "Barney"—the ship loader.

an inclined switchback that automatically delivers it back
into the yards, where it is guided into place by means of
electrical switches and car retarders.

This yard, at Maumee Bay, Toledo, is jointly operated
by the New York Central and the Baltimore and Ohio railroads and has a capacity of 5500 cars. Three "Barneys" are
used to load the ships.

The Fading Emperor

Slightly further west we run into a section of railroading
where the steam locomotive is still king. Here railside
equipment and servicing facilities are simple and direct as
they have been for over the century during which the railroads tied this whole nation together with their immense
networks.

Typical of the commonsense operations of early days is
the high overhead coaling and sanding station shown here.
Awkward and ponderous by modern standards, it provided
a quick answer to a railroading problem. Of course the coal

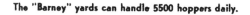

The "Barney" yards can handle 5500 hoppers daily.

hopper had to be pushed high up the trestle into the tower
—high enough so the coal could still roll down into awaiting tender. Sand for the locomotive was delivered in the
same way. Still, the whole operation was operated by gravity, with little fear of broken-down machinery.

Out here, too, are some of the great locomotive shops
that handle colossal steam boilers with the same ease that
a watchmaker handles a balance wheel. Here we see the
great side-rods and driving-rods being repaired and replaced and we understand why high maintenance cost is
making the great steam giant begin to disappear from the
steel rails of the country's roads.

The relatively high cost of repair and maintenance of
steam locomotives is not the only reason for the present
supremacy of the Diesel. Although steam locomotives

could undoubtedly match the speed of Diesels, they cannot do so without serious damage to the running rails. At high speeds the steam locomotive begins to "kink" the rails. You see, when driving and side rods, one each side, come down to their lowest position they have a heavy thrust on the track, which has a tendency to pound dents in the rails. Although counterbalances (those half-moon weights on the driving wheels) compensate somewhat for this thrust, they have never provided a solution to the problem. Diesels, with their gears driving from the center of the axle, roll along smoothly without damage to the rails.

Yes, like a dying soldier, the steam locomotive, long the Emperor of the clicking rails, is slowly fading away. Railroaders watch this transition sadly. Many of us hope we can keep the tradition of that grand machine alive on our model roads.

Repairing the big ones is a real job.

The famed New York Central Hudson 4-6-4 type locomotive, class J1-d, highballing along the Hudson Division. These engines are used for both freight and passenger service.

Sorrowfully granting that the steam locomotive, like the old dot-and-dash telegraph which governed its movements, is destined for the limbo of legend, rail travel is here to stay. So let's hop back to New York City and make a new 1954 streamlined start at Grand Central Station.

If you have never seen New York Central's Grand Central Terminal at New York—but expect to—don't be disappointed by its exterior appearance. Surrounded by the magnificent spires of the mid-town Manhattan buildings, the terminal may seem flat and dwarfed. But wait until you get inside. This beehive of human activity stretches wide and deep in a manner that's even more astonishing than the sky-reaching splendor of its neighboring structures. It is when you walk into the main concourse of Grand Central that you first begin to appreciate its immensity and the ingenuity of its builders.

Construction of the present Grand Central Terminal was begun in 1903. Installation of electric power for train operation was rushed and inaugurated on February 13, 1907, and the new edifice and its equipment was completed on February 2, 1913.

Since then, in spite of New York's sensational suburban growth, and the doubling and redoubling many times over of the main line traffic pouring in on both the New York Central and the New York, New Haven and Hartford, the station's capacity never has been stretched to its limit.

The terminal itself is one of the busiest in the world. It holds 67 tracks, with 41 on its upper level, and 26 on the lower. With its adjuncts the terminal covers 48 acres, and has waiting room floor space to accommodate more than 30,000 people.

An average of 510 trains enter or leave the terminal daily. In 1946, the station handled an all-time record of

A big percentage of Grand Central's human traffic springs from the subway stations deep in the ground. These include the Lexington Ave. subway, an IRT line to Long Island City and a shuttle train to Times Square.

North of the terminal rears the tower of New York Central's office building.

65,156,063 passengers. It has its own medical service, a police force under its own police chief, and employs 200 "Red Cap" porters.

The central concourse, one of the largest and most beautiful rooms in the world, is 125 feet high, 272 feet long and 120 feet wide. In it are the baggage rooms, ticket offices and information booths of both roads.

This upper level waiting room also houses its own art gallery (the third largest in the city), inspires its patrons with music from one of the world's great pipe organs, and its ceiling is decorated by one of the largest and most comprehensive murals in existence. Incongruously, it may be said that so unappreciative is the public, that few of the thousands of daily commuters are even aware the beautiful mural is there.

Just below this huge main concourse is another, just as wide and long, which similarly functions for commuter lines to suburban areas. Deep in these catacombs too, run the subway lines that pick up incoming commuters and carry them on to their places of business.

When Commodore Vanderbilt chose the present site of Grand Central Terminal in 1869, the location was considered to be far "uptown." But with the tremendous expansion of New York's population in the last four decades, the station now is actually at the "center of gravity" of the city, and the New York Central tracks run right down the center of Manhattan's rock-based island.

Back in the old days, and well into the 20th century, steam trains ran clear into the 42nd St. terminal. As electrical power became available and the smoke became offensive to city dwellers, New York Central installed a third rail system all the way to Harmon, 40 miles away, which permitted covering the tracks to form a tunnel arrangement under 50 city blocks north of the terminal.

Today, a large section of fashionable Park Avenue, including its luxurious apartments, sits astride the maze of New York Central's tracks. As you pass through the lower floors of these huge buildings you can hear the rumble of trains passing underneath.

Years ago Grand Central Terminal's maze of trackage ran uncovered all the way to 42nd Street.

Grand Central's Business Section

There is an old story which says that you could take an unkempt hobo into Grand Central, bathe him, shave and shampoo him, dress him in the finest clothes, feed him, equip him with luggage and send him forth in a limousine, without leaving the station.

This is literally true. It really is a city within a building. The myriad of passageways which branch out of the concourse contain every imaginable kind of business establishment. To mention a few: There are two large restaurants, several lunch-rooms, twenty-two newsstands, six bootblack stands, six cigar stores, two barber shops, a ladies' hairdressing parlor, two book shops, two drug stores, a clothing and haberdashery store, print shop, jewelry shop, candy store, cutlery shop, a car renting agency, a clothes-weaving shop, and even an air-cooled movie. Several of the large midtown hotels have direct underground tunnels to the station. Many commuters in offices several blocks from the main station, can walk under shelter to their offices in inclement weather.

New York Central trains come out into the sunlight at 96th Street.

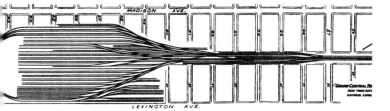

The upper track level handles the through trains.

Underneath It All—the Train Operation

We have talked at length about the general appearance and equipment of the station itself. Now, what about the system and the men who must deliver human cargo in and out daily in almost unbelievable numbers? You will see on these pages simplified versions of the great web-like terminal tracks in the station itself.

Miles out of town is the great Mott Haven switchyard that stores waiting trains. But in between these is the bottleneck, four tracks wide, extending roughly from 57th St. to Mott Haven Avenue at 138th, with two station stops en route. This "throat" of track tightens up with commuter trains in early morning and late afternoon so that trains have only a two-minute headway.

The New York Central has solved this problem by assigning three of the four tracks to incoming traffic in the mornings and, conversely, three tracks outgoing for the evening rush. This system would be completely foolproof if it weren't for people and the weather. At certain times, and for different reasons, passengers may "bunch up" on incoming or outgoing trains, making necessary more cars and longer sidings for arrival.

Snowstorms as far off as Albany or Buffalo may completely upset established routine. These are only a few of

Deep in the station lie the surburban tracks.

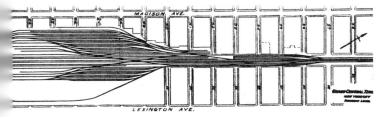

Operating a two-minute headway in these tunnels is a man-sized job.

the headaches that make a dispatcher long for a little cottage in the hills.

Don't forget, you railroaders, that colored signals in this tunnel must work both ways and that the controller in charge is responsible for running all trains in either direction.

Central control of this amazing labyrinth is in a "tower" in the vicinity of 57th St. It is called a tower because it is two stories high, even though it does not reach the street level of the city. The "A" tower, on the top level, controls the main line trains of the upper level tracks. The "B" tower dispatches the commuter trains on the lower level. Obviously, these two controller systems must be perfectly coordinated to handle trains coming through the always congested "throat" of the system.

As you may see from the diagrams of the Grand Central track layouts, most trains come into a dead-end spur. This is not too much of a problem so far as commuter trains are

concerned because most of the cars are motorized and can
be taken out just as they come in. The through trains, however, do present a problem because they are in the terminal
in reverse position, and in need of service. Practically all
of these must be returned to the Mott Haven yards for repairs, clean linen, water, and ice. To the dispatcher this
means sending out an empty train, and bringing it back
ready for the next paying run with little or no appreciable
delay—no mean feat if he does it.

Grand Central's Long Track Fingers

The influence of New York Central's biggest terminal
is felt for many miles out of the station itself. Because of
the electrification necessary to bring trains into the catacombs of New York, outgoing track patterns differ from
those of other cities.

Trains that speed out of the Park Avenue tunnel on the
four-track "throat" or "bottleneck" are destined to go in
many directions. Major slow-down on this stretch is the
125th St. station, where most of them make split-second
stops. Immediately after, at 138th St., these trains begin
to split up and take their separate ways. Here, in a maze
of signal bridges, semaphores and switches, engineers guide
their locomotives to the proper outgoing tracks.

Here, also, at a place vaguely known as "Mott Haven"
is New York Central's passenger storage yard, containing
hundreds of Pullmans and coaches awaiting service and
"make-up" for outgoing runs.

These signal bridges will bewilder anyone but a railroader.

A Pennsylvania Mountain 4-8-2 type locomotive hauls a solid coal train. Huge tenders, having a capacity of 22,000 gallons of water, are used on long runs.

THEORETICALLY, for the purposes of this narrative, we have described the facilities of the New York Central Railroad and its ultra-modern "new look." However, we might just as well have walked westward a few blocks and started eulogizing the many New Era innovations installed by the Central's principal rival, the Pennsylvania Railroad —the "longest" (in miles of trackage) railroad in the world.

New York's Pennsylvania Station takes off its hat to no one—not even its magnificent rival, Grand Central. The "Pennsy" is undoubtedly the world's busiest railway station, as well as being one of the two principal gateways to the world's largest and richest metropolis.

More than 100,000,000 people use its facilities annually.

The main station, bordered by 7th and 8th avenues and 31st and 33rd streets, is an imposing, colonnaded, polished-marble structure, covering a scant eight acres, but its adjacent underground trackage spreads out over an area almost four times that size.

It cost more than $125,000,000 to build.

Design of the station was inspired by some of the great

buildings of ancient Rome, particularly the Baths of Emperors Caracalla, Titus and Diocletian and the Basilica of Constantine the Great. The "new" station was opened to the public on September 8, 1910.

Since that date an estimated two billion men, women and children (the entire population of the world) have passed through its doors.

Pennsylvania's train concourse is a skylighted area frequently used as "location" for travel scenes by Hollywood movie productions.

The main waiting room is 277 feet long, 103 feet wide and 150 feet high. It is comparable in size to the nave of St. Peter's in Rome.

Traffic movements in and out of the station, both human and mechanical, are even more complicated and amazing than those in the more expansive Grand Central.

This is the "front parlor" of Penn Station. It contains the central information booth and the ticket offices for all main line trains.

The second section of Pennsylvania's big terminal contains all train gates for main line passenger traffic. Stairs lead down to the train tunnels underneath. Incoming passengers can use escalators coming up.

While the latter, owned by the New York Central Railroad, services two major railroads on 67 tracks, the Pennsylvania, with only 21 tracks, is the terminal for four major railroad systems, including the famous Long Island commuter railroad. With the exception of New York City's network of subways, the Long Island Railroad has the heaviest commuter traffic in the world.

In addition to all this, the station houses platforms, tracks and caters to the needs of the multi-millions who annually ride four subway lines—the IRT, BMT, Independent and the Hudson-Manhattan tubes.

Daylight Time is always a source of trouble to both travelers and railroad personnel. Railroads which pass through several time zones must retain Standard Time on their schedules and interpret the schedules to the public in Daylight Time.

Besides the Pennsylvania and the Long Island, which was until recently a subsidiary of the Pennsylvania, the station also serves the Boston-Washington service of the New York, New Haven and Hartford Railroad, which passes through another 1,500,000 passengers every year.

Other roads using the Pennsylvania tracks and servicing facilities such as repairs, cleaning, etc., are the Lehigh Valley, the Atlantic Coast Line, the Seaboard Airline Railway and the Southern Railway. These roads also use Pennsylvania's locomotive power entering and leaving the Terminal.

No steam locomotives now run into the mammoth web of Pennsylvania's tracks. All four mainline tracks to Washington are electrified with catenary systems, as are the tracks to Harrisburg. Through trains are delivered to Washington and points West of New York by the famous Pennsylvania GG-1's, where they are subsequently picked up by other types of locomotion.

Eastward from the station the Pennsylvania has four tunnels under the East River, through which pass the Long Island trains. This road uses the electrical, outside third rail.

The crack Boston-to-Washington New Haven trains change crews and locomotives at Penn Station. From here the New Haven crosses under the East River to Long Island, then over Hell Gate Bridge to the Bronx, and thence upward through New York State and Connecticut. The whole transfer takes little more than 15 minutes. The New Haven's electric locomotives are equipped with both pantographs for the catenary system and shoes for the third rail so they can operate on Pennsylvania's dual system.

An average of 750 trains daily are handled in and out of the station, operating at times on only a two-minute headway. A large number of these trains, obviously, are those of the Long Island commuters. During the morning and evening rush hours 7 of the system's 21 tracks are entirely turned over to handling this service.

Like Grand Central, the Pennsylvania has two passenger levels, with the Northern half of the lower level assigned to the accommodations of its Long Island patrons. This lower level also houses the two subway stations and platforms.

Because of the necessary fast pace of passenger traffic through Penn Station, it does not lend itself to the installation of many business establishments. While the station has a number of specialty shops and restaurants on both levels, the shopping area is not so widely diversified—there are no "on-the-premise" movies.

Some of the other features of the terminal include a Telephone Information which handles up to 1,000 questions an hour, with the correct answer in about 30 seconds, and mail-handling facilities capable of moving more than 5,000,000 pouches a month. Ten miles of underground, endless belting conveys these to and from New York General Post Office next door.

The Director's Room in the main station is the control

Crew dispatchers in station set up crews for both Pennsylvania Railroad and Long Island. The Pennsylvania is one of the few railroads to use women on passenger train crews. They are called "trainmen" and their duties consist of collecting tickets and handling passenger traffic.

center for all power transmission in and out of the huge depot, handling the 660 volt, D.C. third rails and the 11,000 volt, A.C. catenary (overhead) system. Tower "A" on a Westerly platform controls movement of trains on the entire 21 tracks. It is the nerve center for operation of switches and signals.

Eastbound and Westbound Outgoing Trains

As all New York City stations are fed by electrically powered locomotion, no terminal story is complete without extending it out to where steam and Diesel power take over.

Westward out of Penn Station the big GG-1 is king. To Washington, 226 miles away, and carrying passengers and freight to and from the big cities of Philadelphia, Baltimore and Harrisburg, GG-1's roar in and out of the river tunnel constantly.

The GG-1, a unique and exclusive development of the Pennsylvania Railroad, is a wonderful example of efficient locomotive power. Measuring 79 feet in length and weigh-

ing approximately 237 tons, this electric engine is Pennsylvania's workhorse wherever the catenary system goes. As
mentioned before, the GG-1 handles, not only Pennsylvania rolling stock, but that of the New York New Haven
and Hartford, Lehigh Valley, Atlantic Coast Line, the Seaboard Airline and the Southern Railway.

One other delivery job, done through the tunnel by the
GG-1, is to New York and Long Branch Railroad, which
services the New Jersey coastline. This road is operated
jointly by the Pennsylvania and the Central Railroad of
New Jersey. GG-1's take cars to South Amboy, where they
are picked up by steam or Diesel.

Running over the main line out of Penn Station are the
multiple-unit commuter trains, that run down as far as
Trenton. These trains, too, use catenary operation.

Eastward Is the Long Island

Eastward from Penn Station, through four tunnels under the river, runs the Long Island Rail Road—the Long
Island, as far as is known, carries more passengers per day
than any railroad in the world.

To use the expression of a Division Operator, the Long
Island "can be compared to a great tree, the Jamaica Station the trunk from which the branches extend." Through
the network of these tracks there run, daily, 630 regular
trains and 242 extra trains. As the Island is rich in produce,
a number of these extras are freights. In a limited area
there are 30 interlocking stations, 11 block stations and 15
block-limit stations.

In addition to the main line, which runs clear to the end
of the Island, there are 11 branch commuter lines that run
through or to Jamaica. Some of these originate or terminate at the station.

The Jamaica Station is mentioned here because it, too,
is one of the points where electrified trains, outbound from
the Pennsylvania Station, are converted to other power.
At this terminal, in the past, Long Island's third-rail-pow-
ered electric trains were coupled to steam locomotives.
Today, the conversion is almost entirely to Diesel locomotives and, in a short time, will be completely so.

Heavy traffic conditions of the Long Island led to the construction of this double-decker, a rarity in railroading. Not to be confused with the streamlined vistadome cars, these are regular commuter coaches with seats "staggered" up and down to increase car capacity. Result: the double-deckers carry 132 passengers as compared to 72 for the ordinary coach. Long Island has 60 of these air-conditioned cars in service.

This Santa Fe four unit Diesel is painted in blue and yellow. These colors are used on freight engines while silver and red are used on passenger locomotives.

PHOTOGRAPHING MODEL RAILROADS

Nᴏᴛ to compete with proud fathers who show off baby pictures at the drop of a hat, but with equal pride, model railroaders have taken to photographing their pikes and trains and displaying the results to one and all at every opportunity. Reports of the growing numbers of modelers bitten by the camera bug, indicate that this is a movement to be reckoned with and is, therefore, worthy of attention. As you know, the essence of model railroading is realism. For this reason, no photograph does the job if it doesn't capture that realism right down to the last rivet.

Because of the differences in size between the average person and his model railroad, problems of proportion, distance, perspective, depth, lighting, etc. present them

selves for solution before shooting begins. In this chapter
are a few tips on how to overcome these problems and
enjoy an entirely new and interesting activity in connection with your model railroad.

In pursuing this hobby within a hobby, always bear in
mind the importance of size relationship. In an 0 gauge
model, for instance, everything is constructed on the scale
of ¼ inch to the foot. By this proportioning, if you hold
your camera 5 feet above the model, you are making an
aerial shot from a height of 240 feet. If you are 6 feet tall,
by the standards of the model you would measure but 1½
inches. This factor is vitally important if you want to
get the utmost in realism.

In attempting to achieve an eye level view with dramatic
lighting of any of your subjects, as in the photograph at
the bottom of the page, you might be faced with the following problem. Even with the camera set on the floor
of your layout, the center of the lens may be higher than
the top of the engine and cars. This would give you an
overhead perspective that would throw the entire picture
out of focus. One way to overcome this difficulty is to pose
your trains on the edge of your layout so that you can line
the camera up to get the correct angle, slightly below
"floor" level if necessary.

Another point that warrants consideration is that of
lighting. Here again you are after realism. To simulate a
bright day, use either flash or flood, with one lamp repre-

Low angle and dramatic lighting make a realistic scene.

senting sunlight and the second taking the place of light that normally would come from the sky itself. This latter may be "bounced" from walls or ceiling so that it will have no definite direction. If you use "bounce" light alone, it will give the effect of an overcast day. If walls are too far away, or the ceiling too high, the light may be bounced from a card held above your subject.

A loco alongside a coaling station, an engine on the turntable, or one coming under a signal bridge are all good subjects because they provide a tie-in with some of your equipment. And your accessories are the "extras" that will give atmosphere and an air of reality to your photographs.

Look at the photo on p. 345. No accessories have been used but it is an excellent example of how effectively you can pose your picture to bring out some of the more dramatic aspects of your pike. The rough terrain and tunnels in this case lend a feeling of open-air railroading that has the look of the real thing. Just be sure to bring out vividly all your background details.

As soon as you start taking close-ups of anything in your

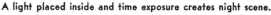

A light placed inside and time exposure creates night scene.

Study your composition and lighting well.

layout, you will discover that the depth of field almost vanishes. Try to avoid this in shots where everything from nearby to far away is sharp and clear. The way to get around it is to use the smallest possible diaphragm opening consistent with the shutter speed necessary to stop motion. For example, if you want to make a long shot of a train you will have to get far enough back so that the depth of field provided by your lens will cover the whole train vividly. This will result in a smaller size image on the film which can be enlarged when the print is made. For this type of shooting a short-focal length lens is better because of its greater depth.

An excellent way to increase depth which gives your whole picture more body and strength, is to photograph a mirror image of your subject. You'll find this an aid particularly when you can't get the camera into the picture that you want. In addition, another advantage is that because the focusing distance is equal to the distance between the lens and the mirror plus the distance from the mirror to your subject, you can pick up a few extra inches or feet, as may be needed.

The manner in which you handle your lighting can

Which is the real train and which is the model? Lower picture, a model, is carefully set up and studied before photographing.

oftentimes make or break the picture. All the lighting, however, does not have to be on the set. You can get excellent results with a flash shot with the flash off the camera. To change a day shot to a dramatic night shot, print the area around the focal point of your subject normally, then shield this part while giving a definite overexposure to the rest of the picture area. The result is a night scene with subdued shadows and startling lighting effects.

When placing your lighting, make sure that light will fall on all parts that are shown in the picture. A flash shot that has an overbright foreground and a fading-off-to-black

Tricks in photography.

background cannot make a very realistic daytime picture. If your lighting is not sufficient to cover the area you need, then set the camera on a tripod and make a time exposure by existing light.

To do this, the rolling stock cannot be in motion and in almost every case, unless the lighting is of the speedlight variety, it is better to "pose" the trains. On a close-up shot it will take your highest shutter speed to stop the movement on the film when flash is used.

As most of your shots will be made close-up, it will be well for you to invest in a supplementary close-up lens if your camera cannot be worked at less than three feet from the subject. If the close-up lens is not used, it means that you must blow up the image to a greater extent and perhaps lose some of the wealth of fine detail that is predominant in present-day models.

Naturally, if you plan to keep a record of your work as it progresses, a general shot of the whole layout is necessary. But remember, it is the details and sections of the whole which make the more interesting pictures. The more unusual the props that make up your scenes, the more in-teresting will be your picture.

For an idea of the realism you can achieve by applying some of the tips you have read here, look at the photos on p. 348. You'll agree that the lower picture of a model rivals the top photo in true-to-life detailing and that exciting action look. You probably found yourself asking which is real and which is the model. Sufficient depth of field is, of course, highly important here. You must get everything in sharp focus from nearest to farthest distance. For best re-sults, pose your trains where you want to and then stop the lens down for maximum sharpness and depth of field. As mentioned previously, the lighting effects play a vital part in adding to the effect which you are seeking to obtain.

Don't get the impression that an elaborate array of equipment is needed to set up shop to photograph your layout. On the contrary, you can achieve most of the effects you will want by a clever use of only four or five items. You must have, of course, a camera. And even this can be as simple as you want to make it. But just be sure that you know how to use it to make up for its shortcomings if it is a very inexpensive one. A ground glass lens is recom-mended for best results. Floodlights are very important for those extra-special lighting effects that really lend a touch of drama and action to your photographs. Two will be enough to get you rolling. And they will give you night and day shots that set each picture off and keep them from resembling each other if you are posing the same model against the same background more than once.

You might also find a use for reflectors that reflect back and lighten up shadow areas so that they won't be too dark. These can be used very effectively and easily with a little practice. Filters may also be added as a part of your equipment but not until you have mastered the techniques that are involved in the simpler stages of photography. They will help you to change the appearance of back-ground and scenery. For example you can use a filter to make a light blue sky almost black and you can change the color of the grass on your pike from a dark to a light green. This lends variety to your backgrounds. And you'll be able to use the same scenery over and over again for all of your trains and accessories.

Once you've really gotten the knack of taking your pictures to make them look exactly as you want them to, you can employ various tricks of photography for emphasis and drama. To bring out the intricate detailing and scaling of one of your favorites, use the magnifying glass trick on page 349. Here, an ordinary magnifying glass was held before the section to receive special attention, and the photographer took special pains with his lighting effects to be sure that there was no glare or streak from a light shining on the magnifying glass.

Various tricks can be used with lighting and camera angles once you get the feel of your new hobby. You can focus floodlights to catch interesting shadows on the ground or on walls of your subject and even of smoke-puffs from your engines. By removing a patch from the floor of a waist-high layout, you can catch trains passing overhead or, with a little more effect and ingenuity, you can create the illusion of a picture having been taken from an airplane. Just get high above your subject, with a light directly on the train but slightly beneath you. Then suspend a model airplane below the light but directly over the train. In this way, your shadow is out of the picture but the shadow of the plane falls across the train. If done carefully with particular attention to proportions, the effect can be very unique and interesting. You'll find yourself inventing all different ways of presenting your trains in their most interesting aspects once you get started. As a matter of fact, you can exchange tips amongst your fellow railroaders. There are thousands of possible variations.

But remember when making your shots, to keep these few principles in mind:

1. Select a viewpoint that will dramatize your subjects.

2. Make your lighting consistent with the time of day you want to show.

3. Secure maximum sharpness by stopping down the lens as far as possible.

4. Use your imagination. The results are worth the effort.

WIRING FOR EFFECT

THERE ARE unlimited special effects available on model railroads. So long as model railroaders model, there will be new ones cropping up.

One modeler, for instance, came by a locomotive smoke unit. He promptly concealed it in an industrial stack, and now, by turning a switch, can generate smoke in one of his factories. His blower is a small motor with a tiny fan, and it works fine.

For modelers, there seems to be only the limit of time and ability—imagination abounds.

Below is the wiring diagram of an automatic railroad on which two opposing trains can run indefinitely, never colliding. The secret, of course, is in letting the trains con-

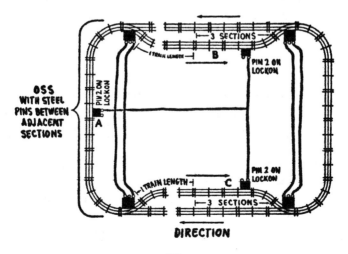

trol each other. Such a wiring system can be made to cut off and run by customary hand methods.

On this automatic system, ground rails on the sidings are insulated so that a train always halts on them. A train at point A will provide a ground circuit through an OSS section and start the train at point B. Train A goes into the siding C and stops. Train B goes on to complete the circuit and start train A again. B takes the siding until A completes the cycle and the whole procedure continues indefinitely.

The switches are wired so that when one is open, its opposite number automatically closes.

A similar system is used on the double-loop system below. Here, a train emerging from the siding activates the train that has been deadened on the other siding. At the same time, it throws the switches in the proper manner.

The method is simple enough and requires little work. Insulating tracks takes only a moment (by prying off the rail and inserting light cardboard), or OSS track can be obtained. Matches or fiber pins can be used at the ends of rails. If you remember to have insulated sections long enough to hold your longest train—or insulate your loco-

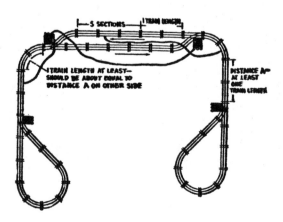

motive from your tender—it is difficult to go wrong.

This is a useful method, and of course, does not need to be applied to layouts in this exact way. It can be used to run a set of trains on one part of the track while you shift cars around your yard areas or in your terminals.

Many model railroaders, certainly a large proportion of hobbyists, like to work up a night scene for their road. The gleam of a few house lights which go out one by one, the streetlights with their faint glow, and a rousing headlight from a speeding locomotive—it seems to evoke a feeling of nostalgia. Many hobbyists have a rheostat on the main lights, and so the "sun" can rise and set. Thus the streetlights go on on schedule.

One possibility is an electrical storm as pictured on page 352. A sky painting on your scenic background can be made of tissue backed up by heavier paper. Some jagged lightning streaks are cut from it, and colored light bulbs are placed behind it. These are wired as shown, and a turn of the switch across and back will produce flashes. A cloud placed a bit out from the painting will add to the illusion.

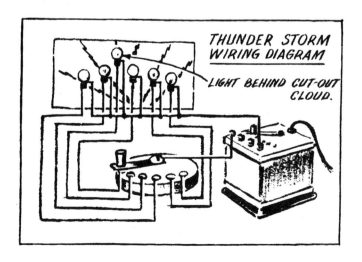

THUNDER STORM WIRING DIAGRAM

LIGHT BEHIND CUT-OUT CLOUD.

A rather common trick can be done with a standard city background scene or with the suburban scene, both of which are available in Skyline sets. These can be laid on a drawing board or other smooth work surface. Then with a hobby knife, and with liberal doses of patience, the small windows in some of the homes and office buildings are cut out. Not all windows are cut out of any one building, and an occasional home is quite dark. Similarly, not all the windows in one building or on one floor are cut out—although one whole floor can be dark.

This scene is mounted as usual on lath and tacked into position, but with three or four inches space behind it. A few small light bulbs behind it will make the windows glow. Over some windows, if further effect is desired, translucent tracing paper may be cemented. Here and there a bit of red or blue cellophane will look like curtains, but use that only in one or two spots.

With one or more of these effects, a variety of views is obtained that will liven your road.

Water of all sorts seems to fascinate model railroaders, almost without exception. There is good reason for the streams and lakes on model layouts. They justify the bridges, they add variety and interest to landscapes, they may even add industrial possibilities to a region.

You can make this waterfall with the usual materials and a bit of wiring, plus patience. Any real water on a model layout produces a great many problems, and almost all modelers avoid use of it.

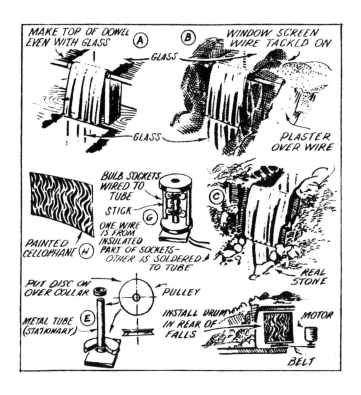

Many modelers experiment with real water. All but the most meticulous soon give it up. You can use real water, but your tinsmithing must be topnotch. The water must be continually inspected to make sure that no moss or cloth is hanging into it—if so, it will siphon water onto the other parts of the layout. Engines or cars dropped into water by a wreck may be ruined or out of commission for some time. In short, it is a continuous headache and rarely worth the bother.

One of the things that seems to make water so desirable to so many people is that a waterfall can then be made. That is true—but a falls can be made without water. If one is expertly made and put in the proper setting, it is very deceptive to onlookers.

Locate it at the far side of your layout, farthest from visitors. Avoid glaring lights directly on it. The setting should be among hills, and should be a blend of hills, trees, rocks, and water. The falls should not be conspicuous in any way, just visible to the casual view.

To make it, create streams just as usual, but on two levels. The best method for streams is careful modeling in plaster of the underwater detail; then glass which has been lightly rubbed with water color blue and green is placed over it. Some modelmakers use a glass that is plain on one side and wavy on the other, and this can be placed on flat, painted board.

To the top of the falls, a dowel rod is cemented so that frosted cellophane can be cemented over it and onto the glass. The dowel gives the curve to the water as it runs over the lip of the falls. At the bottom, the cellophane is tugged so that it wrinkles vertically. Then it is tacked to a board so that the wrinkles touch the lower glass. Thin water colors may be used to color the cellophane slightly.

Proper scenery of rocks and plaster and lichen and so on is added, and bits of cotton (or glass wool, if you don't object to handling it) are added at the bottom of the falls.

Back of the falls, a drum is installed. It is a cellophane drum with wavy lines painted in varying intensity. Lights are concealed inside it. Thus, if the drum is rotated, the lights penetrate the two layers of cellophane just enough to throw hazy waving lines down the falls. The lights should be dim enough that they do not give a luminous glow to the falls; and they should only be bright enough to show some motion, as if from reflected light.

The mechanics of making the cylinder and wiring it are shown in the drawings. Collector rings for the light bulbs are necessary; and any sort of pulley arrangement will do to turn it. Its speed should be very, very slow, of course.

You can make yourself a set of northern lights, a special effect that is highly dramatic. Using low hills to conceal the lights, arrange your background as shown below. It is painted with clouds so that it will pick up reflected light from the bulbs. If desired, the background can curve so that it blends with the ceiling.

The colored bulbs are arranged in a direct line across the base of the backdrop. The wiring is shown below, and it can be seen that if the hand switch is slowly turned in complete circles, the lamps will light in an irregular sequence.

Each time the switch touches a contact it will light lamps of various colors, and the effect will be that of the odd and mysterious northern lights. The changing and shifting must not be too rapid; a bit of practice will enable you to give a convincing demonstration.

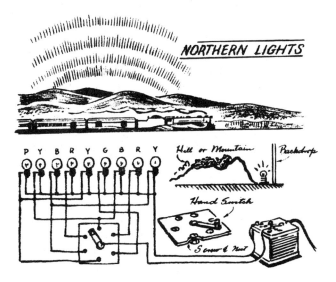

CLUBS: FOR AND AGAINST

CHAPTER TWENTY-THREE

T HE DIFFICULT thing about clubs is not how to form one, but whether to form one.

For every benefit of club activity, there is a corresponding problem. The decision depends on the person.

The arguments pro and con are about like this:

There is pleasure in group activity—the fun of working and pursuing one's hobby with people who feel basically the same about an avocation. This pleasure cuts across social and economic lines, and a whip-smart advertising man or broker may find himself playing apprentice to a mechanic or machinist who has the cunning fingertips of his calling. A well-to-do banker may find that his youngest clerk knows more railroading than he ever will. And for most men, there is a sincere warmth in group give-and-take.

Group activity has its drawbacks, though. The top-notch craftsman may feel he is dragged down to the group level, while the rank beginner may feel shunned and useless. A medium is hard to strike, and petty difficulties tend to be magnified. Unless it is especially well organized, a group tends to break into factions and bitter bickering.

Learning in a large group is easy. If you need or want to know about soldering, for instance, there is always someone around who knows about it and can teach you. The group tends to pool its knowledge, bringing everyone to a high level of skill in their chosen activity.

Yet, the argument works the other way. In a group, one person—usually the most skillful—does all of the soldering, to continue the foregoing example. On the other hand, a lone workman is forced to become a jack-of-all-trades, learning by trial and error. He makes mistakes, but he learns from them, and is not completely overshadowed by someone who has no need of the experience.

In a group, the railroading is better. It is more fun to run a large layout than a small one; there is more variety in a big spread. Also, big layouts mean a longer running program or timetable. The development of dispatching skills and other similar techniques demands a large road.

However, size does not always indicate quality, and a big road may not be as railroad-like as a small one. And in any case, each operator is subject to group rulings, whether right or wrong, wise or unwise. And, finally, space for a big layout is not always so easy to find.

And so it goes. The arguments could continue indefinitely. Anyone with experience can argue either side convincingly.

But the truth is that the case is not so black and white as it appears above. Knowing the pitfalls above—and others—model railroad clubs have set themselves up to avoid the obvious traps. Also, the perfectly competent lone operator is a rarity. Let's face it: Many of us need our fellow men.

If you want to work alone, fine. Nobody disputes the right, and some of the finest layouts are one-man jobs. But if so, there is little of interest in the rest of this chapter. What follows will interest the model railroader who wants to work with two or three others, or with enough others to form an organized club.

The Informal Group

There is, actually, a middle way between the lone operator and the formal, organized group.

Many railroaders own and maintain their own roads in their own home. Recognizing the pleasure of companionship, and because their layout is unwieldy if run single-handed, they invite a select few in to help.

Naturally, there are no hard-and-fast rules about such a group—it depends on the owner. He is in charge at all times; and decisions are made by him, democratically or arbitrarily, as his judgment and temperament decree.

To cite an example or two, let's first consider Henry Abraham, who operates a splendid road on Long Island. Hank is pretty well known among hobbyists by now, having written about the subject at length in *Model Builder* and *Model Railroader.*

The Abraham household has (due to amazing tolerance which is necessary on the part of model railroad families) turned over a large cellar to the railroad. About 300-and-some feet of track occupy the tables. The road can be run single-handed, but there are a few people who drop in regularly to help out and to try out their own cars and locomotives.

Many of the visitors also try out ideas. One friend may have a hot idea for a relay system and work with Hank until it is perfected. Another friend may build, just for kicks, a large and cunningly constructed steel mill to which Hank adds trackage. Still another friend may be the person who helps Hank run the road during his "open-house" week when visitors are permitted to drop a contri-

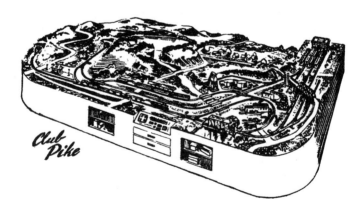

Club
Pike

bution into a jar for one charity or another. (Hank usually raises several hundred dollars each year for some charitable group, and the "open house" is now something of a community institution.)

But many of Hank's friends, which seem to include most people who know him, just drop in and kibitz. They sit unobtrusively in corners and watch the trains run. They ask plenty of questions. But, of course, they are invariably careful of the layout and the rolling stock on it.

It is so informal that it hardly is a group at all, and yet many people come regularly, drawn together by the common love of railroads and model railroads.

A bit more organized is the railroad of Bob McKeand in Westchester County, outside New York City. Bob works for the New York Central, but, not wholly satisfied with that, he runs a miniature New York Central in his cellar.

It's not exactly in his cellar, either. As a matter of fact, Bob runs the most amazing road in the U. S. If that is a brash statement, let me elaborate a moment.

In the large cellar of a large house, one terminal of the road is located on a shoulder-high platform. From there it descends in a series of dazzling loops to the floor. The track on the floor has been cemented to place with concrete, and so can be trodden without damage. There is a large branch line which occupies most of the cellar floor area.

From the floor, the main line rises in steep curving grades, passing through several rooms until it runs right out through a hole which Bob tediously cut through the 14" stone wall. Under the porch is trackage along almost two whole sides of the house and forming a loop and turnaround with storage tracks.

But that's not all. From the porch, the tracks go clear around the remaining two sides of the house and on into the garage. These are stainless steel rails set into concrete.

The terminals are shortened miniatures of New York and Chicago, and operators at various points are in telephonic communication. Also, there are lights which enable an operator to run things alone.

There is a difference of over ten feet in elevation between the low and high points of the road, and there is about 750' of trackage. The neighbors, including me, will not be much astonished if Bob figures out a way to run the road up to the porch roof where an operator can be stationed in a bedroom to run that division.

I have seen prettier roads, and many ones easier to understand; but never have I seen or heard of a road of equal accomplishments. And I've seen, too, many veteran model railroaders gasp at Bob's road and his casual, but accurate operations. The layout is, incidentally, a tribute to the performing powers of Lionel equipment— he makes it do things the manufacturer would never dare to claim for fear of ridicule.

But—having wandered—what about his informal group? Bob McKeand holds operating night every Friday. A bunch of regulars attend, often bringing a locomotive or two along (although Bob has plenty of rolling stock). Assignments are passed out, and the fellows go to their various posts, some scrambling under the porch, others deploying to the garage. Each is in charge of a division, but since much of the road is single track, each must be aware of the other's movements.

Some nights there is strict timetable operation, other nights a series of tests to set up a new variation. To the visitor it is as mysterious as the workings of the real New York Central, but the proof is in the fact that after a few tests, Bob and his gang invariably settle into a routine that results in a steady calling out of "Number 22—on time at tower AY."

That, of course, is the time to remake the schedule so that it is a little more difficult.

It is not a club in the sense that the New York Society of Model Engineers is a club, and yet it is a group that gives a great many people a very enjoyable time.

The Formal Club

There is a handy book on clubs by Lawrence W. Sagle, the genial B. and O. public relations man who is also a confirmed model railroad hobbyist. His *Book of Rules for Model Railroaders* is a brief but very instructive tract on club organization. It will answer all of the questions you can think of—and a great many that would not occur to you until later.

Most clubs are organized with a club structure and a railroading structure. The club structure includes a president or chairman, a secretary, a treasurer, and one or two other officers who may be concerned with the library, the club rooms and so on. These are club officers whose duty is to run club matters and make policy decisions.

It is surprising how quickly a club is known, and there will be many matters to be dealt with that do not concern the direct operation of the railroad. It may be a question of joining a local hobby show; it may be a charitable exhibit. There will be duties enough for all the officers.

Separate from these officers are the railroad officers—however, one man may hold posts in both groups. In most clubs, a superintendent is the ranking operating person, as would be found in a division of a real road. The super may have an aid in a large club, usually designated as secretary to the super.

Under the superintendent are four categories: signals, engineering, maintenance, and operating. The number of people in each group depend on the size of the club and the railroad.

Signaling responsibility may be divided so that there is a signal engineer, a signal supervisor, and a signal maintainer. This is the maximum, and if your road is small or your signaling limited, all functions may be combined into one.

Engineering divides into track, structures, and scenery, and any of these three groups may be as large or small as necessary. A division engineer will head the group, and three other men will have responsibility for one part. Naturally, if you are just laying track and have no scenery, you omit one group and enlarge another.

Rolling stock maintenance should be provided, as well as a group to inspect and approve additions by club members. It may be that this function will be covered by the individuals. But it is useful to have someone delegated to check the oiling and cleanliness of all locomotives, to see that cars roll freely and couplers are working. By trial and error, a club can determine how many men can be useful in this capacity.

The operating section will normally be the largest on any nights the trains run. Even on nights when work is being done on circuits and track, you will want a standby crew to run test trains along various sections of track.

The operating group consists, in order of their rank, of a trainmaster, a train dispatcher, and under him, train conductors, engineers and brakemen and a yardmaster and yard crew.

The mechanics of running the operating club can be handled in several ways. Many clubs have one operating night per month, and other nights are devoted to building and maintenance. Some clubs appoint a superintendent for this period; other clubs appoint him for two, three, or four such periods, or for one year.

During a superintendent's tenure, he is fully responsible for running the road, and he therefore has power to appoint persons and to promote and demote them. Many clubs have a grievance board, so that a member who feels unjustly treated may have his punishment reviewed.

In most clubs, a novice begins as a brakeman working with a conductor until he knows the ropes and the rules. In a short period, he is promoted to conductor, thence to engineer and so on up the line until he is capable of being trainmaster. He should have experience on signals, engineering, and maintenance during or preceding this training. Finally he may be qualified as superintendent.

Qualification does not carry any privilege. A qualified trainmaster may find himself working as an engineer or conductor, or he may be put in as yardmaster or a member of the yard crew.

Jobs may be given out by seniority or by rotation. Under seniority, members automatically move up only as the road expands or as members at the top drop out. Membership by-laws should be very specific about reasons for dropping members and leaves of absence. Thus the senior members can bid for any open job for which they are qualified, the opportunity to bid running right down the roster—which should be posted by the club. The job of superintendent should be elective under this system.

Under a rotational system, members are automatically jumped one step at regular intervals. However, no member may be promoted into a job for which he has not qualified. In this way, after a given number of operating nights, all members at the top would drop to the bottom of the list and begin all over again.

The choice of the two systems is up to the club membership, but most large, well-organized clubs use the former method. It is, of course, more railroad-like.

Perhaps the biggest thing to remember about a club is that it is a means to an end. The objective is not the club, but the model railroading. Officers must keep the objective in mind and interpret club by-laws for the best interest of all in model railroading. In the long run, the club will prosper from intelligent and liberal interpretation of its constitution and by-laws.

TOOLS

CHAPTER TWENTY-FOUR

For a model railroader, hand tools are a necessity. Power tools are a luxury, for at best there is little skilled carpentry to be done. Not too many hand tools are absolutely essential, but like other collections, tools tend to grow. You may start with a hammer, screwdriver, and small saw, and wind up with a collection housed in a large room.

Here we will consider only the model railroader's tools that are especially useful to him.

First, a word of warning: Any tool is potentially dangerous. The danger invariably lies in misuse of the tools. The wrong wrench can slip and crack knuckles; a nail wrongly held can cause a broken thumb; a screwdriver used as a prying tool can snap with explosive force and put out an eye. Use each tool for its intended purpose only—it will last longer and so may you.

As to power tools, a drill press or a hand-power drill is useful, but they are not necessary for model railroad demands. A power saw is a wonderful asset for a carpenter, but rarely necessary or particularly useful except on the largest roads. A grindstone is the best thing for sharpening hand tools, but requires skill and constant use of tools to justify it.

Hand tools group conveniently into these divisions: fastening, cutting, measuring, holding, and finishing.

Fastening tools include hammers, screwdrivers, wrenches, and some odds and ends like wire, cotter keys, corrugated fasteners, and clamps with glue.

The common claw hammer is a necessity in any household, and for craft work of any kind should be a good name brand. (Most craftsmen, incidentally, admire and use the products of the major mail-order houses—they are usually of superior quality.) A good hammer is a wise buy, for it will last longer. But the biggest reason for quality is in the safety. Cheap hammers may break or the head may slip off the handle, and if it happens at the top of the swing, the head flies with great force.

Swing any hammer by grasping it at the end and using the entire forearm. It takes a bit of time to learn, but it is more effective than a wrist motion.

Add a rather heavy ball pein hammer to your tools. An upholsterer's hammer (magnetized) is useful. Small tack hammers are rarely useful; if you want to remove tacks, get a magnetized tack puller.

Buy a collection of nails, and keep them in jars or cans. You will want some finishing nails and some regular nails. They should be bought by the pound. One of the home assortments will supply tiny nails for your model buildings.

With a nail set—which drives nails home without damaging the wood—and a punch for marking locations, you are all fixed.

WORK BENCH

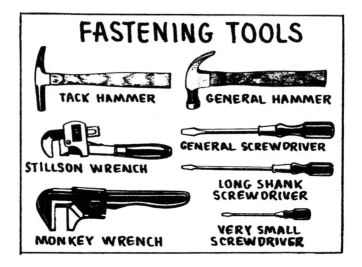

FASTENING TOOLS

TACK HAMMER   GENERAL HAMMER

STILLSON WRENCH   GENERAL SCREWDRIVER

LONG SHANK
SCREWDRIVER

MONKEY WRENCH   VERY SMALL
SCREWDRIVER

In screwdrivers, get three sizes: one quite small; a medium size, say 4"; and one large one about 6" or 8". In addition, you may want a set of Phillips screwdrivers for the four-corner slotted screws found in many home appliances. By all means get a screwdriver bit for your brace; and you may want a ratchet screwdriver if you do very much work.

When sinking screws, keep a fairly hard piece of soap near. Draw large screws over the soap so they pick up some chips, and they will drive home much more easily.

Occasionally there will be a bolt to be drawn up tight, so that an 8" adjustable wrench is useful. There are many types, but the Crescent wrench seems to be the most adaptable to common situations encountered.

Cutting tools include saws, chisels, planes, drills and files and rasps.

If you do relatively little carpentry, a combination crosscut and rip saw is best. It will do a fair job of each, but

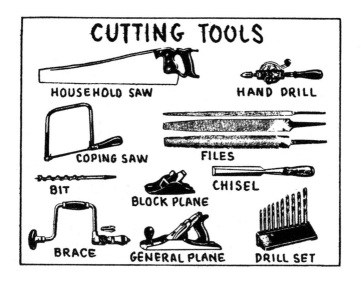

CUTTING TOOLS

HOUSEHOLD SAW   HAND DRILL

COPING SAW   FILES

BIT   BLOCK PLANE   CHISEL

BRACE   GENERAL PLANE   DRILL SET

of course cannot match the specialized saws. A 20″ blade is long enough for most home use.

There are specialized saws without number, but the next most useful saw for any home-owner is a coping saw (often called, in error, a jig saw). Not only will it cut around corners, but it can be used on metal. Metal will damage the blades, of course, but they do not cost much. Blades vary greatly, so it is best to get an adjustable saw.

A keyhole saw is handy for getting into small spaces in the middle of large boards where the coping saw cannot reach.

A set of at least three wood chisels can be used by anyone who does much wood work. They should be sized about ¼″, ½″, and 1″ for most jobs. In using them, always point the tool away from the body (your stomach is pretty soft) and do not strike hard. If possible, use a wooden mallet, or put a rubber crutch tip over your hammer—it's easier on the chisels.

Keep chisels hanging so that the point touches nothing, and sharpen it only on the beveled side.

A spoke plane and a 10″ plane are plenty for most needs. When using the plane, remember that most wood has a preferred direction, depending on the grain. This may change on a long piece. Never lay the plane with cutting edge down—it hurts the blade. Always mind your fingers as you run the plane along—it will take skin off, too. Hang the plane up when not in use.

A drawknife is one of the handiest tools for removing an edge from a board. It is used when there is too much wood remaining to be planed, and not enough to justify a saw cut. Drawknives work only with the grain, never across it. They are one of the handier "extra" tools.

Files and rasps are much more useful than most people know. A smooth file will finish a piece almost as well as medium-grade sandpaper. A rasp will remove wood almost as fast as a plane. There are only two real tricks to know (besides keeping your fingers out from under rasps). First, use handles with files and rasps. They cost only ten or fifteen cents, and make the work much better and easier. Second, remember that these tools cut only on the forward stroke. Always lift them on the return stroke, otherwise the teeth will be damaged.

Files and rasps are cleaned with a file card. The name is odd, for actually it is a brush with heavy wire bristles.

Half-round files and rasps seem most useful, but in time you may want a complete collection that will include a dozen or more.

You will certainly want a set of drills and a small hand drill (or speed drill). These will give you flexibility in working, and with a set of drills ranging from ¼″ down, you will have enough variety to begin.

A brace and bit is used in carpentry, and you should have a number of bits. Get a screwdriver bit—it will handle anything you are likely to encounter in size or stubbomness . An adjustable bit is very useful, since it can be gauged to holes from about ⅝″ up to 1½″. It is especially useful in fitting dowel into wood.

Measuring tools include rulers, try-squares, calipers, and scratch awls. The latter is used for marking. Get a steel tape measure, but also have a steel ruler. In model making, the ruler is used with hobby knives or razors to cut model building material.

A combination square will provide the steel ruler. It will also gauge right angles and 45° angles, and it usually has a level in it. Some are adjustable for measuring bevels.

Calipers are most useful for modelers who do delicate work. Of course they are a necessity to machinists. A pair of inside and outside calipers will save time and increase accuracy on your models.

Holding tools include vises, clamps, and pliers. For heavy work, a large steel-jawed vise is best. One of the small detachable vises is satisfactory for purely model work, though. A woodworking vise is very handy, but a large steel vise can be used for wood if some wooden faces are used to avoid scarring the work.

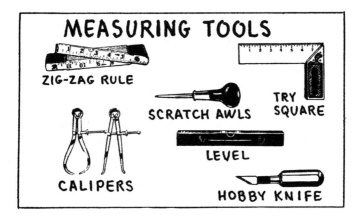

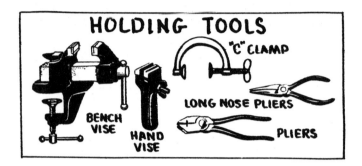

A 6″ or 8″ C-clamp is useful for carpentry, but for most model work, tiny C-clamps are much better. They can hold a ruler in place and they can hold material while glue is setting firmly. Pairs should be bought in several sizes.

Have at least two pairs of pliers. Use an electrician's pair for your wiring job, and have a pair of long-nosed pliers for fine work and for clamping loose track ends. The adjustable pliers with teeth in the jaws are very useful too.

Have a supply of different grades of sandpaper, and also some fine emery cloth. These will be used to finish work before painting.

A recurring problem of model railroaders is soldering. It is unquestionably useful. The only drawbacks are that a bit of skill is required and there is also the possibility of burning things. At least, consider learning to solder if you don't do it now. Get a manufacturer's pamphlet and study it. It is not difficult; it just doesn't seem to be a natural skill (or, as you may gather, it isn't for me). In buying equipment, an electric iron is considered easiest to use, and you will need fine soldering tips for model work.

Take good care of your tools. Keep them in place on a board near your work bench. Don't jumble them in drawers or work boxes. They'll last many years if well treated.

ENGINE WHISTLE SIGNALS

With most engines today, a whistle is provided. Most standard whistle signals are listed below. With practice, you can communicate with friends or imaginary crews.

"0"	Illustrates short blast.
"_____"	Illustrates long blast.
0	Apply brakes. Stop.
— —	Release brakes. Proceed.
—— 000	Flagman protect rear of train.
— — — —	Flagman return from West or South.
— — — — —	Flagman return from East or North.
000	When train is standing, back.
—— 00	To call attention to Yard engines, extra trains, trains of same or inferior class at night, to signals displayed for following section.
— — 0 —	Approaching grade crossings or obscure places.
———————	Approaching stations, junctions, railroad crossings, and tunnels.
0 ——	Inspect train for air line leak or brakes sticking. Succession of short sounds: Alarm for persons or animals on track.

COMMUNICATION SIGNALS

Inside a passenger train, the conductor can signal the engineer with a small cord that blows a soft air whistle. Next time you ride, listen for these communication signals.

"0"	Illustrates short sound.
"____"	Illustrates long sound.
00	When standing, start.
00	When running, stop immediately.
000	When standing, back.
000	When running, stop at next passenger station.
0000	When standing, apply or release air brakes.
0000	When running, reduce speed.
00000	When standing, recall flagman.
00000	When running, increase speed.
———	When running, brakes sticking; look back for hand signals.

TRAIN MARKER LIGHTS

| Engine running forward by day as an extra. | Engine running forward by night as extra. | Engine by day with signals for second section. | Engine by night with signals for second section. |

| Engine backing at night, alone or train's rear. | Deadhead tender has red lamps at rear. | Rear car of train by day has lamps which are unlit. | Rear car of train by night has red lamps to rear. |

Letter beside drawing indicates: W—white light or flag; G—green light or flag; R—red light.

HAND, FLAG AND LAMP SIGNALS

| PROCEED | REDUCE SPEED | TRAIN HAS PARTED | BACK | STOP |

Hand, flag and lamp signals can all be used on your own model pike when you are working with anyone else. Let one person operate the transformer, the other give hand-signals from across the room as if it were too far to speak. A train can be directed very accurately in this way.

A GLOSSARY OF TERMS AND PHRASES INCLUDING RAILROAD SLANG

Abutment—An anchoring foundation supporting the end-thrust of a bridge.

AC—Alternating current; electric current of the reversing type.

Accommodation—A local train which makes all stops.

Alley—A clear track, usually in a yard.

Articulated Locomotive—An engine in which two sets of wheels and cylinders are used and pivoted on separate frames.

Ash Cat—A locomotive fireman.

Ash Pan—A tray under the firebox which accumulates ashes until an ash pit is reached.

Aspect—One of the indications of a signal light.

Automatic Block Signal—A signal actuated by the movements of trains.

Bad Order Track—A track on which cars are set out for repairs.

Baggage Smasher—A baggage handler.

Ballast—The cinders or crushed rock or gravel used to hold ties in place.

Balloon Stack—A wide flaring stack used to prevent sparks from escaping.

Bascule Bridge—A general term for counterbalanced lift bridges.

Belt Line—A connecting line between two or more railroads, so-called because it often encircles a city like a belt.

Big Hook—A wrecking crane.

Big Wheel—A rotary snowplow.

Bill of Lading—A form describing freight, its charges and destination in detail.

Bleed—To drain the air from a car or cars.

Blind Siding—A siding without telephone or telegraph connections to the dispatcher; no order can be received on it.

Block—A section of track which is controlled as a unit.

Block Signal—The signal, usually automatic, which controls a block.

Board—A fixed signal or marker.

Board, Call—Bulletin board where crew assignments are posted.

Boiler—The part of the locomotive where steam is generated.

Bolster—A plate or beam across the top of trucks to which the body or chassis is attached.

Boom Car—Car next to derrick car on which the crane boom is rested while traveling.

Brakeman—A member of a freight or passenger train crew. His duties are to assist the conductor in any way necessary.

Brass Hat—Top railroad executive.

Brownies—Demerits issued by the superintendent for infractions of rules; a certain number means suspension, and a greater number may mean dismissal.

Bug—A telegraph key.

Buggy—Caboose.

Buggy Track—Caboose track.

Bump—To exercise seniority in replacing a man in his position.

Bunker—A bin, usually elevated, for storing coal.

Butcher—A person selling papers, candy, etc., in passenger cars.

Cab—The section of the locomotive which contains the controls and where the engineer rides.

Caboose-Way Car—A caboose with a section for freight.

Call Boy, Caller—A boy, or man, whose duty is to summon crews.

Camelback—A locomotive with the cab astride the boiler, the fireman riding under a hood at the rear; also called a "Mother Hubbard."

Cap—A torpedo put on the tracks for signaling purposes.

Car Knocker—A car inspector, so-called from the men who tap the wheels of cars to test soundness.

Cinder Pit—An ash pit.

Circuit—A complete path for the flow of electricity.

Circuit Breaker—A device which interrupts a circuit if an overload occurs.

Class—Groups into which trains are divided, from two to four, depending on the railroad; see chapter on Operations.

Class I Railroad—A railroad in the U. S. with operating revenue over $1 million per year.

Classification Yards—A freight yard or yards where trains are broken up and made up by shifting of cars or by a hump.

Clear Board—A go-ahead signal.

Conductor—A crew member on freight or passenger trains, in charge of train at all stops or while the train is at terminals or stations.

Consist—The cars which make up a train, usually used in connection with freight train.

Converter—An electrical device for changing Direct Current (DC) to AC.

Coupler—The device which joins two cars.

Crew—The men who run a particular train.

Crossing—An intersection of two tracks on the same level.

Crossing, Grade—An intersection between a crossing and tracks on the same level.

Crossover—Track and switches which enables trains to cross from one parallel track to another.

Culvert—A passageway under tracks for drainage of water.

Cut—A number of cars coupled together, an excavated section through a hill so that tracks remain level.

DC—Direct current; electrical current which flows only in one direction.

Dead Man's Control—Automatic control which an engineer must hold in "on" position against a spring; if he dies or is hurt, it is automatically released and stops the train.

Deadhead—An empty car; a passenger riding on a pass; a locomotive traveling without cars.

Departure Yard—An arrangement of yard tracks from which cars are forwarded.

Diamond Stack—(see Balloon Stack) A diamond-shaped smoke stack.

Dinky—Any small, undersized locomotive.

Dispatcher—An employee who coordinates all train movements in his area, usually one division; he may issue special orders to keep traffic moving.

Distant Signal—A signal to indicate the aspect of a signal some distance ahead.

Division—That portion of a railroad managed by a superintendent.

Dome—A round protrusion on the boiler of a locomotive; it houses steam controls or sand.

Double—To take a train up a hill one half at one time.

Double-header—A train pulled by two locomotives.

Dowel—A round wooden stick, in various sizes.

Drawbar—The bar connecting an engine with the tender.

Drill—To switch cars in a yard.

Driving Wheels—The wheels of a locomotive which are powered.

E Unit—A reversing device in model locomotives.

Engine Yard—The yard in which engines are stored and serviced.

Engineer—A crew member who controls the locomotive; he is in charge of the train while it is moving.

Extra—A train not shown on schedules; it operates on train orders.

Facing Switch—A turnout with the points facing traffic.

Fill—Earth used to make a level roadbed across a valley or depression.

Fireman—Crew member whose job is to keep the fire and

steam up in the locomotive; on a Diesel he services the motors.

Fish Plate—A bar which joins ends of rails.

Flag—To protect the rear of the train by having a brakeman walk back with a flag while it is halted; to have any person not on the crew stop the train by waving hands, hat, etc.

Flange—A protruding lip on a girder or wheel; the edging of the wheel which keeps it on the tracks.

Frog—The portion of a switch which is grooved for the wheel flanges; named for its resemblance to a frog.

Gangway—The space between the locomotive and the tender through which the crew enters and leaves.

Gauge—The distance between heads of running rails.

Goat—A locomotive, almost always a small yard engine.

Hack—A caboose.

Helper—The second, or added locomotive on a double-header.

High Iron—Main line; track on which travel is only by schedule or order.

Highball—To speed; a sign to go ahead; so called from old ball signals.

Home Cars—Freight cars owned by a road.

Home Signal—The signal protecting the immediate block.

Hoop—A cane loop used to pass orders up to moving trains; the fireman puts his arm through the large loop.

Horsepower—The measuring unit of power; the power necessary to continuously raise 550 pounds one foot in one second.

Hostler—A roundhouse worker who cares for locomotives after each trip.

Hot-box—An overheated journal or bearing on a freight car wheel.

Hump—An elevated section of track down which freight cars can be coasted for classification in the yards below.

Johnson Bar—The reversing lever of a locomotive.

Ladder Track—A track connecting a number of parallel sidings or stubs in a yard or terminal.

Lead Track—Trackage connecting a yard with the main line.

Low Iron—Yard tracks; anything not the main line.

Main Line (also Main Iron, Main Stem, etc.)—Through trackage; restricted by rules to travel only by scheduled trains or those with train orders.

Mallet—An articulated locomotive named after the designer; often used for any articulated locomotive.

Markers—Flags or lights used on trains to indicate special status or to warn of a following section.

Multiple Unit (MU)—Cars which contain their own power, but which can be controlled from the foremost car; used on commuter runs.

Muzzle Loader—Any hand-fired locomotive.

Nose—Front end of locomotive.

OS—Means "entered on the sheet," often used as a verb to indicate reporting of a train which has passed a tower.

Pantograph—The collapsible and adjustable structure which provides contact with overhead wires; so called from pivoting arrangement.

Passing Siding—A siding specifically for passing of trains in the same or opposite directions; may be several miles long.

Peddler—A way freight.

Pier—A support for the center section of a bridge.

Pilot—Structure at front of locomotive for sweeping tracks; often called a cowcatcher.

Piston—The head which moves inside the cylinder when pressed by steam.

Piston Rod—The rod attached to the piston which transmits power to the connecting rod.

Poling—Moving cars on an adjoining track by using a long spar which is placed in a socket of the car end beam and a socket on the locomotive pilot beam.

Prototype—The actual thing from which a model is patterned.

RCS (Remote Control Section)—A type of Lionel track for unloading and uncoupling; now replaced by UCS.

Rectifier—A device for converting AC into DC.

Reefer—A refrigerator car.

Restricted Track—A track section where train speeds are reduced.

Right-of-Way—The land on which the railroad is built.

Riprap—Large pieces of stone used to prevent washouts in roadbeds.

Road Engine—Locomotive used regularly for main-line service.

Rule G—The railroad rule against drinking.

Running Board—The walkway along the boiler of an engine.

Scale—The ratio in size between a drawing or a model and the prototype.

Section Hand—A track worker.

Semaphore—A signal which uses an arm.

Seniority—Length of service relative to others.

Service Track—Track on which engines take on coal and water.

Shanty—A caboose.

Shunt—To shift or drill cars.

Siding—An auxiliary track which may be entered from either end.

Smoking a Meet—Sending up a column of black smoke to signal an approaching train that another is present.

Spar—The wooden rod used in poling operations.

Spotting—Placing of cars; shifting.

Spur—A divergent track having only one entry; a branch line over which irregular service is offered.

Station—Any stop along the mainline.

Steam Chest—A box containing the valve mechanisms for the cylinders.

Stoker—An automatic firing device; a fireman.

Stub—A short diverging track ending in a bumper; it has a switch only at one end.

Tea Kettle—Any old locomotive, especially a leaky one.

Throat—Entrance tracks to a yard or terminal.

Tie Plate—The steel shoes in which the rail sits when spiked to the wooden tie.

Timetable—A printed schedule of train movements; an employee's timetable is a large bulky affair, much longer than a passenger's timetable.

Tractive Effort—The force with which a locomotive can pull under controlled conditions.

Trailing Switch—A turnout in which the points face away from prevailing traffic.

Train Order— A written order on a form which gives directions for train movements not on the schedule; train orders usually come from the dispatcher.

Trainmaster— An employee who coordinates the work of the yardmaster and roundhouse foreman; he reports directly to the superintendent.

Transformer— A device for changing high-voltage AC into low-voltage AC; also a device which does the reverse.

Trestle— A wooden bridge structure of regularly placed bents.

Turnout—A switch; a British term for switch, often used in this country.

Washout— Track ballast washed away by water action.

Way Car—A freight car carrying local shipments.

Way Freight—A freight making all local stops for which shipments are carried.

Wildcat—A runaway locomotive.

Wye (occasionally given as "Y")—A track system with three switches and three legs which enables a train to turn around.

Yardmaster—A railroad employee in charge of a yard operation.